McGraw-Hill's
Conquering ACT Math

W9-AXM-083

McGraw-Hill's Conquering ACT Math

Steven W. Dulan
and the faculty of
Advantage Education

New York   Chicago   San Francisco   Lisbon   London   Madrid   Mexico City
Milan   New Delhi   San Juan   Seoul   Singapore   Sydney   Toronto

The **McGraw·Hill** Companies

Copyright © 2008 by The McGraw-Hill Companies, inc. All rights reserved. Printed in the United States of America. Except as permitted under the United States Copyright Act of 1976, no part of this publication may be reproduced or distributed in any form or by any means, or stored in a data base or retrieval system, without the prior written permission of the publisher.

1 2 3 4 5 6 7 8 9 0   QPD/QPD   0 1 3 2 1 0 9 8

ISBN 978-0-07-149597-4
MHID 0-07-149597-5

McGraw-Hill books are available at special quantity discounts for use as premiums and sales promotions, or for use in corporate training programs. For more information, please write to the Director of Special Sales, McGraw-Hill Professional, Two Penn Plaza, New York, NY 10121-2298. Or contact your local bookstore.

ACT is a registered trademark of ACT, Inc., which was not involved in the production of, and does not endorse, this product.

Library of Congress Cataloging-in-Publication Data

Dulan, Steven W.
  McGraw-Hill's conquering ACT math / Steven W. Dulan.
     p. cm.
  ISBN 978-0-07-149597-4
    1. Mathematics–Examinations, questions, etc.   2. ACT Assessment–Study guides.   I. Title.
QA43.D835   2008
510.76–dc22

                                           2007048459

CONTENTS

ACKNOWLEDGMENTS

I would like to acknowledge the outstanding contribution of the faculty and staff of Advantage Education. Your hard work and dedication have made this endeavor a success. You are not only the smartest, but also the best.

Special thanks must be given to the following Advantage Education faculty and staff members: Aishah Ali, Lisa DiLiberti, Ryan Particka, Andrew Sanford, Alexander Savinov, and Amanda Thompson.

Most importantly, I would like to acknowledge the single biggest contributor to this work: my wife and colleague Amy Dulan. None of this would have been possible without you.

ABOUT THE AUTHOR

Steven W. Dulan, J.D., has been involved with ACT preparation since 1989, when, as a former U.S. Army Infantry Sergeant, and undergraduate student at Michigan State University, Steve became an ACT instructor. He has been helping students to prepare for success on the ACT, PSAT, SAT, and other standardized exams ever since. Steve scored in the 99th percentile on every standardized test he has ever taken.

After graduating from Michigan State University, Steve attended The Thomas M. Cooley Law School on a full Honors Scholarship. While attending law school, Steve continued to teach standardized test prep classes (including ACT, SAT, PSAT, GRE, GMAT, and LSAT) an average of 30 hours each week, and tutored some of his fellow law students in a variety of subjects and in essay exam writing techniques. Steve has also served as an instructor at Baker University, Cleary University, Lansing Community College, The Ohio State University-Real Estate Institute, and The Thomas M. Cooley Law School. Guest lecturer credits include Michigan State University, University of Michigan, Detroit College of Law, Marquette University, Texas Technical University, University of Miami, and Wright State University.

Thousands of students have benefited from Steve's instruction, coaching, and admissions consulting, and have secured entry to the colleges and universities of their choice. Steve's students have gained admission to some of the most prestigious institutions of higher learning in the world, and have received numerous scholarships of their own. Since 1997, Steve has served as the president of Advantage Education® (www.AdvantageEd.com), a company dedicated to providing effective and affordable test prep education in a variety of settings, including one-on-one tutoring via the Internet worldwide using its Personal Distance Learning® system. The information and techniques included in this book are the result of Steve's experiences with test preparation students at all levels over many years.

McGraw-Hill's
Conquering ACT Math

INTRODUCTION

ABOUT THE ACT

The ACT is the fastest-growing and most widely accepted college entrance exam in the United States. It is designed to assess high school students' general educational development and their ability to complete college-level work. The authors of the ACT insist that the ACT is an achievement test, not a direct measure of abilities. It is not an IQ test, nor is it a measure of your worth as a human being. It is not even a perfect measure of how well you will do in college. Theoretically, each of us has a specific potential to learn and acquire skills. The ACT doesn't measure your natural, inborn ability. If it did, we wouldn't be as successful as we are at raising students' scores on ACT exams.

The ACT actually measures a certain knowledge base and skill set. It is "trainable," meaning that you can do better on your ACT if you work on learning the knowledge and gaining the skills that are tested.

STRUCTURE OF THE ACT

The ACT is made up of four multiple-choice tests—English, Mathematics, Reading, and Science Reasoning—and one optional essay. There are 215 multiple-choice questions on the test. The multiple-choice tests are always given in the same order, followed by the essay. In fact, there is a lot of predictability when it comes to the ACT. The current exam still has very much in common with ACT exams from past years. This means that we basically know what is going to be on your ACT in terms of question types and content.

Following is a table showing a breakdown of the question types, number of each question type, and time allotted for each section of the ACT:

ACT Structure

ENGLISH	
75 Questions 45 Minutes	
Content/Skills	**Number of Questions**
Usage/Mechanics	**40**
Punctuation	10
Grammar/Usage	12
Sentence Structure	18
Rhetorical Skills	**35**
Strategy	12
Organization	11
Style	12

MATHEMATICS	
60 Questions 60 Minutes	
Content	**Number of Questions**
Pre-Algebra and Elementary Algebra	24
Intermediate Algebra and Coordinate Geometry	18
Plane Geometry	14
Trigonometry	4

READING	
40 Questions 35 Minutes	
Passage Type	**Number of Questions**
Prose Fiction	10
Social Science	10
Humanities	10
Natural Science	10

SCIENCE REASONING	
40 Questions 35 Minutes	
Format	**Number of Questions**
Data Representation	15
Research Summaries	18
Conflicting Viewpoints	7
Content Areas: Biology, Physical Sciences, Chemistry, Physics	

Note: There are 7 passages in this section, and the order is not always as shown above. You will generally see 3 Data Representation passages, 3 Research Summaries passages, and 1 Conflicting Viewpoints passage.

WRITING TEST
ACT offers an optional 30-minute Writing Test for students testing within the United States.

Scoring the ACT

Each of the multiple-choice sections of the ACT (English Test, Mathematics Test, Reading Test, Science Reasoning Test) is given a score on a scale of 1 to 36. These four "scaled scores" are then averaged and rounded according to normal rounding rules to yield a Composite Score. It is this Composite Score that is most often meant when someone refers to your ACT score.

You don't have to be perfect to get a good score on the ACT. The truth is that you can miss a fair number of questions and still get a score that places you in the top 1 percent of all test takers. In fact, this test is so hard and the time limit is so unrealistic for most test takers that you can get a score that is at or above the national average (about a 21) even if you get almost half of the questions wrong.

The practice tests in this book are simulations created by experts to replicate the question types, difficulty level, and content areas that you will find on your real ACT Mathematics Test. The scoring worksheets provided are guides to computing approximate scores. Actual ACT exams are scored from tables that are unique to each test. The actual scaled scores depend on a number of factors: the number of students who take the test, the difficulty level of the items (questions and answer choices), and the performance of all of the students who take the test. Do not get too hung up on your test scores while you practice; the idea is to learn something from each practice experience and to get used to the "look and feel" of the ACT Mathematics Test.

Who Writes the ACT?

There is a company called ACT, Inc., that decides exactly what is going to be on your ACT exam. The experts at ACT, Inc., consult with classroom teachers at the high school and college level. They look at high school and college curricula, and they employ educators and specialized psychologists called "psychometricians" (measurers of the mind), who know a lot about the human brain and how it operates under various conditions. Later in this book, we'll lay out the details of how you will be tested so that you can get yourself ready for the "contest" on test day.

Why Do ACT Exams Exist?

Colleges use the ACT for admissions decisions and sometimes for advanced placement. The test is also used to make scholarship decisions. Because there are variations in grading standards and requirements among high schools around the country, the admissions departments at colleges use the ACT, in part, to help provide a standard for comparison. There are studies that reveal a fair amount of "grade inflation" at some schools; therefore, colleges cannot simply rely upon grade-point averages when evaluating academic performance.

How Do I Register for the ACT?

You should register for the ACT in advance. Do not just show up on test day with a Number 2 pencil and dive right in. The best source of information for all things ACT is, not surprisingly, the ACT web site: **www.act.org.** There is also a very good chance that a guidance counselor and/or pre-college counselor at your school has an ACT Registration Book, which includes all of the information that you need for your test registration.

◾◾◾ HOW TO USE THIS BOOK

This book contains general information about the ACT and chapters on the specific mathematics content areas tested, mathematics exercises, and in-format practice questions.

In a perfect situation, you will be reading this book at least several weeks before you take your actual ACT exam. If that is not the case, you can still benefit from this book. Look at the General Test-Taking Strategies section in this chapter first, and then take the Diagnostic Test in Chapter 2, which will help you to pinpoint areas of strength and weakness in your knowledge base and skill set. Even just a few hours of study and practice can have a beneficial impact on your ACT score.

If you are reading this only days before your ACT exam, it is important to mention that you should not preorder any ACT score reports. As of the writing of this book, ACT, Inc., allows you to pick and choose which scores you send out to colleges. So, you should only send scores after you have a chance to review them yourself. If your score is not acceptable, you can always retake the ACT and only send the scores from your best testing day to your schools of choice. This is especially important if you are unsure of how you will score and if you are going in with only minimum preparation.

As you work with the practice questions in this book, be aware that most of them are simulated to match actual ACT Mathematics Test items. If you work through all of the material provided, you can rest assured that there won't be any surprises on test day. Be aware, though, that ACT exams are sensitive to factors such as fatigue and stress; the time of day that you take the practice tests, your surroundings, and other things going on in your life can have an impact on your scores. Don't get worried if you see some variations due to an off day or because the practice test exposed a weakness in your knowledge base or skill set. Just use the information that you gather as a tool to help you improve.

In our experience, the students who see the largest increase in their scores are the ones who put in consistent effort over time. Try to keep your frustration to a minimum if you struggle with the practice tests and aren't doing as well as you had hoped. Similarly, try to keep yourself from becoming overconfident when you have a great practice-testing day.

There is an explanation for each of the practice questions in this book. You will probably not need to read all of them. Sometimes, you can tell right away why you answered a particular question incorrectly. We have seen countless students smack themselves on the forehead and say "stupid mistake." We try to refer to these errors as "concentration errors." Everyone makes them from time to time, and you should not worry when they occur. There is a good chance that your focus will be a little better on the real test as long as you train yourself properly with the aid of this book. You should distinguish between concentration errors and any holes in your knowledge base or understanding. If you have the time, it is worth reading the explanations for any of the questions that were at all challenging for you. Sometimes, students get questions correct for the wrong reason, or because they guessed correctly. While you are practicing, you should mark any questions that you want to revisit and be sure to read the explanations for them.

> **Study Tip**
>
> Your score will improve with practice! Decide when you are going to take the ACT and allow for sufficient practice time leading up to the test. We recommend 6–8 weeks of preparation before the test.

◾◾◾ GENERAL TEST-TAKING INFORMATION AND STRATEGIES

Now it's time to take a look at some general test-taking information and strategies that should help you approach the ACT with confidence. We'll start by discussing the importance of acquiring the skills necessary to maximize your ACT scores, and finish with some tips on how to handle stress before, during, and after the test. Additional chapters in this book include strategies and techniques specific to the ACT mathematics section.

KSA (Knowledge, Skills, Abilities)

Cognitive psychologists who study learning and thinking use the letters KSA to refer to the basic components of human performance in all human activities, from academics to athletics, playing music to playing games. The letters stand for Knowledge, Skills, and Abilities. As mentioned previously, the ACT measures a specific set of skills that can be improved through study and practice. You probably already understand this since you are reading this book. In fact, many thousands of students over the years have successfully raised their ACT scores through study and practice.

Learning Facts vs. Acquiring Skills

The human brain stores and retrieves factual knowledge a little differently from the way it acquires and executes skills. Knowledge can generally be learned quickly and is fairly durable, even when you are under stress. You learn factual information by studying, and you acquire skills through practice. There is some overlap between these actions; you will learn while you practice, and vice versa. In fact, research shows that repetition is important for both information storage and skills acquisition.

As we just mentioned, repetition is necessary to acquire and improve skills: knowing *about* a skill, or understanding how the skill should be executed, is not the same as actually *having* that skill. For instance, you might be told *about* a skill such as driving a car with a standard transmission, playing the piano, or typing on a computer keyboard. You might have a great teacher, have wonderful learning tools, and pay attention very carefully. You might *understand* everything perfectly. But, the first few times that you actually attempt the skill, you will probably make some mistakes. In fact, you will probably experience some frustration because of the gap between your understanding of the skill and your actual ability to perform the skill. Perfecting skills takes practice. When skills are repeated so many times that they can't be further improved, psychologists use the term *perfectly internalized skills,* which means that the skills are executed automatically, without any conscious thought. You need repetition to create the pathways in your brain that control your skills. Therefore, you shouldn't be satisfied with simply reading this book and then saying to yourself, "I get it." You will not reach your full ACT scoring potential unless you put in sufficient time practicing in addition to understanding and learning.

Practicing to Internalize Skills

We hope that you will internalize the skills you need for top performance on the ACT so that you don't have to spend time and energy figuring out what to do during the introduction to the exam. We are hoping that you will be well into each section while some of your less-prepared classmates are still reading the directions and trying to figure out exactly what they are supposed to be doing. We suggest that you practice sufficiently so that you develop your test-taking skills, and, specifically, good ACT-taking skills. While you practice, you should distinguish between practice that is meant to serve as a learning experience and practice that is meant to be a realistic simulation of what will happen on your actual ACT.

During practice that is meant for learning, it is okay to "cheat." You should feel free to disregard the time limits and just think about how the questions are put together; you can stop to look at the explanations included in this book. It is even okay to talk to others about what you are learning during your "learning practice." However, you also need to do some simulated testing practice, where you time yourself carefully and try to control as many variables in your environment as you can. Some research shows that you will have an easier time executing your skills and remembering information when the environment that you are testing in is similar to the environment where you studied and practiced.

There is a psychological term, *cognitive endurance*, which refers to your ability to perform difficult mental tasks over an extended period of time. Just as with your physical endurance, you can build up your cognitive endurance through training. As you prepare yourself for the ACT, you should start off with shorter practice sessions and work up to the point where you can easily do a 60-minute ACT Mathematics Test with no noticeable fatigue.

Now, let's explore the skills and strategies important to ensuring your success on the ACT.

Do the Easy Stuff First

First, you should get familiar with the format of each section of the ACT so that you can recognize questions that are likely to give you trouble. The format of the ACT Mathematics Test is covered in Chapter 1.

All of the questions on an ACT test are weighted exactly equally to one another. When you are taking the test, we suggest that you "bypass pockets of resistance." Go around trouble spots and return to them later. It is a much better use of your time and energy to pick up all of the correct answers that you can early on, and then go back and work on the tougher questions. Learn to recognize the question types that are likely to give you trouble and be sure not to get goaded into a fight with them.

There will be some time-consuming questions that show up early on the Mathematics Test designed to lure you into wasting time that would be better spent answering some more reasonable questions later. Don't get caught up in these. Move on and come back to them later. By the time you take the test, you will have learned to recognize the question types that are likely to give you trouble. When you see them, don't be surprised. Just recognize them and work on the easier material first. If time permits, you can always come back and work on the challenging problems in the final minutes before the proctor calls, "Time!"

This book contains specific suggestions for which question types you should probably skip. You'll also develop "likes and dislikes" while practicing, meaning you will know that certain question types are always going to be tough for you. By test day you will have done enough timed practice that you will also develop a "feel" for how long you should be spending on each question. Be flexible. Even if a question is of a type that you can usually answer easily, do not spend more time than you should on it. There is usually time to come back if you leave a question too soon. However, once you waste a second of time, you cannot get it back.

Stay "On Point"

Most *incorrect* ACT answers are incorrect because they are irrelevant. This applies to all of the different question types on all of the various sections.

Study Tip

Do not attempt any timed practice tests when you are mentally or physically exhausted. This will add unwanted stress to an already stressful situation. You must be realistic about how you spend your time and energy during the preparation process.

Study Tip

Because what is easy for some is not necessarily easy for others, do enough practice to quickly recognize the question types that will be easy for *you*. Answer those questions first, then go back to work on the more difficult questions if time allows.

For example, if you get very good at spotting and eliminating answer choices that are too big or too small on the ACT Mathematics Test, you'll go a long way toward improving your score. This can be more difficult than it sounds because some of the incorrect choices will contain numbers from the question, or will be the result of a small miscalculation.

Manage the Answer Sheet

Be certain to avoid the common mistake of marking the answer to each question on your answer document (bubble sheet) as you finish the question. In other words, you should NOT go to your answer sheet after each question. This is dangerous and wastes time. It is dangerous because you run an increased risk of marking your answer sheet incorrectly and perhaps not catching your error on time. It wastes time because you have to find your place on the answer sheet and then find your place back in the test booklet over and over again. The amount of time that is "wasted" is not large as you mark each question. But, it adds up over the course of an entire test section and could cost you the amount of time you need to answer a few more questions correctly.

Instead, you should mark your answers in the test booklet and transfer your answers from the test booklet to the answer sheet in groups. On any of the sections, filling in circles (bubbles) on your answer sheet can be a good activity to keep you busy when you simply need a break to clear your head. Be sure to practice this technique until you are comfortable with it.

Use the Test Booklet

The ACT test booklets are meant to be used by one test taker only. You will not have any scratch paper on test day for the Mathematics Test. You are expected to do all note-taking and figuring on the booklet itself. Generally, no one ever bothers to look at the test booklet since you cannot receive credit for anything that is written there. Your score comes only from the answers that you mark on the answer sheet. Therefore, you should feel comfortable marking up the questions, crossing off incorrect answer choices, making calculations, and so on, to help you to stay focused on relevant information.

Guess Wisely

Since there is no added scoring penalty for incorrect answers on the ACT, you should never leave a bubble blank on your answer sheet. We counted all of the correct answers on three recently released ACT exams and found that the distribution of answers by position on the answer sheet was almost exactly even. This means that there is no position that is more likely to be correct than any other. We use the term *position* when referring to the answer sheet because the letter assigned to the positions changes depending on whether you are working on an odd or even question. On the Mathematics Test, the odd-numbered questions have answer choices labeled A through E and the even-numbered questions have answer choices that are labeled F through K. This system allows you to stay on track on your answer sheet.

Make educated guesses by eliminating answer choices. It's a good idea to add a symbol or two to the common repertoire to help distinguish between the answer choices that you eliminate, and those that could be correct.

> **Study Tip**
> The answers are distributed fairly evenly across the positions, so you should always guess the same position if you are guessing at random. Of course, if you can eliminate a choice or two, or if you have a hunch, then this advice doesn't apply.

For example, when you eliminate an answer choice, make a mark through the letter so that you no longer consider it a viable choice:

If a rectangle measures 18 meters by 24 meters, what is the length, in meters, of the diagonal of the rectangle?
F. 18
G. 24
H. 30
J. 42
K. 900

The step shown above is fairly common. If you think that an answer choice *may* be correct, but want to consider the remaining choices before you make your final decision, underline the answer choice, as shown below. This might be a new step in your standard process:

If a rectangle measures 18 meters by 24 meters, what is the length, in meters, of the diagonal of the rectangle?
F. 18
G. 24
H. 30
J. 42
K. 900

Once you've decided on your final answer, circle it for later transfer to the answer sheet:

If a rectangle measures 18 meters by 24 meters, what is the length, in meters, of the diagonal of the rectangle?
F. 18
G. 24
H. 30
J. 42
K. 900

If you have eliminated one or more of the answer choices and still don't feel comfortable guessing among those that remain, place a large **X** next to the question, leave the circle empty on your answer sheet, and come back to the question later if you have time. Try to budget your time so that you have at least a minute or two left at the end of each section to locate the questions you've marked with an **X**; because you will be making an educated guess, select one of the answer choices that you did not already eliminate and fill in the corresponding circle on your answer sheet.

You also need to find out whether you are an answer-changer; if you change an answer, are you more likely to change it *to* the correct answer, or *from* the correct answer? You can only learn this about yourself by doing practice exams and paying attention to your tendencies. In general, we recommend sticking with your first choice.

Some students worry if they notice strings of the same answers on their answer sheets. This does not necessarily indicate a problem. While analyzing actual, released ACT exams, we counted strings of up to five questions long, all marked with the same answer position on the answer sheet, and all correct. You should not be too concerned even if you find a string of five answer choices that are all in the same position on the answer sheet.

Manage Stress

In college, stress arises from sources such as family expectations, fear of failure, heavy workload, competition, and difficult subjects. The ACT is designed to create similar stresses. The psychometricians we mentioned earlier, who contribute to the design of standardized tests, use artificial stressors to test how you will respond to the stress of college. In other words, they are actually trying to create a certain level of stress in you.

The main stressor is the time limit. The time limits are set on the ACT so that most students cannot finish all of the questions in the time allowed. Use the specific strategies mentioned in Chapter 7 to help you select as many correct answers as possible in the time allowed. Also, be sure to read Chapter 4 for a complete review of the concepts and subject matter tested on the ACT Mathematics Test.

Remember, if you practice enough, there should be no surprises on test day!

Relax to Succeed

Probably the worst thing that can happen to a test taker is to panic. When you panic, you can usually identify a specific set of easily recognizable symptoms: sweating, shortness of breath, muscle tension, increased pulse rate, tunnel vision, nausea, lightheadedness, and, in rare cases, even loss of consciousness. These symptoms are the results of chemical changes in the brain brought on by some stimulus. The stimulus does not have to be external. Therefore, we can panic ourselves just by thinking about certain things. The stress chemical in your body called epinephrine, more commonly known as adrenaline, brings on these symptoms. Adrenaline changes the priorities in your brain activity. It moves blood and electrical energy away from some parts of the brain and to others. Specifically, it increases brain activity in the areas that control your body and decreases blood flow to the parts of your brain that are involved in complex thinking. Therefore, panic makes a person stronger and faster—and also less able to perform the type of critical thinking that is important on the ACT. It is not a bad thing to have a small amount of adrenaline in your bloodstream due to a healthy amount of excitement about your exam, but you should be careful not to panic before or during your test.

You can control your adrenaline levels by minimizing the unknown factors in the testing process. The biggest stress-inducing questions are: "What do the test writers expect?"; "Am I ready?"; and "How will I do on test day?"

If you spend your time and energy studying and practicing under realistic conditions before test day, you will have a much better chance of controlling your adrenaline levels and handling the exam with no panic.

The goals of your preparation should be to learn about the test, acquire the skills that are being measured by the test, and learn about yourself and how you respond to the different parts of the test. You need to be familiar with the material that is tested on each section of your test. Decide which questions you'll attempt to solve on test day and which ones you'll simply guess on. As you work through this book, make an assessment of the best use of your time and energy. Concentrate on the areas that will give you the highest score in the amount of time that you have until you take the ACT. This will give you a feeling of confidence on test day even when you are facing very challenging questions.

Relaxation Techniques

The following are suggestions to help you feel as relaxed and confident as possible on test day.

Be Prepared

The more prepared you feel, the less likely it is that you'll be stressed on test day. Study and practice consistently during the time between now and your test day. Be organized. Have your supplies and lucky testing clothes ready in advance. Make a practice trip to the test center before your test day.

Know Yourself

Get to know your strengths and weaknesses on the ACT and the things that help you to relax. Some test takers like to have a slightly anxious feeling to help them focus. Other folks do best when they are so relaxed that they are almost asleep. You will learn about yourself through practice.

Have a Plan of Attack

Know how you are going to work through each part of the exam. There is no time to create a plan of attack on test day. Practice enough that you internalize the skills you need to do your best on each section, and you won't have to stop to think about what to do next.

Breathe

If you feel yourself tensing up, slow down and take deeper breaths. This will relax you and get more oxygen to your brain so that you can think more clearly.

Take Breaks

You cannot stay sharply focused on your ACT for the whole time in the testing center. You are certainly going to have distracting thoughts, or times when you just can't process all the information. When this happens, close your eyes, clear your mind, and then start back on your test. This process should take only a minute or so. You could pray, meditate, or just visualize a place or person that helps you relax. Try thinking of something fun that you have planned to do after your test.

Be Aware of Time

Time yourself on test day. You should have timed yourself on some of your practice exams, so you will have a sense of how long each section should take you. We suggest that you use an analog (dial face) watch. You can' turn the hands on your watch back from noon to allow enough time for the section that you are working on. For example, set your watch to 11:00 for the 60-minute ACT Mathematics Test.

Clear Your Head

Remember, all that matters during the test is your test. All of life's other issues will have to be dealt with after your test is finished. You might find this attitude easier to attain if you lose track of what time it is in the "outside world"—another benefit of resetting your watch.

Eat Right

Sugar is bad for stress and brain function in general. Consuming refined sugar creates biological stress that has an impact on your brain chemistry. Keep it to a minimum for several days before your test. If you are actually addicted to caffeine (you can tell that you are if you get headaches when you skip a day), get your normal amount. Don't forget to eat regularly while you're preparing for the ACT. It's not a good idea to skip meals simply because you are experiencing some additional stress.

A Note on Music

Some types of music increase measured brain stress and interfere with clear thinking. Specifically, some rock, hip-hop, and dance rhythms, while great for certain occasions, can have detrimental effects on certain types of brain waves and interfere with learning and optimal test taking. Other music seems to help to organize brain waves and create a relaxed state that is conducive to learning and skills acquisition.

The Impact of Mozart

There is a great debate raging among scientists and educators about a study that was done some years ago, which seemed to show that listening to Mozart made students temporarily more intelligent. While not everyone agrees that it helps, no one has ever seriously argued that it hurts. So, get yourself a Mozart CD and listen to it before practice and before your real test. It might help. In the worst-case scenario, you will have listened to some good music and maybe broadened your horizons a bit. You cannot listen to music *during* your ACT, so do not listen to it during your practice tests.

■■■ WHAT TO DO ON TEST DAY

If you work through the material in this book and do some additional practice on released ACT items (visit act.org), you should be more than adequately prepared for the test. Use the following tips to help the entire testing process go smoothly.

Do a Dry Run

Make sure that you know how long it will take to get to the testing center, where you will park, alternative routes, and so on. If you are testing in a place that is new to you, try to get into the building between now and test day so that you can absorb the sounds and smells, find out where the bathrooms and snack machines are, and so on.

Rest Up and Wake Up Early

You generally have to be at the testing center by 8:00 a.m. Set two alarms if you have to. Leave yourself plenty of time to get fully awake before you have to run out the door. Be sure to get enough rest the night before the test. The better rested you are, the better things seem. When you are fatigued, you are more likely to look on the dark side of things and worry more, which hurts your test scores.

Dress for Success

Wear loose, comfortable clothes in layers so that you can adjust to the temperature. Remember your watch. There might not be a clock in your testing room. (See page 10 for more information on timing!)

Fuel Up

It is important to eat something before you take the test. An empty stomach might be distracting and uncomfortable on test day. Foods without too much sugar are probably best. Get your normal dose of caffeine, if any. (Test day is not the time to "try coffee " for the first time!)

Bring Supplies

Bring your driver's license (or passport), your admission ticket, several sharpened Number 2 pencils, erasers, a timepiece, and your approved calculator. If you need them, bring your glasses or contact lenses. You won't be able to eat or drink while the test is in progress, but you can bring a snack for the break time.

Warm Up Your Brain

Read a newspaper or something similar, or review some practice material so that the ACT isn't the first thing you read on test day. If you review ACT material, make sure that it is something that you have worked through before and focus on the part of the test that you tend to be best at. This is certainly the time to accentuate the positive!

Plan a Mini-Vacation

Most students find it easier to concentrate on their test preparation and on their ACT if they have a plan for some fun right after the test. Plan something that you can look forward to as a reward for all the hard work and energy that you're putting into preparing for and taking the test.

◼◼ WHAT'S NEXT?

The remaining chapters in this book include more detailed information about the format and scoring of the ACT Mathematics Test, a diagnostic test to evaluate your current readiness for the ACT Mathematics Test, strategies specific to the ACT Mathematics Test, exercises to hone your mathematics skills, and practice questions in ACT format.

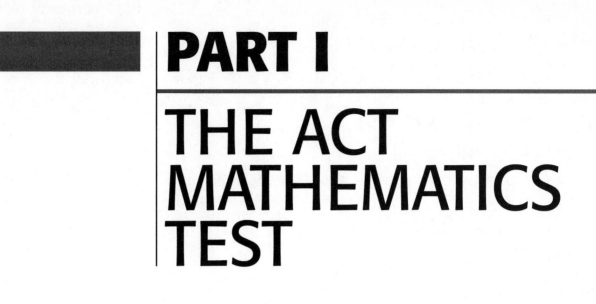

PART I

THE ACT MATHEMATICS TEST

CHAPTER 1

FORMAT AND SCORING

As mentioned in the Introduction, the ACT is made up of four multiple-choice tests (English, Mathematics, Reading, and Science Reasoning) and an optional essay. This chapter will provide more information on the format of the ACT Mathematics Test and briefly discuss how this test is scored.

■■■ FORMAT

The ACT Mathematics Test includes 60 questions that are designed to measure your ability to reason mathematically, to understand basic math terminology, and to recall basic mathematics formulas and principles. You will have 60 minutes to answer these questions. You should be able to solve problems and apply relevant mathematics concepts in the following areas:

- *Pre-Algebra*: approximately 23 percent of the total number of questions will cover basic mathematical operations, place value, square roots, factors, ratio, proportion, percent, linear equations, and simple probability.
- *Elementary Algebra*: approximately 17 percent of the total number of questions will be based on properties of exponents, substitution, functions, and quadratic equations.
- *Intermediate Algebra*: approximately 15 percent of the total number of questions will focus on rational and radical expressions, absolute value, inequalities, sequences, systems of equations, roots of polynomials, and complex numbers.
- *Coordinate Geometry*: approximately 15 percent of the total number of questions will cover graphing equations, graphing inequalities, slope, parallel and perpendicular lines, distance, and midpoint.
- *Plane Geometry*: approximately 23 percent of the total number of questions will focus on the properties and relations of plane figures, including circles, rectangles, triangles, and parallelograms.
- *Trigonometry*: approximately 7 percent of the total number of questions will be based on trigonometric concepts.

Each of these content areas will be further discussed in Chapter 4. In Chapter 5, you will have an opportunity to practice and build the skills necessary for success on the ACT Mathematics Test.

Anatomy of an ACT Mathematics Question

As mentioned earlier in this book, each multiple-choice mathematics question includes five answer choices (A, B, C, D, E for odd-numbered questions) or (F, G, H, J, K for even-numbered questions). The answer choices correspond to the bubbles on your answer sheet. You may use an approved calculator to assist you in answering any of the multiple-choice questions, but none of the questions actually requires the use of a calculator to solve.

The basic structure of an ACT mathematics question is illustrated below.

1. If $5x - 6 = 14$, then what is the value of $8x$? } **Question**

A. $\dfrac{8}{5}$

B. 4

C. $\dfrac{64}{5}$ } **Answer Choices**

D. 20
E. 32

▰▰ SCORING

As noted earlier, each of the ACT multiple-choice tests is given a score on a scale of 1–36. In 2006, the average ACT Mathematics Test score in the United States was 20.8. Your score will be rounded to the nearest whole number before it is reported. The schools that you select to receive score reports will get four ACT Mathematics Test scores: your total score based on all 60 questions, a subscore based on the Pre-Algebra/Elementary Algebra questions, a subscore based on the Algebra/Coordinate Geometry questions, and a subscore based on the Plane Geometry/Trigonometry questions. Because most colleges and universities focus only on the total score, we have not included specific information on calculating subscores. Check with the admissions departments at your schools of choice to find out how (or if) they use Mathematics subscores.

Your ACT Mathematics Test score will be used along with the scores from the other ACT multiple-choice tests to calculate your composite score. Refer to the Scoring Worksheets provided with the answers to the Practice Tests in this book to calculate your approximate scaled score (1–36) for each test.

▰▰ WHAT'S NEXT?

Chapter 2 includes a Diagnostic Test, which you should use to determine your current readiness for the ACT Mathematics Test. Then, read Chapter 3, "Strategies and Techniques," to learn the best approach to answering the questions on the simulated tests included in this book, as well as on your actual ACT.

CHAPTER 2

ACT MATHEMATICS DIAGNOSTIC TEST

The following Diagnostic Test will assist you in evaluating your current readiness for the ACT Mathematics Test. Make an honest effort to answer each question, then review the explanations that follow. Don't worry if you are unable to answer many or most of the questions at this point. The rest of the book contains information and resources to help you to maximize your ACT Mathematics scores. Once you have identified your areas of strength and weakness, you should review those particular sections in the book.

ACT MATHEMATICS DIAGNOSTIC TEST
Answer Sheet

MATHEMATICS

1 Ⓐ Ⓑ Ⓒ Ⓓ Ⓔ	16 Ⓕ Ⓖ Ⓗ Ⓙ Ⓚ	31 Ⓐ Ⓑ Ⓒ Ⓓ Ⓔ	46 Ⓕ Ⓖ Ⓗ Ⓙ Ⓚ
2 Ⓕ Ⓖ Ⓗ Ⓙ Ⓚ	17 Ⓐ Ⓑ Ⓒ Ⓓ Ⓔ	32 Ⓕ Ⓖ Ⓗ Ⓙ Ⓚ	47 Ⓐ Ⓑ Ⓒ Ⓓ Ⓔ
3 Ⓐ Ⓑ Ⓒ Ⓓ Ⓔ	18 Ⓕ Ⓖ Ⓗ Ⓙ Ⓚ	33 Ⓐ Ⓑ Ⓒ Ⓓ Ⓔ	48 Ⓕ Ⓖ Ⓗ Ⓙ Ⓚ
4 Ⓕ Ⓖ Ⓗ Ⓙ Ⓚ	19 Ⓐ Ⓑ Ⓒ Ⓓ Ⓔ	34 Ⓕ Ⓖ Ⓗ Ⓙ Ⓚ	49 Ⓐ Ⓑ Ⓒ Ⓓ Ⓔ
5 Ⓐ Ⓑ Ⓒ Ⓓ Ⓔ	20 Ⓕ Ⓖ Ⓗ Ⓙ Ⓚ	35 Ⓐ Ⓑ Ⓒ Ⓓ Ⓔ	50 Ⓕ Ⓖ Ⓗ Ⓙ Ⓚ
6 Ⓕ Ⓖ Ⓗ Ⓙ Ⓚ	21 Ⓐ Ⓑ Ⓒ Ⓓ Ⓔ	36 Ⓕ Ⓖ Ⓗ Ⓙ Ⓚ	51 Ⓐ Ⓑ Ⓒ Ⓓ Ⓔ
7 Ⓐ Ⓑ Ⓒ Ⓓ Ⓔ	22 Ⓕ Ⓖ Ⓗ Ⓙ Ⓚ	37 Ⓐ Ⓑ Ⓒ Ⓓ Ⓔ	52 Ⓕ Ⓖ Ⓗ Ⓙ Ⓚ
8 Ⓕ Ⓖ Ⓗ Ⓙ Ⓚ	23 Ⓐ Ⓑ Ⓒ Ⓓ Ⓔ	38 Ⓕ Ⓖ Ⓗ Ⓙ Ⓚ	53 Ⓐ Ⓑ Ⓒ Ⓓ Ⓔ
9 Ⓐ Ⓑ Ⓒ Ⓓ Ⓔ	24 Ⓕ Ⓖ Ⓗ Ⓙ Ⓚ	39 Ⓐ Ⓑ Ⓒ Ⓓ Ⓔ	54 Ⓕ Ⓖ Ⓗ Ⓙ Ⓚ
10 Ⓕ Ⓖ Ⓗ Ⓙ Ⓚ	25 Ⓐ Ⓑ Ⓒ Ⓓ Ⓔ	40 Ⓕ Ⓖ Ⓗ Ⓙ Ⓚ	55 Ⓐ Ⓑ Ⓒ Ⓓ Ⓔ
11 Ⓐ Ⓑ Ⓒ Ⓓ Ⓔ	26 Ⓕ Ⓖ Ⓗ Ⓙ Ⓚ	41 Ⓐ Ⓑ Ⓒ Ⓓ Ⓔ	56 Ⓕ Ⓖ Ⓗ Ⓙ Ⓚ
12 Ⓕ Ⓖ Ⓗ Ⓙ Ⓚ	27 Ⓐ Ⓑ Ⓒ Ⓓ Ⓔ	42 Ⓕ Ⓖ Ⓗ Ⓙ Ⓚ	57 Ⓐ Ⓑ Ⓒ Ⓓ Ⓔ
13 Ⓐ Ⓑ Ⓒ Ⓓ Ⓔ	28 Ⓕ Ⓖ Ⓗ Ⓙ Ⓚ	43 Ⓐ Ⓑ Ⓒ Ⓓ Ⓔ	58 Ⓕ Ⓖ Ⓗ Ⓙ Ⓚ
14 Ⓕ Ⓖ Ⓗ Ⓙ Ⓚ	29 Ⓐ Ⓑ Ⓒ Ⓓ Ⓔ	44 Ⓕ Ⓖ Ⓗ Ⓙ Ⓚ	59 Ⓐ Ⓑ Ⓒ Ⓓ Ⓔ
15 Ⓐ Ⓑ Ⓒ Ⓓ Ⓔ	30 Ⓕ Ⓖ Ⓗ Ⓙ Ⓚ	45 Ⓐ Ⓑ Ⓒ Ⓓ Ⓔ	60 Ⓕ Ⓖ Ⓗ Ⓙ Ⓚ

MATHEMATICS TEST

60 Minutes—60 Questions

DIRECTIONS: Solve each of the problems in the time allowed, then fill in the corresponding bubble on your answer sheet. Do not spend too much time on any one problem; skip the more difficult problems and go back to them later. You may use a calculator on this test. For this test you should assume that figures are NOT necessarily drawn to scale, that all geometric figures lie in a plane, and that the word *line* is used to indicate a straight line.

1. For each of four months, the table below gives the number of games a basketball team played, the number of free throws the team attempted, and the number of free throws the team made.

Month	Games	Free throws attempted	Free throws made
September	4	78	69
October	6	107	93
November	8	120	102
December	5	83	76

To the nearest tenth, what is the average number of free throws that the team made per game in November?
A. 8.5
B. 10.2
C. 12.8
D. 15.0
E. 17.3

DO YOUR FIGURING HERE.

2. For the polygon below, the lengths of 2 sides are not given. Each angle between adjacent sides measures 90°. What is the polygon's perimeter, in centimeters?

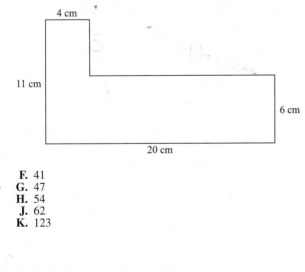

F. 41
G. 47
H. 54
J. 62
K. 123

GO ON TO THE NEXT PAGE.

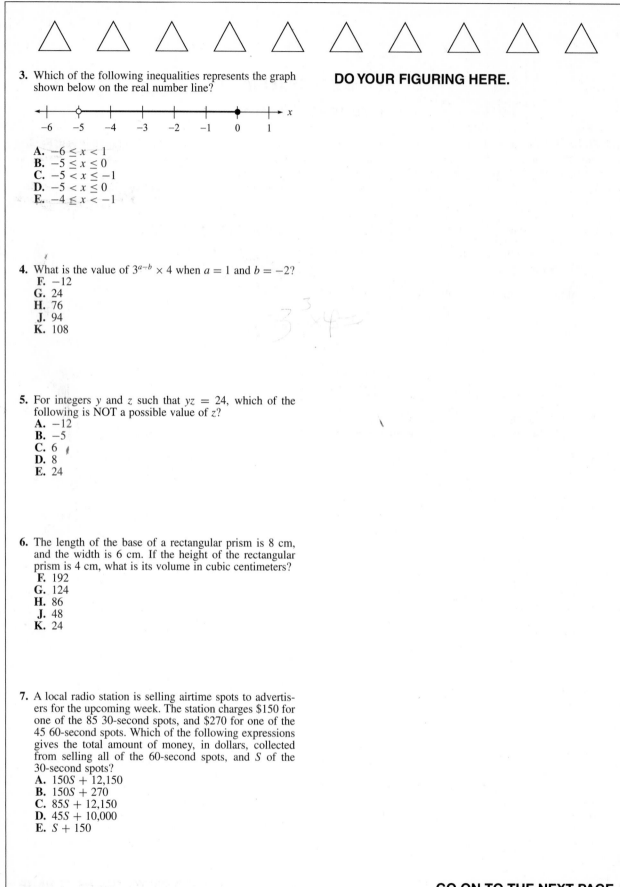

3. Which of the following inequalities represents the graph shown below on the real number line?

DO YOUR FIGURING HERE.

A. $-6 \leq x < 1$
B. $-5 \leq x \leq 0$
C. $-5 < x \leq -1$
D. $-5 < x \leq 0$
E. $-4 \leq x < -1$

4. What is the value of $3^{a-b} \times 4$ when $a = 1$ and $b = -2$?
  F. -12
  G. 24
  H. 76
  J. 94
  K. 108

5. For integers y and z such that $yz = 24$, which of the following is NOT a possible value of z?
  A. -12
  B. -5
  C. 6
  D. 8
  E. 24

6. The length of the base of a rectangular prism is 8 cm, and the width is 6 cm. If the height of the rectangular prism is 4 cm, what is its volume in cubic centimeters?
  F. 192
  G. 124
  H. 86
  J. 48
  K. 24

7. A local radio station is selling airtime spots to advertisers for the upcoming week. The station charges $150 for one of the 85 30-second spots, and $270 for one of the 45 60-second spots. Which of the following expressions gives the total amount of money, in dollars, collected from selling all of the 60-second spots, and S of the 30-second spots?
  A. $150S + 12{,}150$
  B. $150S + 270$
  C. $85S + 12{,}150$
  D. $45S + 10{,}000$
  E. $S + 150$

GO ON TO THE NEXT PAGE.

8. In the figure below, W, X, and Y are colinear, the measure of angle WXZ is $4x°$, and the measure of angle YXZ is $8x°$. What is the measure of angle WXZ?

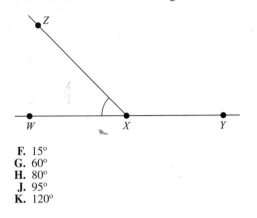

   F. 15°
   G. 60°
   H. 80°
   J. 95°
   K. 120°

9. Mickey is living in a house with 11 other people, and each person gets his own room. There are 3 bedrooms on the first floor, 5 on the second, and 4 on the third. The housemates are deciding who gets what room by drawing numbers out of a hat. If Mickey draws first, what is the probability that he will get a room on the third floor?

   A. $\dfrac{1}{12}$

   B. $\dfrac{1}{6}$

   C. $\dfrac{1}{4}$

   D. $\dfrac{1}{3}$

   E. $\dfrac{5}{12}$

GO ON TO THE NEXT PAGE.

DO YOUR FIGURING HERE.

10. A new video game arrived in toy stores, and initially the sales were slow. The game's popularity increased dramatically a few months after its release. Then sales slowly declined for a few months. After about a year, sales began to decline more rapidly. Which one of the following graphs could represent the number of video games sold each month as a function of time after the game initially arrived in stores?

DO YOUR FIGURING HERE.

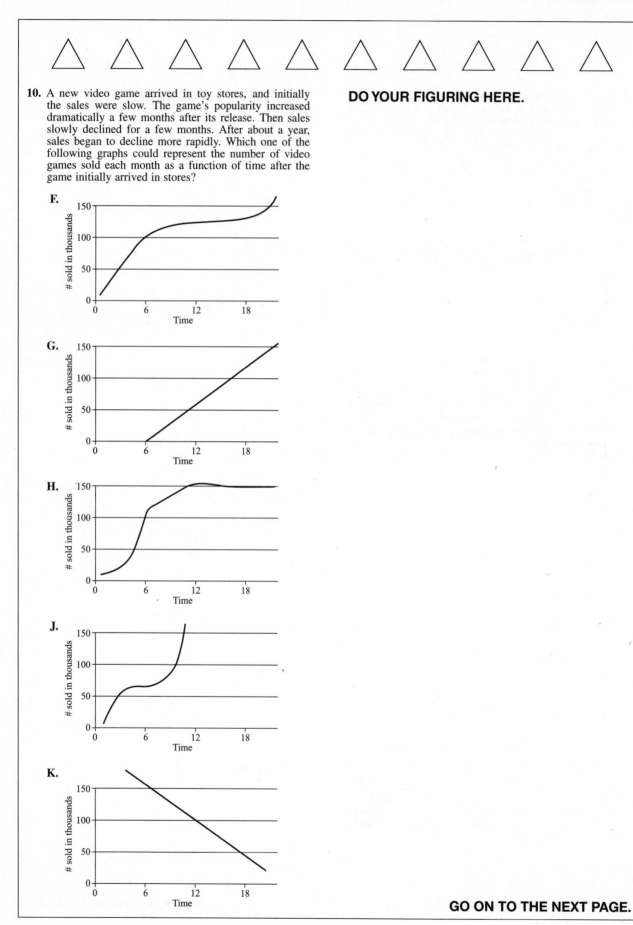

GO ON TO THE NEXT PAGE.

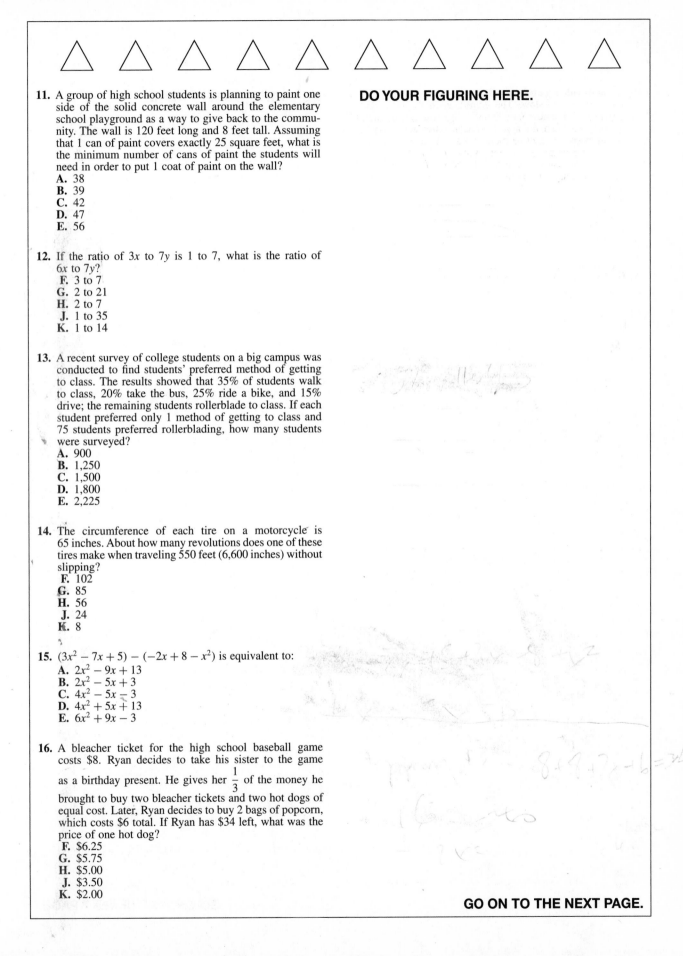

11. A group of high school students is planning to paint one side of the solid concrete wall around the elementary school playground as a way to give back to the community. The wall is 120 feet long and 8 feet tall. Assuming that 1 can of paint covers exactly 25 square feet, what is the minimum number of cans of paint the students will need in order to put 1 coat of paint on the wall?
- **A.** 38
- **B.** 39
- **C.** 42
- **D.** 47
- **E.** 56

DO YOUR FIGURING HERE.

12. If the ratio of $3x$ to $7y$ is 1 to 7, what is the ratio of $6x$ to $7y$?
- **F.** 3 to 7
- **G.** 2 to 21
- **H.** 2 to 7
- **J.** 1 to 35
- **K.** 1 to 14

13. A recent survey of college students on a big campus was conducted to find students' preferred method of getting to class. The results showed that 35% of students walk to class, 20% take the bus, 25% ride a bike, and 15% drive; the remaining students rollerblade to class. If each student preferred only 1 method of getting to class and 75 students preferred rollerblading, how many students were surveyed?
- **A.** 900
- **B.** 1,250
- **C.** 1,500
- **D.** 1,800
- **E.** 2,225

14. The circumference of each tire on a motorcycle is 65 inches. About how many revolutions does one of these tires make when traveling 550 feet (6,600 inches) without slipping?
- **F.** 102
- **G.** 85
- **H.** 56
- **J.** 24
- **K.** 8

15. $(3x^2 - 7x + 5) - (-2x + 8 - x^2)$ is equivalent to:
- **A.** $2x^2 - 9x + 13$
- **B.** $2x^2 - 5x + 3$
- **C.** $4x^2 - 5x - 3$
- **D.** $4x^2 + 5x + 13$
- **E.** $6x^2 + 9x - 3$

16. A bleacher ticket for the high school baseball game costs $8. Ryan decides to take his sister to the game as a birthday present. He gives her $\frac{1}{3}$ of the money he brought to buy two bleacher tickets and two hot dogs of equal cost. Later, Ryan decides to buy 2 bags of popcorn, which costs $6 total. If Ryan has $34 left, what was the price of one hot dog?
- **F.** $6.25
- **G.** $5.75
- **H.** $5.00
- **J.** $3.50
- **K.** $2.00

GO ON TO THE NEXT PAGE.

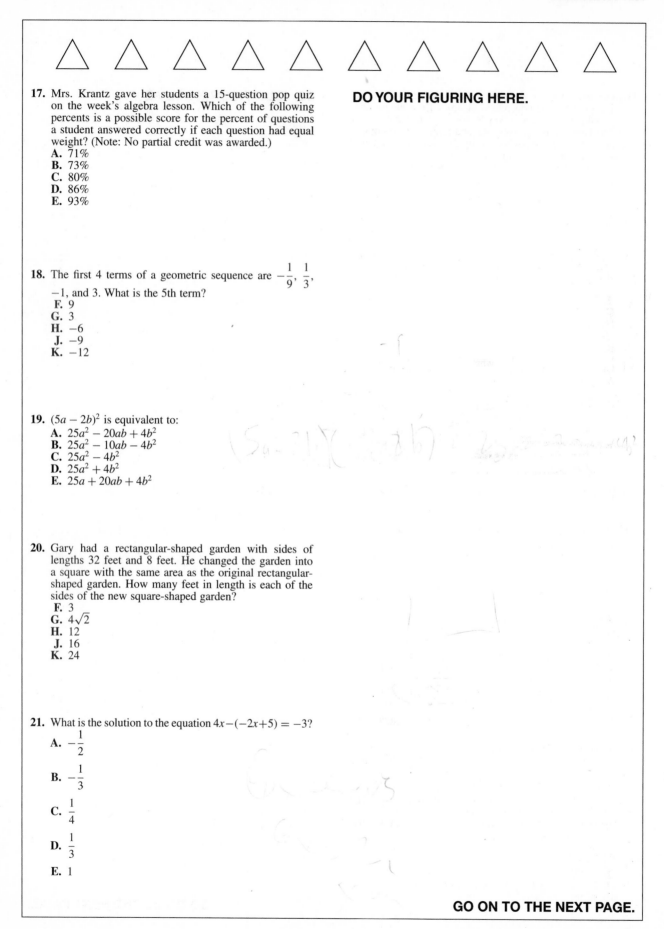

17. Mrs. Krantz gave her students a 15-question pop quiz on the week's algebra lesson. Which of the following percents is a possible score for the percent of questions a student answered correctly if each question had equal weight? (Note: No partial credit was awarded.)
  A. 71%
  B. 73%
  C. 80%
  D. 86%
  E. 93%

DO YOUR FIGURING HERE.

18. The first 4 terms of a geometric sequence are $-\frac{1}{9}, \frac{1}{3}$, -1, and 3. What is the 5th term?
  F. 9
  G. 3
  H. -6
  J. -9
  K. -12

19. $(5a - 2b)^2$ is equivalent to:
  A. $25a^2 - 20ab + 4b^2$
  B. $25a^2 - 10ab - 4b^2$
  C. $25a^2 - 4b^2$
  D. $25a^2 + 4b^2$
  E. $25a + 20ab + 4b^2$

20. Gary had a rectangular-shaped garden with sides of lengths 32 feet and 8 feet. He changed the garden into a square with the same area as the original rectangular-shaped garden. How many feet in length is each of the sides of the new square-shaped garden?
  F. 3
  G. $4\sqrt{2}$
  H. 12
  J. 16
  K. 24

21. What is the solution to the equation $4x - (-2x + 5) = -3$?
  A. $-\frac{1}{2}$
  B. $-\frac{1}{3}$
  C. $\frac{1}{4}$
  D. $\frac{1}{3}$
  E. 1

GO ON TO THE NEXT PAGE.

22. The area of $\triangle ABC$ below is 42 square inches. If $\overline{BD}$ is 7 inches long, how long is $\overline{AC}$, in inches?

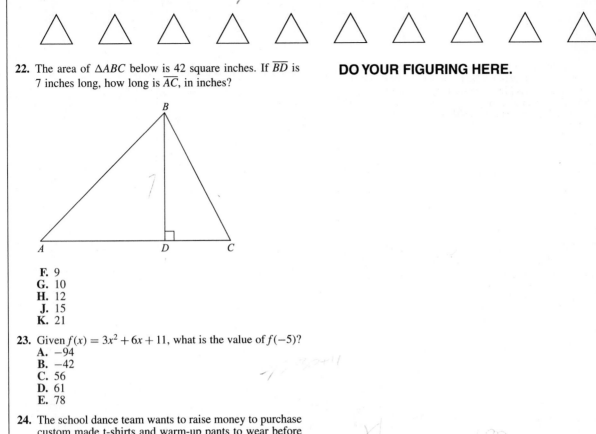

DO YOUR FIGURING HERE.

F. 9
G. 10
H. 12
J. 15
K. 21

23. Given $f(x) = 3x^2 + 6x + 11$, what is the value of $f(-5)$?
A. -94
B. -42
C. 56
D. 61
E. 78

24. The school dance team wants to raise money to purchase custom made t-shirts and warm-up pants to wear before competitions. The team decides to sell boxes of cookies for $2.50 each. For each of the first 100 boxes sold, the team will receive $0.60. For each of the next 200 sold, the team will receive $0.75. For each additional box of cookies sold, the team will receive $0.95. How many boxes must the team sell in order to reach its goal of raising $400.00?
F. 200
G. 383
H. 450
J. 500
K. 542

25. The table below shows the age distribution of the varsity football team at Washington High School.

Age, in years	15	16	17	18
Percent of team	8	22	32	38

What percent of the team is at least 17 years old?
A. 32%
B. 38%
C. 54%
D. 65%
E. 70%

26. What percent of $\frac{4}{8}$ is $\frac{1}{8}$?
F. 20%
G. 25%
H. 30%
J. 50%
K. 60%

GO ON TO THE NEXT PAGE.

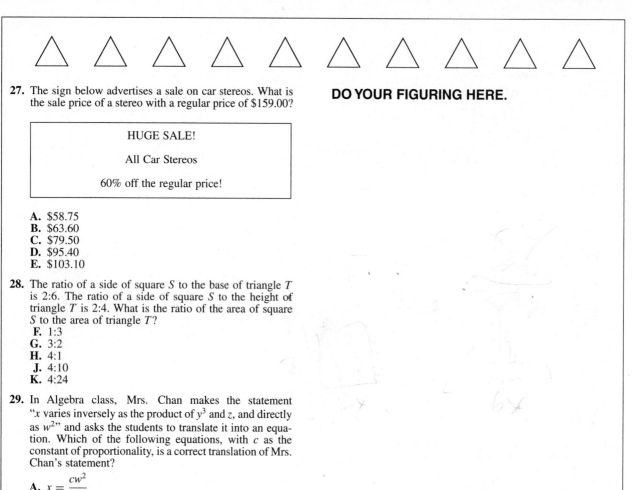

27. The sign below advertises a sale on car stereos. What is the sale price of a stereo with a regular price of $159.00?

> **HUGE SALE!**
>
> All Car Stereos
>
> 60% off the regular price!

- **A.** $58.75
- **B.** $63.60
- **C.** $79.50
- **D.** $95.40
- **E.** $103.10

28. The ratio of a side of square S to the base of triangle T is 2:6. The ratio of a side of square S to the height of triangle T is 2:4. What is the ratio of the area of square S to the area of triangle T?

- **F.** 1:3
- **G.** 3:2
- **H.** 4:1
- **J.** 4:10
- **K.** 4:24

29. In Algebra class, Mrs. Chan makes the statement "x varies inversely as the product of y^3 and z, and directly as w^2" and asks the students to translate it into an equation. Which of the following equations, with c as the constant of proportionality, is a correct translation of Mrs. Chan's statement?

- **A.** $x = \dfrac{cw^2}{y^3 z}$

- **B.** $x = \dfrac{cy^3 z}{w^2}$

- **C.** $x = \dfrac{w^2 y^3 z}{c}$

- **D.** $x = \dfrac{w^2}{cy^3 z}$

- **E.** $x = cw^2 y^3 z$

30. In a given isosceles triangle, the measure of each of the base angles is four times the measure of the vertex angle. What is the measure, in degrees, of the vertex angle?

- **F.** 20°
- **G.** 30°
- **H.** 45°
- **J.** 70°
- **K.** 80°

31. Two friends have formed their own business where they perform magic shows. For a single month, when x number of shows are performed, the friends' profit, P dollars, can be modeled by $P = x^2 - 30x - 1,000$. What is the least number of shows that the friends must perform in order for them not to lose money in any given month?

- **A.** 20
- **B.** 35
- **C.** 50
- **D.** 62
- **E.** 71

DO YOUR FIGURING HERE.

GO ON TO THE NEXT PAGE.

Use the following information to answer Questions 32–34.

DO YOUR FIGURING HERE.

A student is taking a course in speed reading. The results of different reading tests to determine reading speed (words per minute) over an 8-week period are plotted on the graph below, which also shows the line of best fit based on those results.

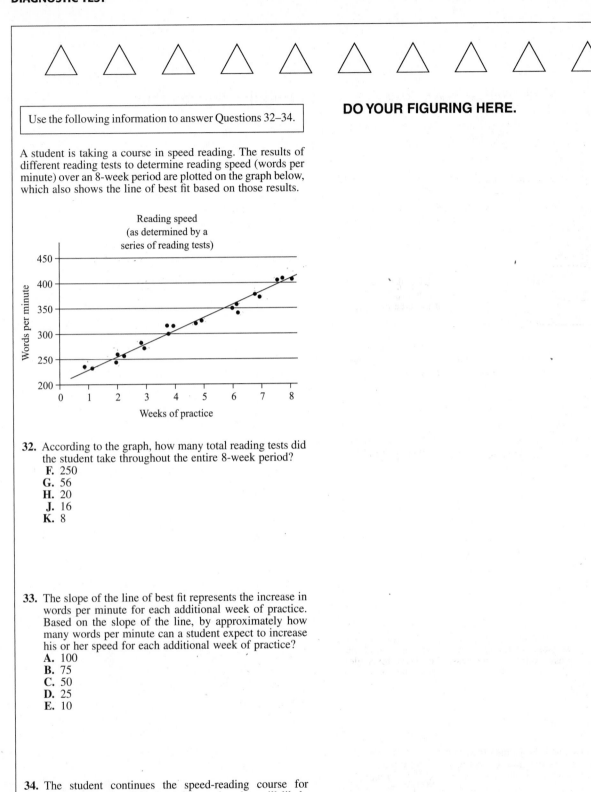

Reading speed
(as determined by a
series of reading tests)

32. According to the graph, how many total reading tests did the student take throughout the entire 8-week period?
  F. 250
  G. 56
  H. 20
  J. 16
  K. 8

33. The slope of the line of best fit represents the increase in words per minute for each additional week of practice. Based on the slope of the line, by approximately how many words per minute can a student expect to increase his or her speed for each additional week of practice?
  A. 100
  B. 75
  C. 50
  D. 25
  E. 10

34. The student continues the speed-reading course for another 8 weeks. Based on the graph, what will likely be the student's reading speed (words per minute) at the end of 16 weeks?
  F. 200
  G. 600
  H. 800
  J. 1600
  K. Cannot be determined from the given information.

GO ON TO THE NEXT PAGE.

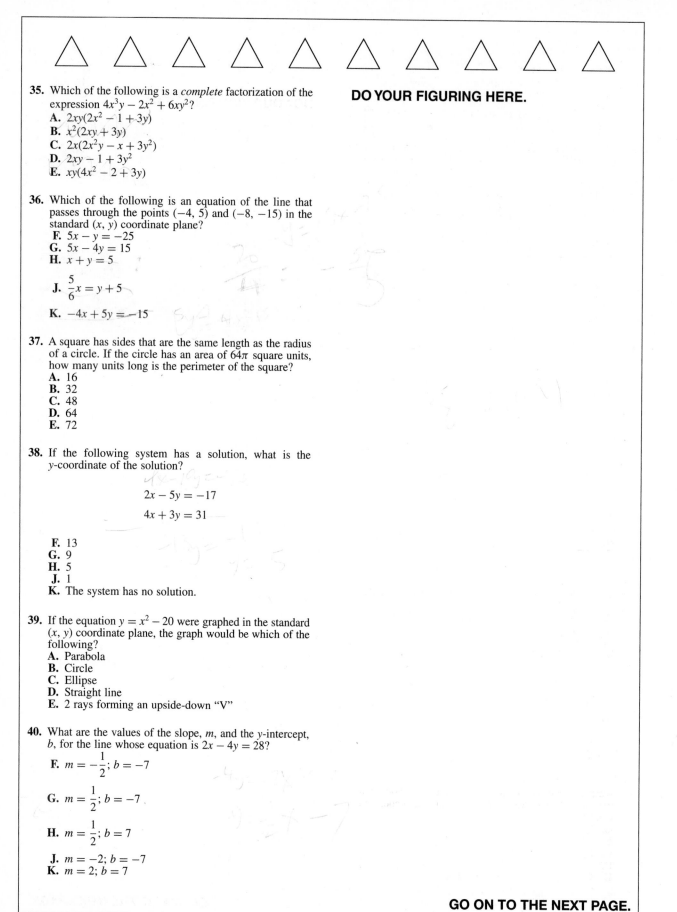

35. Which of the following is a *complete* factorization of the expression $4x^3y - 2x^2 + 6xy^2$?

A. $2xy(2x^2 - 1 + 3y)$
B. $x^2(2xy + 3y)$
C. $2x(2x^2y - x + 3y^2)$
D. $2xy - 1 + 3y^2$
E. $xy(4x^2 - 2 + 3y)$

36. Which of the following is an equation of the line that passes through the points $(-4, 5)$ and $(-8, -15)$ in the standard (x, y) coordinate plane?

F. $5x - y = -25$
G. $5x - 4y = 15$
H. $x + y = 5$

J. $\dfrac{5}{6}x = y + 5$

K. $-4x + 5y = -15$

37. A square has sides that are the same length as the radius of a circle. If the circle has an area of 64π square units, how many units long is the perimeter of the square?

A. 16
B. 32
C. 48
D. 64
E. 72

38. If the following system has a solution, what is the y-coordinate of the solution?

$$2x - 5y = -17$$

$$4x + 3y = 31$$

F. 13
G. 9
H. 5
J. 1
K. The system has no solution.

39. If the equation $y = x^2 - 20$ were graphed in the standard (x, y) coordinate plane, the graph would be which of the following?

A. Parabola
B. Circle
C. Ellipse
D. Straight line
E. 2 rays forming an upside-down "V"

40. What are the values of the slope, m, and the y-intercept, b, for the line whose equation is $2x - 4y = 28$?

F. $m = -\dfrac{1}{2}; b = -7$

G. $m = \dfrac{1}{2}; b = -7$

H. $m = \dfrac{1}{2}; b = 7$

J. $m = -2; b = -7$
K. $m = 2; b = 7$

DO YOUR FIGURING HERE.

GO ON TO THE NEXT PAGE.

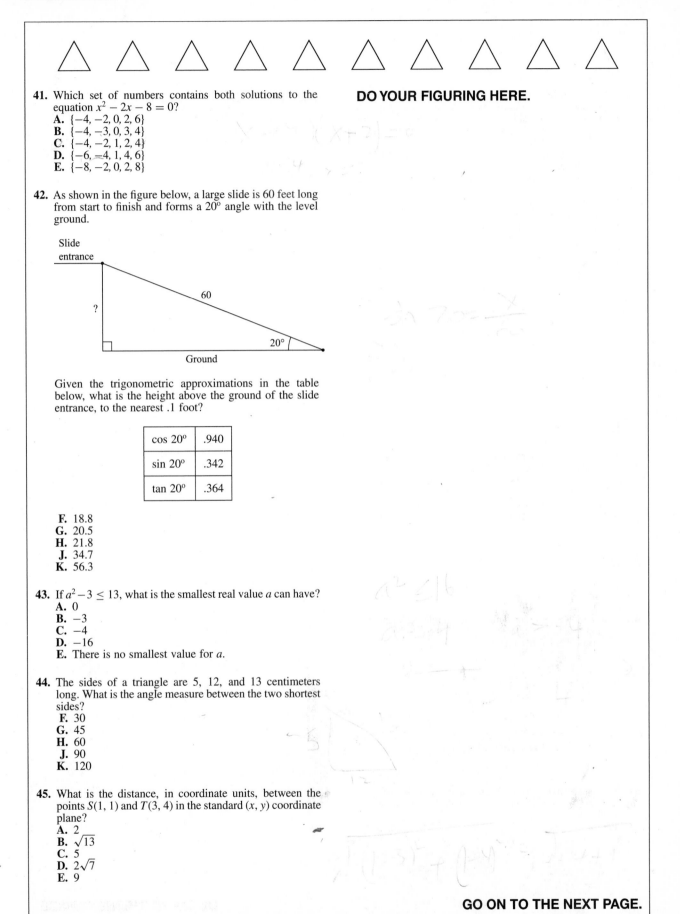

41. Which set of numbers contains both solutions to the equation $x^2 - 2x - 8 = 0$?
   A. $\{-4, -2, 0, 2, 6\}$
   B. $\{-4, -3, 0, 3, 4\}$
   C. $\{-4, -2, 1, 2, 4\}$
   D. $\{-6, -4, 1, 4, 6\}$
   E. $\{-8, -2, 0, 2, 8\}$

42. As shown in the figure below, a large slide is 60 feet long from start to finish and forms a 20° angle with the level ground.

Slide entrance

60

?

20°

Ground

Given the trigonometric approximations in the table below, what is the height above the ground of the slide entrance, to the nearest .1 foot?

cos 20°	.940
sin 20°	.342
tan 20°	.364

   F. 18.8
   G. 20.5
   H. 21.8
   J. 34.7
   K. 56.3

43. If $a^2 - 3 \le 13$, what is the smallest real value a can have?
   A. 0
   B. -3
   C. -4
   D. -16
   E. There is no smallest value for a.

44. The sides of a triangle are 5, 12, and 13 centimeters long. What is the angle measure between the two shortest sides?
   F. 30
   G. 45
   H. 60
   J. 90
   K. 120

45. What is the distance, in coordinate units, between the points $S(1, 1)$ and $T(3, 4)$ in the standard (x, y) coordinate plane?
   A. 2
   B. $\sqrt{13}$
   C. 5
   D. $2\sqrt{7}$
   E. 9

DO YOUR FIGURING HERE.

GO ON TO THE NEXT PAGE.

46. Two friends, Erin and Pete, leave in separate cars at the same time from the same location to go on a ski trip. An hour into the drive, Erin stops to get gas, while Pete continues at a constant speed of 62 mph. By the time Erin gets back on the freeway, Pete is 8 miles ahead of her. Erin drives at 69 mph to catch up to Pete. Which of the following equations, when solved for t, gives the number of minutes it will take Erin to catch up to Pete?
　F. $62t + 8 = 69t$
　G. $1.03t + 8 = 1.15t$

　H. $\dfrac{8 + 1.15t}{1.15t} = 1.03t$

　J. $1.03t - 8 = 1.15t$
　K. $1.15t = 10$

47. Which of the following defines the solution set for the system of inequalities shown below?

$$3x - 5 > 4$$
$$x + 2 \le 10$$

　A. $x \le 8$
　B. $x > 9$
　C. $9 < x \le 10$
　D. $-3 < x \le 8$
　E. $3 < x \le 8$

48. At Northern College, 42 juniors are enrolled in a theater class and 29 juniors are enrolled in a computer graphics class. Of these juniors, 18 are enrolled in both classes. How many of the 104 juniors at Northern College are NOT enrolled in either a theater or a computer graphics class?
　F. 4
　G. 25
　H. 33
　J. 46
　K. 51

49. If two lines in the standard (x, y) coordinate plane are parallel and the slope of one of the lines is -2, what is the slope of the other line?
　A. -2

　B. $-\dfrac{1}{2}$

　C. 0

　D. $-\dfrac{1}{2}$

　E. 2

50. In the standard (x, y) coordinate plane, $(6, 10)$ is half-way between $(c, 2c - 5)$ and $(3c, c + 16)$. What is the value of c?
　F. -2
　G. 0
　H. 3
　J. 5
　K. 9

DO YOUR FIGURING HERE.

GO ON TO THE NEXT PAGE.

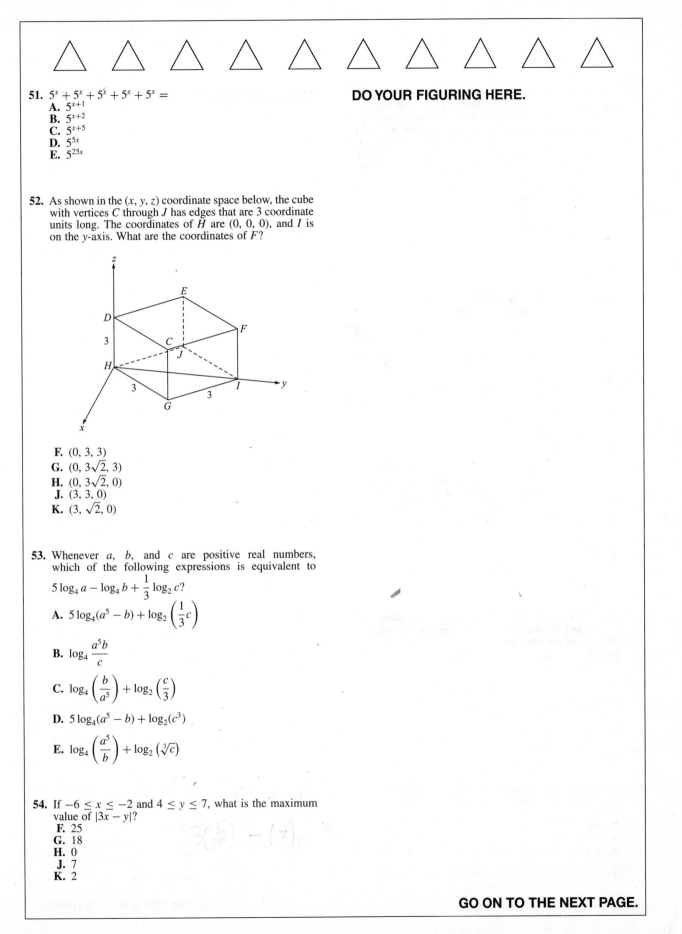

51. $5^x + 5^x + 5^x + 5^x + 5^x =$
   A. 5^{x+1}
   B. 5^{x+2}
   C. 5^{x+5}
   D. 5^{5x}
   E. 5^{25x}

DO YOUR FIGURING HERE.

52. As shown in the (x, y, z) coordinate space below, the cube with vertices C through J has edges that are 3 coordinate units long. The coordinates of H are $(0, 0, 0)$, and I is on the y-axis. What are the coordinates of F?

   F. $(0, 3, 3)$
   G. $(0, 3\sqrt{2}, 3)$
   H. $(0, 3\sqrt{2}, 0)$
   J. $(3, 3, 0)$
   K. $(3, \sqrt{2}, 0)$

53. Whenever a, b, and c are positive real numbers, which of the following expressions is equivalent to $5 \log_4 a - \log_4 b + \dfrac{1}{3} \log_2 c$?

   A. $5 \log_4(a^5 - b) + \log_2\left(\dfrac{1}{3}c\right)$

   B. $\log_4 \dfrac{a^5 b}{c}$

   C. $\log_4\left(\dfrac{b}{a^5}\right) + \log_2\left(\dfrac{c}{3}\right)$

   D. $5 \log_4(a^5 - b) + \log_2(c^3)$

   E. $\log_4\left(\dfrac{a^5}{b}\right) + \log_2\left(\sqrt[3]{c}\right)$

54. If $-6 \le x \le -2$ and $4 \le y \le 7$, what is the maximum value of $|3x - y|$?
   F. 25
   G. 18
   H. 0
   J. 7
   K. 2

GO ON TO THE NEXT PAGE.

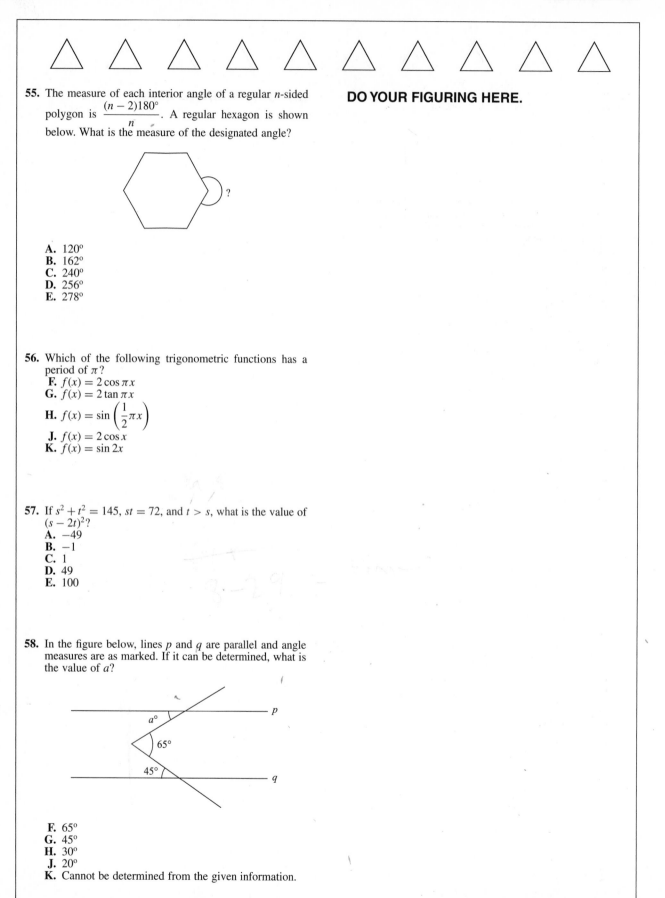

55. The measure of each interior angle of a regular *n*-sided polygon is $\dfrac{(n-2)180°}{n}$. A regular hexagon is shown below. What is the measure of the designated angle?

A. 120°
B. 162°
C. 240°
D. 256°
E. 278°

56. Which of the following trigonometric functions has a period of π?

F. $f(x) = 2\cos \pi x$
G. $f(x) = 2\tan \pi x$
H. $f(x) = \sin\left(\dfrac{1}{2}\pi x\right)$
J. $f(x) = 2\cos x$
K. $f(x) = \sin 2x$

57. If $s^2 + t^2 = 145$, $st = 72$, and $t > s$, what is the value of $(s - 2t)^2$?

A. −49
B. −1
C. 1
D. 49
E. 100

58. In the figure below, lines *p* and *q* are parallel and angle measures are as marked. If it can be determined, what is the value of *a*?

F. 65°
G. 45°
H. 30°
J. 20°
K. Cannot be determined from the given information.

DO YOUR FIGURING HERE.

GO ON TO THE NEXT PAGE.

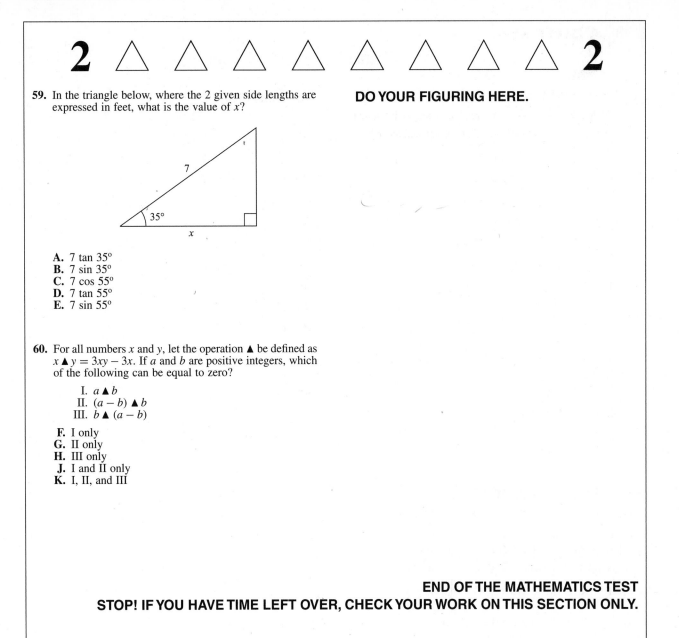

2 △ △ △ △ △ △ △ △ **2**

59. In the triangle below, where the 2 given side lengths are expressed in feet, what is the value of *x*?

DO YOUR FIGURING HERE.

A. 7 tan 35°
B. 7 sin 35°
C. 7 cos 55°
D. 7 tan 55°
E. 7 sin 55°

60. For all numbers *x* and *y*, let the operation ▲ be defined as $x \blacktriangle y = 3xy - 3x$. If *a* and *b* are positive integers, which of the following can be equal to zero?

    I. $a \blacktriangle b$
    II. $(a - b) \blacktriangle b$
    III. $b \blacktriangle (a - b)$

F. I only
G. II only
H. III only
J. I and II only
K. I, II, and III

END OF THE MATHEMATICS TEST
STOP! IF YOU HAVE TIME LEFT OVER, CHECK YOUR WORK ON THIS SECTION ONLY.

ANSWER KEY

Mathematics Test

1. C	16. K	31. C	46. G
2. J	17. C	32. H	47. E
3. D	18. J	33. D	48. K
4. K	19. A	34. G	49. A
5. B	20. J	35. C	50. H
6. F	21. D	36. F	51. A
7. A	22. H	37. B	52. G
8. G	23. C	38. H	53. E
9. D	24. J	39. A	54. F
10. H	25. E	40. G	55. C
11. B	26. G	41. C	56. K
12. H	27. B	42. G	57. E
13. C	28. F	43. C	58. J
14. F	29. A	44. J	59. E
15. C	30. F	45. B	60. K

SCORING WORKSHEET

On each ACT multiple-choice test (English, Mathematics, Reading, and Science Reasoning) you will receive a SCALED SCORE on a scale of 1 to 36. Use the following guidelines to determine your approximate SCALED SCORE on the ACT Mathematics Diagnostic Test that you just completed.

Step 1   Determine your RAW SCORE.

Your RAW SCORE is the number of questions that you answered correctly. Because there are 60 questions on the ACT Mathematics Test, the highest possible RAW SCORE is 60.

Step 2   Determine your SCALED SCORE using the following Scoring Worksheet.

Mathematics   _____ × **36** = _____ ÷ **60** = _____
                        RAW SCORE   **+ 1**   (*correction factor)

                                                                                    _____
                                                                                    SCALED SCORE

   *The correction factor is an approximation based on the average from several recent ACT tests. It is most valid for scores in the middle 50% (approximately 16–24 scaled composite score) of the scoring range. The scores are all approximate. Actual ACT scoring scales vary from one administration to the next based upon several factors.

Your SCALED SCORE should be rounded to the nearest number according to normal rules. For example, $31.2 \approx 31$ and $31.5 \approx 32$. If you answered 51 questions correctly on the Mathematics Test, for example, your SCALED SCORE would be 31 (30.6 rounded up).

ANSWERS AND EXPLANATIONS

1. **The correct answer is C.** This question asks you to calculate the average number of free throws that the team made per game in November. The number of free throws that the team attempted has no impact on the answer. Since the team played 8 games in November and made 102 free throws, the average number of free throws made per game is $102 \div 8$, which is 12.75. Round to the nearest 10th to get 12.8.

2. **The correct answer is J.** Perimeter is the sum of the lengths of all sides of a polygon. There are 2 sides of the polygon that are not given, so you must first find the lengths of these 2 sides. To find the first unknown subtract 6 from 11 to get 5 cm. The final unknown is $20 - 4 = 16$. Add up all of the sides to get the perimeter of the figure: $11 + 4 + 5 + 16 + 6 + 20 = 62$.

3. **The correct answer is D.** On this number line, the open circle at –5 and the line going to the right signifies that the number is *strictly greater than* –5. Eliminate answer choices A, B, and E. The line connects with a closed circle at 0, which signifies that the number is *less than or equal to* 0. Therefore, the inequality can be expressed as $-5 < x \leq 0$.

4. **The correct answer is K.** To solve this problem follow these steps:

   Substitute the values given for a and b, then perform the subtraction of the exponents:
   $1 - (-2) = 3$
   Compute the exponent: $3^3 = 27$
   Multiply 27 by 4: $27 \times 4 = 108$

5. **The correct answer is B.** This problem deals with factors of 24. Because –5 is not a factor of 24, it is not a possible value of z.

6. **The correct answer is F.** The formula for the volume of a rectangular prism is Volume = Length × Width × Height. Substitute the given values into the formula: $8 \times 6 \times 4 = 192$.

7. **The correct answer is A.** If the radio station sold all of the 45 60-second spots it would collect 270×45, or \$12,150. Eliminate answer choices B, D, and E. Since the 30-second spots each cost \$150, the amount the station collects from selling S of them would be $150S$. Therefore, in total, the radio station would collect $150S + 12,150$.

8. **The correct answer is G.** In this problem, angle *WXZ* ($4x°$) and angle *YXZ* ($8x°$) must add up to $180°$ because they form a straight line. Therefore, you can set up an equation and solve for x:

   $4x + 8x = 180$
   $12x = 180$
   $x = 15$

   You are given that the measure of angle *WXZ* equals $4x°$, so angle *WXZ* must equal 4×15, or $60°$.

9. **The correct answer is D.** If Mickey is the first to draw a number from the hat, he has a chance to get any 1 of the 12 rooms available in the house. The probability that he will draw a room on the third floor can be expressed by $\frac{4}{12}$, since 4 out of the 12 rooms in the house are on the third floor. Simplifying this fraction gives a probability of $\frac{1}{3}$.

10. **The correct answer is H.** The correct representation of the toy store's sales on a graph should show low sales when the new game first came out. Eliminate answer choice K because it shows initial sales higher than the other answer choices. Answer choice G shows a steady increase in sales, which does not correspond to the information given in the question. Only answer choice H shows low initial sales, followed by a period of growth, with sales tapering off and showing no growth after about 12 months.

11. **The correct answer is B.** The first step in solving this problem is to determine the area of one side of the wall (Area = Length × Height): $120 \times 8 = 960$ square feet. Because one can of paint covers 25 square feet, the students would need $960 \div 25$, or 38.4 cans of paint. The students need more than 38 cans, so they will have to purchase at least 39 cans of paint to have enough to paint the entire wall.

12. **The correct answer is H.** Remember that ratios can be expressed as fractions; $3x$ to $7y = \frac{3x}{7y}$, and $6x$ to $7y = \frac{6x}{7y}$. Therefore, you can set up an equation using fractions to compare the ratios given in the question:

   $$\text{If } \frac{3x}{7y} = \frac{1}{7}, \text{ then } \frac{6x}{7y} = ?$$

Notice that the denominator is the same on the left side of both equations ($7y$). This means that the denominator will be the same on the right side of both equations as well. Now you know that the denominator will be 7, and you can eliminate answer choices G, J, and K. Notice that the numerator in the second fraction ($6x$) is two times the numerator in the first fraction ($3x$). If $3x = 1$, then $6x = 2$. The final ratio is $\frac{2}{7}$, or 2 to 7.

13. **The correct answer is C.** To solve this problem, you must first calculate the percentage of students who prefer to rollerblade to class. Do this by adding up the percentage from the other preferred methods ($35 + 20 + 25 + 15 = 95$), and subtracting it from 100 ($100 - 95 = 5$). This shows that 5% of the students prefer to rollerblade. To solve for the total number of students surveyed, set up a proportion (75 students represent 5% of those surveyed, and x students represent 100%):

$$\frac{75}{5} = \frac{x}{100}$$
$$5x = 7,500$$
$$x = 1,500$$

14. **The correct answer is F.** This problem requires simple division and approximation. The number of revolutions that the tire will make can be expressed by the distance the motorcycle traveled (6,600 inches) divided by the circumference of the tire (65 inches). $6,600 \div 65 = 101.54$. Round up to 102.

15. **The correct answer is C.** To solve this problem, distribute the subtraction (negative sign) over the second quantity ($-2x + 8 - x^2$) to get $2x - 8 + x^2$, then group like terms together:

$$3x^2 + x^2 - 7x + 2x + 5 - 8$$

Add like terms:

$$4x^2 - 5x - 3$$

16. **The correct answer is K.** To most easily solve this problem, start at the end and work your way back. Ryan is left with $34 after all of the purchases. The 2 bags of popcorn cost $6 total, which means he had $40 before buying them. The $40 represents $\frac{2}{3}$ of the money Ryan started with, since he gave his sister $\frac{1}{3}$ of his total amount to buy tickets and hot dogs. To determine how much money he started with, set up an equation:

$$\frac{2}{3}x = 40$$

Multiply both sides by the inverse of the fraction to isolate x on the left side

$$\frac{3}{2}\left(\frac{2}{3}x\right) = 40\left(\frac{3}{2}\right)$$
$$x = 60$$

This means that Ryan's sister spent $20 ($60 - 40$) on tickets and hot dogs. You are given that the bleacher seats cost $8 each, so she spent $16 ($8 \times 2$) on them. That leaves $4 to be spent on the two hot dogs, so each hot dog must have cost $2.

17. **The correct answer is C.** This problem can be solved by testing each of the possible answers. The correct answer should indicate a whole number of questions answered correctly, as there is no way to answer a fraction of a question correctly on the quiz.

Answer choice A: $0.71 \times 15 = 10.65$
Answer choice B: $0.73 \times 15 = 10.95$
Answer choice C: $0.80 \times 15 = 12$
Answer choice D: $0.86 \times 15 = 12.9$
Answer choice E: $0.93 \times 15 = 13.95$

This shows that the only possible percentage of questions answered correctly is 80%, which is 12 out of 15 questions answered correctly.

18. **The correct answer is J.** A geometric sequence is a sequence such that each successive term is obtained from the previous term by multiplying that term by a fixed number called a common ratio. To get from $-\frac{1}{9}$ to $\frac{1}{3}$, you need to multiply $-\frac{1}{9}$ by -3. To make sure that this is the correct common ratio, try it for remaining numbers ($\frac{1}{3} \times -3 = -1$, and $-1 \times -3 = 3$.) The 5th term will be 3×-3, or -9.

19. **The correct answer is A.** In this problem, $(5a - 2b)^2$ can be expressed as $(5a - 2b)(5a - 2b)$. Use the FOIL method to solve:

$$25a^2 - 10ab - 10ab + 4b^2$$
$$25a^2 - 20ab + 4b^2$$

20. **The correct answer is J.** To calculate the area of the rectangular-shaped garden, multiply the length by the width: $32 \times 8 = 256$. You are given that the new square-shaped garden also has an area of 256. Since the area of a square with side x is x^2, the side of a square with area 256 can be found by taking the square root of 256; $\sqrt{256} = 16$.

21. **The correct answer is D.** To solve this problem, follow these steps, and remember the negative signs:

$$4x - (-2x + 5) = -3$$
$$4x + 2x - 5 = -3$$

Combine like terms and add 5 to both sides

$6x = 2$

Divide both sides by 6

$x = \dfrac{1}{3}$

22. **The correct answer is H.** The area of a triangle is given by the formula $A = \dfrac{1}{2}bh$, where b represents the base and h represents the height of the triangle. In this particular triangle, $\overline{AC}$ is the base, and $\overline{BD}$ (7 inches) is the height. Given this information, you can set up an equation to solve for $\overline{AC}$.

$42 = \dfrac{1}{2}(b)(7)$

Multiply by the inverse of $\dfrac{1}{2}$ on both sides.

$(2)42 = (2)\dfrac{1}{2}(b)(7)$
$84 = 7b$

Divide both sides by 7.

$b = 12$

The length of $\overline{AC}$ is 12 inches.

23. **The correct answer is C.** To determine the value of $f(-5)$, simply replace each instance of x in the equation with -5:

$f(-5) = 3(-5)^2 + 6(-5) + 11$
$f(-5) = 3(25) - 30 + 11$
$f(-5) = 75 - 30 + 11$
$f(-5) = 56$

24. **The correct answer is J.** To determine how many boxes the team must sell to meet its goal, you must calculate the total amount of money earned from possible sales:

For the first 100 boxes, the team will earn $100 \times 0.60 = \$60.00$

For the next 200, the team will earn $200 \times 0.75 = \$150.00$

If the team sells 300 boxes of cookies it will earn $210.00, which is $190.00 short of its goal. You are given that for each additional box the team sells, it will earn $0.95. Set up an equation to see how many more boxes the team needs to sell:

$0.95x = 190$
$x = 200$

In total, the team needs to sell $100 + 200 + 200$, or 500 boxes of cookies to meet its goal.

25. **The correct answer is E.** This question asks what percent of the team is *at least* 17 years old, so the only ages that apply would be 17 and 18. Since 32% of the team is 17, and 38% is 18, the percent that is at least 17 is given by $32 + 38$, or 70% of the team.

26. **The correct answer is G.** To answer this question, recognize that $\dfrac{1}{8}$ goes into $\dfrac{4}{8}$ four times, so $\dfrac{1}{8}$ is 25 percent of $\dfrac{4}{8}$. Alternatively, you could convert the fractions to their decimal equivalents and set up a proportion:

$\dfrac{1}{8} = 0.125$

$\dfrac{4}{8} = 0.50$

0.125 is to 0.50 as x is to 100

$\dfrac{0.125}{0.5} = \dfrac{x}{100}$

$0.5x = 0.125 \times 100$
$0.5x = 12.5$
$x = 25$

27. **The correct answer is B.** This problem can be solved in two different ways. First, you can calculate the amount that is being deducted from the original price during the sale and then subtract this amount from the original price. If the stereo is normally $159.00 and is being sold at 60% off, that means the price is reduced by 159×0.6, or $95.40. The stereo would then sell for $159 − \$95.4$, or $63.60. Alternatively, because the stereo is 60% off the original price, you could simply say that it is being sold for 40% of its regular price: $159 \times 0.4 = \$63.60$.

28. **The correct answer is F.** This problem deals with area and ratios. You are given that the ratio of one side of the square to the base of the triangle is 2:6, and that the ratio of another side of the square to the height of the triangle is 2:4. The area of the square is 2×2, or 4 because the area of a square is reached by multiplying two sides. The area of the triangle is $\dfrac{1}{2}(6)(4)$, or 12, since the area for a triangle is given by $A = \dfrac{1}{2}bh$. Therefore, the ratio of the area of the square to the area of the triangle would be 4:12, which can be reduced to 1:3.

29. **The correct answer is A.** In this problem, you are given an inverse variable expression and also a direct variable expression. The answer will be in the form of a fraction, with the direct expression as the numerator and the inverse expression as the denominator. To find the numerator, multiply

by the constant of proportionality, which gives you cw^2. The denominator is "the product of y^3 and z", which is y^3z. Therefore, the answer is expressed as:

$$x = \frac{cw^2}{y^3z}$$

30. The correct answer is F. In an isosceles triangle, two of the sides and two of the angles have the same measurement. This particular triangle has base angles that are 4 times greater than the vertex angle. Since the 3 angles must still add up to $180°$, you can set up an equation:

$$4x + 4x + x = 180$$
$$9x = 180$$
$$x = 20$$

The vertex angle measures $20°$.

31. The correct answer is C. To solve this problem, calculate the number of magic shows the friends must perform each month in order not to lose money on their business. Recognize that this means they will "break even"; that is, their profit will be $0. The equation giving their profit ($P = x^2 - 30x - 1,000$) must equal 0. Try each answer choice to see which one yields a profit of $0:

Answer choice A: $20^2 - 30(20) - 1000 = -1200$; 20 shows gives a loss of $1,200

Answer choice B: $35^2 - 30(35) - 1000 = -825$; 35 shows gives a loss of $825

Answer choice C: $50^2 - 30(50) - 1000 = 0$; 50 shows gives no loss or profit

There is no need to go any further because you have found the number of performances which yields zero loss and zero profit. Therefore, the friends are not losing money.

32. The correct answer is H. According to the information provided, the results of each test are plotted on the graph. There are 20 different points plotted on the graph, each corresponding to the results of a different reading test.

33. The correct answer is D. Looking at the values on the y-axis of the graph, you can see that the student's reading speed increases by approximately 50 words per minute every 2 weeks (Week 1 = 225 wpm, Week 2 = 250 wpm, and so on). Thus, each week the student will increase his or her reading speed by approximately 25 words per minute.

34. The correct answer is G. According to the graph, the student's reading speed increases by 50 words per minute every 2 weeks. Therefore, after an additional 8 weeks, it is likely that the student's reading speed will have increased by 200 words per minute

(50×4), meaning that the student should be able to read at $400 + 200$, or 600 words per minute.

35. The correct answer is C. To properly factor this expression, you must first find the Greatest Common Factor (GCF). Determine the largest monomial that can be divided out of each of the terms. Looking strictly at the numbers (4, 2, 6), the GCF is 2. Looking at the variables (x^3y, x^2, xy^2), the GCF is x. So $2x$ is the GCF for the expression. Now perform the necessary multiplication to match the original expression:

First term: $4x^3y = 2x \times \mathbf{2x^2y}$
Second term: $2x^2 = 2x \times \mathbf{-x}$
Third term: $6xy^2 = 2x \times \mathbf{3y^2}$

Therefore, the answer is $2x(2x^2y - x + 3y^2)$.

36. The correct answer is F. To find the equation of a line passing through two points, you must first determine the slope of the line, given by $\dfrac{(y_2 - y_1)}{(x_2 - x_1)}$:

$$\frac{(-15 - 5)}{(-8 - (-4))}$$
$$= \frac{(-15 - 5)}{(-8 + 4)}$$
$$= \frac{-20}{-4} = 5$$

Next, choose one of the points on the line and write an equation in slope-intercept form ($y = mx + b$, where m is the slope), to find the y-intercept (b). Using the point $(-4, 5)$ will yield an equation that looks like this:

$$y = 5x + b$$
$$5 = 5(-4) + b$$
$$5 = -20 + b$$
$$25 = b$$

This gives you an equation of $y = 5x + 25$ in slope-intercept form. Convert this to standard form ($Ax + By = C$):

$$y = 5x + 25$$
$$5x = y - 25$$
$$5x - y = -25$$

37. The correct answer is B. Since you are given that the sides of the square are the same length as the radius of the circle, you must first calculate this radius. The area of the circle is given as 64π, and the formula for area of a circle is given by $A = \pi r^2$. Use this equation to solve for the radius:

$$64\pi = \pi r^2$$
$$64 = r^2$$
$$r = 8$$

Now you know that each side of the square equals 8 units. Therefore, the perimeter of the square would be $8 + 8 + 8 + 8$, or 32.

38. The correct answer is H. One way to solve this system of equations is to multiply one of them by a number which would allow you to eliminate one of the variables and isolate the other. In this system multiply the top equation by -2:

$$-2(2x - 5y = -17)$$
$$-4x + 10y = 34$$

Now, when you add the two equations together, you can solve for y.

$$-4x + 10y = 34$$
$$\underline{+4x + 3y = 31}$$
$$0 + 13y = 65$$
$$13y = 65$$
$$y = 5$$

39. The correct answer is A. The formula for the classic parabola is $y = x^2$; therefore, the equation $y = x^2 - 20$ is the same parabola translated down by 20 units.

40. The correct answer is G. To solve, convert the equation $2x - 4y = 28$ to slope-intercept form ($y = mx + b$, where m is the slope and b is the y-intercept) by solving for y:

$$2x - 4y = 28$$
$$-4y = -2x + 28$$
$$y = \frac{-2}{-4}x + \frac{28}{-4} \qquad y = \frac{1}{2}x - 7$$

Now that the equation is in slope-intercept form, it is easy to see that $m = \dfrac{1}{2}$ and $b = -7$

41. The correct answer is C. To solve, find the values of x for which $x^2 - 2x - 8 = 0$ is true. There are several ways to solve quadratic equations such as this. In this case, factoring is probably the most efficient. To factor $x^2 - 2x - 8$, think of two numbers that multiply to get -8 and add to get -2. Two such numbers are -4 and 2. The factored form is then $(x - 4)(x + 2)$. Now think about the values of x that make $(x - 4)(x + 2) = 0$ true; $(x - 4) = 0$ or $(x + 2) = 0$. Solving both of these equations yields $x = 4$ or $x = -2$. The only list that contains both the numbers 4 and -2 is $\{-4, -2, 1, 2, 4\}$, or answer choice C.

42. The correct answer is G. In this problem, you are given the length of the slide (60 ft) and the angle it forms with the level ground ($20°$). You are asked to solve for the height of the slide entrance. Since this side of the triangle is opposite to the $20°$ angle,

you can use the sin function of this angle to find the height:

$$\sin 20° = \frac{x}{60} \qquad \text{(sin} = \text{opposite/hypotenuse)}$$

$$0.342 = \frac{x}{60} \qquad \text{(you are given that}$$
$$\sin 20° = 0.342)$$

$$20.52 = x \qquad \text{(multiply both sides by 60)}$$

Rounding to the nearest 0.1 foot, the slide entrance is approximately 20.5 feet high.

43. The correct answer is C. If $a^2 - 3 \leq 13$, then $a^2 \leq 16$. The values of a for which $a^2 = 16$ are $a = 4$ and $a = -4$. Therefore $-4 \leq a \leq 4$. The smallest value that a can have is -4.

44. The correct answer is J. To solve this problem quickly, recognize that the triangle described is a right triangle, where $a^2 + b^2 = c^2$. Therefore, the longest side (13 cm) is the hypotenuse, and the right angle will be between the 2 shortest sides, which are the legs (5 cm and 12 cm).

45. The correct answer is B. The formula for the distance between two points on the x, y coordinate plane is given by $\sqrt{(x_2 - x_1) + (y_2 - y_1)}$. Substitute the numbers from the given points into this equation:

$$\sqrt{(3 - 1)^2 + (4 - 1)^2}$$
$$\sqrt{(2)^2 + (3)^2}$$
$$\sqrt{4 + 9}$$
$$\sqrt{13}$$

The distance between the two points is $\sqrt{13}$.

46. The correct answer is G. In order to determine how many minutes it will take Erin to catch up to Pete, you must first convert their respective driving speeds into minutes. (The answer choices should give you a clue.) If Pete is driving 62 miles per hour, he is driving $\dfrac{62}{60}$, or 1.03 miles per minute. Likewise, if Erin is driving 69 mph, she is driving at $\dfrac{69}{60}$, or 1.15 miles per minute. When Erin gets back on the freeway, Pete is 8 miles ahead of her, so the equation can be expressed as $1.03t + 8 = 1.15t$.

47. The correct answer is E. To find the solution set for this system of inequalities, simply solve each of the inequalities:

$$\left.\begin{array}{l} 3x - 5 > 4 \\ 3x > 9 \\ x > 3 \end{array}\right\} \text{First inequality}$$

$$\left.\begin{array}{l} x + 2 \leq 10 \\ x \leq 8 \end{array}\right\} \text{Second inequality}$$

After solving both inequalities, you are left with $3 < x \leq 8$, which represents the solution set for both inequalities.

48. **The correct answer is K.** There are 42 juniors enrolled in a theater class, and 29 enrolled in a computer graphics class. This gives a total of 71 juniors enrolled in one or both of the classes. However, since 18 juniors are enrolled in *both* classes, there are really only 53 individual juniors total enrolled in these classes (subtract 18 from 71). Since there are 104 juniors at Northern College, $104 - 53$, or 51 juniors are not enrolled in either class.

49. **The correct answer is A.** Lines that are parallel have the same slope, whereas lines that are perpendicular have slopes that are opposite reciprocals. Since these two lines are parallel, both have a slope of -2.

50. **The correct answer is H.** The formula for finding the midpoint on a line segment is given by $\left(\dfrac{x_1 + x_2}{2}, \dfrac{y_1 + y_2}{2}\right)$. In this problem, you are given the coordinates of the midpoint, and are asked to solve for c. To solve, set up an equation for either x or y (we've chosen x):

$\dfrac{x_1 + x_2}{2} = 6$ (6 is the x coordinate of the given midpoint)

$\dfrac{c + 3c}{2} = 6$ (c and $3c$ are the x coordinates of the two given points on the line)

$\dfrac{4c}{2} = 6$

$2c = 6$

$c = 3$

51. **The correct answer is A.** To solve this problem, you must recall the rules governing exponents. First, simplify the equation, as shown below:

$5^x + 5^x + 5^x + 5^x + 5^x = 5(5^x)$

5 is equivalent to 5^1, and when you multiply like coefficients with exponents, you must add the exponents. Therefore, $5^1(5^x) = 5^{x+1}$.

52. **The correct answer is G.** Within the cube, HI bisects the side $HGIJ$ and forms two equal triangles. Since you are given that two of the sides of the triangle each measure 3, you can use the Pythagorean theorem to find the length of HI:

$3^2 + 3^2 = x^2$
$9 + 9 = x^2$
$18 = x^2$
$\sqrt{x^2} = \sqrt{18}$
$x = \sqrt{9 \times 2}$
$x = 3\sqrt{2}$

The length of HI is $3\sqrt{2}$. This means that I is located at $3\sqrt{2}$ on the y-axis. As for point F, it is located directly above point H which is on the y-axis, so its x-coordinate is 0. It is similar to I as it is located at $3\sqrt{2}$ on the y-axis, and is similar to D as it is located at 3 on the z-axis. Therefore, the coordinates for F are $(0, 3\sqrt{2}, 3)$.

53. **The correct answer is E.** To simplify $5\log_4 a - \log_4 b + \dfrac{1}{3}\log_2 c$, first recall the properties of logarithms. The expression $5\log_4 a$ can be written as $\log_4 a^5$. Likewise, $\dfrac{1}{3}\log_2 c$ can be written as $\log_2 c^{1/3}$, or $\log_2\left(\sqrt[3]{c}\right)$. Also because $5\log_4 a - \log_4 b$ are both logs of base 4, they can be combined to make $\log_4\left(\dfrac{a^5}{b}\right)$. Therefore the expression $5\log_4 a - \log_4 b + \dfrac{1}{3}\log_2 c$ can be written as $\log_4\left(\dfrac{a^5}{b}\right) + \log_2\left(\sqrt[3]{c}\right)$.

54. **The correct answer is F.** To find the maximum value in this problem, you simply need to get the highest number possible (within the limits set by the inequalities) within the absolute value signs. Because the absolute value will be positive, select a value for x that will result in the greatest value when multiplied by 3; $3 \times -6 = -18$. Likewise, select 7 for y because subtracting 7 from -18 will result in the largest possible number within the absolute value signs:

$|3x - y|$
$|3(-6) - 7|$
$|-18 - 7|$
$|-25| = 25$

55. **The correct answer is C.** Here you are given that the measure of each interior angle of an n-sided polygon is $\dfrac{(n-2)180}{n}$. Since this figure is a hexagon (6 sides), substitute 6 for n to find the measure of each interior angle:

$\dfrac{(6-2)180}{6} =$

$\dfrac{4 \times 180}{6} =$

$\dfrac{720}{6} = 120$

The measure of each interior angle is 120°; however, the question is asking for the measure of the exterior angle. Since the two must add up to

$360°$, the exterior angle can be found with a simple equation:

$$120 + x = 360$$
$$x = 240$$

56. The correct answer is K. By definition, $f(x) = a \times \sin(bx + c)$. The period of this function is given by $\frac{2\pi}{b}$. For $f(x) = \sin 2x$, the period is $\frac{2\pi}{2}$, which is equal to π.

57. The correct answer is E. To solve, first determine all of the factors of 72: 1 and 72, 2 and 36, 3 and 24, 4 and 18, 6 and 12, and 8 and 9. Only 8 and 9 satisfy the second requirement that $s^2 + t^2 = 145$ ($8^2 = 64$ and $9^2 = 81$; $64 + 81 = 145$). Since $t > s$, then $t = 9$ and $s = 8$. Therefore, $(s - 2t)^2 = [8 - 2(9)]^2 = (8 - 18)^2 = (-10)^2 = 100$.

58. The correct answer is J. Suppose the line that creates the $45°$ angle was extended to intersect line p, as shown below.

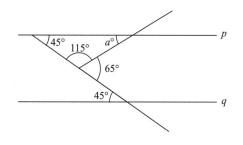

A triangle that includes the angle with measure $a°$ is created. The triangle also has angles $45°$ (alternate interior angles) and $180° - 65° = 115°$ (supplementary angles). Since there are $180°$ within a triangle, $a = 180 - 115 - 45 = 20°$.

59. The correct answer is E. To solve this problem, it makes sense to first find the missing angle measure. The three angles of a triangle must add up to $180°$:

$$35 + 90 + ? = 180$$
$$125 + ? = 180$$
$$? = 55$$

The missing angle measures $55°$. Using this angle, x represents the opposite side, while 7 is the hypotenuse. The trigonometric function using the opposite and hypotenuse sides is the sine function:

$$\sin = \text{opp/hyp}$$
$$\sin 55° = \frac{x}{7}$$
$$7 \sin 55° = x$$

60. The correct answer is K. To solve this problem, substitute the values a and b for x and y in each Roman numeral. Set the equations equal to zero, since you are asked to determine which of the Roman numerals can be equal to zero.

Roman Numeral I: Substitute a for x and b for y and set it equal to zero: $3ab - 3a = 0$. Factor out a $3a$: $3a(b - 1) = 0$. Since a cannot equal zero (it must be positive based on the information given in the problem), then $(b - 1) = 0$. Solving for b gives you $b = 1$. Since b is a positive integer, Roman numeral I can equal 0. Eliminate answer choices G and H, because they do not include Roman numeral I.

Roman Numeral II: Substitute $(a - b)$ for x and b for y and set it equal to zero: $3(a - b)b - 3(a - b) = 0$. Factor out $3(a - b)$: $3(a - b)(b - 1) = 0$. This is true if $a = b$ or if $b = 1$. Since either a or b can be a positive integer, Roman numeral II can equal 0. Eliminate answer choice F because it does not include Roman numeral II.

Roman Numeral III: Substitute b for x and $(a - b)$ for y and set it equal to zero: $3b(a - b) - 3b = 0$. Factor out $3b$: $3b[(a - b) - 1] = 0$. Since b cannot equal zero (it must be positive based on the information given in the problem), then $(a - b - 1) = 0$. Solving for a gives you $a = b + 1$, which can be a positive integer. Solving for b gives you $b = 1 - a$, which can also be a positive integer. So, Roman numeral III can equal 0. Eliminate answer choice J because it does not include Roman numeral III.

By the process of elimination, you are left with answer choice K.

CHAPTER 3

STRATEGIES AND TECHNIQUES

As mentioned in Chapter 1, the ACT Mathematics Test is designed to test your ability to reason mathematically, to understand basic math terminology, and to recall basic mathematics formulas and principles.

You will not receive credit for anything that you write in your test booklet, but you should work through the problems in the available space so that you can check your work. Be sure to do enough practice to determine just how much space you need to solve various problems. You can use whatever space is available, but you cannot move to another test section in search of blank space to solve your math problems.

If you don't know the answer to a question, mark it in your test booklet and come back to it later if you have time. Cross off answer choices that you are able to eliminate. Make an educated guess if you are able to eliminate even one answer choice. The answer choices correspond to the bubbles on your answer sheet.

You are not penalized for incorrect answers, so it is in your best interest to fill in every bubble on your answer sheet.

You can use an approved calculator to assist you in answering any of the multiple-choice questions, but none of the questions actually require the use of a calculator. If you do use your calculator, be sure that you are using it in the most efficient way possible; do not just accept an answer from your calculator as correct. Always try to predict the answer, and if the result of your calculations is nowhere close to what you predicted, then consider trying the problem again.

The following strategies and techniques will help you to correctly answer as many of the questions on your ACT Mathematics Test as possible:

- Apply Logic
- Draw Pictures
- Answer the Question That You Are Asked
- Don't Quit Early
- Test the Answers
- Substitute Numbers for the Variables
- Read the Questions Carefully

APPLY LOGIC

Even though you can use a calculator, most of the actual calculations are fairly simple. In fact, the ACT test writers are just as likely to test your logical reasoning ability or your ability to follow directions as they are to test your

Study Tip
Please visit www.act.org for a list of approved calculators. Generally, calculators with memory and print functions are not allowed. The list of approved calculators is periodically updated, so check the website a couple of weeks before your test.

ability to plug numbers into an equation. Consider the following example question:

> If $b - c = 2$, and $a + c = 16$, then $a + b = $?
> **A.** 8
> **B.** 14
> **C.** 16
> **D.** 18
> **E.** 32
>
> **The correct answer is D.** To solve this problem, first recognize that $(b - c) + (a + c) = a + b$. This is true because the c values cancel each other out, leaving you with $b + a$, which is equivalent to $a + b$. Therefore, $a + b$ must equal $2 + 16$, or 18.

▬▬ DRAW PICTURES

Many seemingly complex story-problems will become considerably easier if you are able to visualize them. This strategy should not take a lot of time and can help you avoid making careless errors. Your sketch doesn't have to be beautiful; it just has to accurately depict the relationships in the problem. Sometimes, you are given a figure or a table that you can work with (and write on); sometimes, you just have to make your own. Consider the following example question:

> The diagonal of a rectangular garden is 15 feet, and one side is 9 feet. What is the perimeter of the garden, in feet?
> **A.** 135
> **B.** 108
> **C.** 68
> **D.** 48
> **E.** 42
>
> **The correct answer is E.** To solve this problem, it is helpful to draw a picture, as shown below:

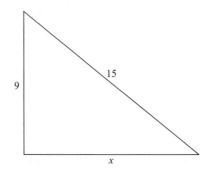

If a rectangular garden has a side of 9 feet and a diagonal of 15 feet, it forms a right triangle with leg 9 and hypotenuse 15. Using the Pythagorean Theorem, the length of the other leg, x, can be determined in the following equation:

$$15^2 = 9^2 + x^2$$
$$x^2 = 225 - 81$$
$$x^2 = 144$$
$$x = 12$$

The perimeter of the rectangle is therefore $2(9) + 2(12)$, or 42, answer choice E.

◼◼◼ ANSWER THE QUESTION THAT YOU ARE ASKED

If the problem requires three steps to reach a solution and you only completed two of the steps, it is likely that the answer you arrived at will be one of the choices. However, it will not be the correct choice! Consider the following example question:

The rectangular garden shown in the figure below has a stone border 2 feet in width on all sides. What is the area, in square feet, of that portion of the garden that excludes the border?

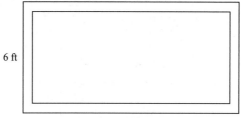

6 ft

12 ft

A. 4
B. 16
C. 40
D. 56
E. 72

The correct answer is B. This problem is asking for the area of the middle portion of the garden. To solve this problem, perform the following calculations, and remember that the border goes around the entire garden and therefore it should be deducted twice from each dimension. First, subtract the border width from the length of the garden:

$$12 - 2(2) = 8$$

Next, subtract the border width from the width of the garden:

$$6 - 2(2) = 2$$

The area (Length × Width) of the portion of the garden that excludes the border is 8 × 2, or 16.

If you only accounted for the border along one length and one width of the garden, you would have gotten answer choice C. Answer choice D is the area of the border around the garden. Answer choice E is the area of the entire garden, including the stone border.

◼◼◼ DON'T QUIT EARLY

Some of the questions on the ACT Mathematics Test will appear quite difficult the first time you look at them. Often though, you will be able to reason your way through the problem so that it makes sense. Keep in mind that these questions do not usually involve intensive calculations or complicated manipulations. Consider the following example question:

If $0 < pr < 1$, then which of the following CANNOT be true?
A. $p < 0$ and $r < 0$
B. $p < -1$ and $r < 0$
C. $p < -1$ and $r < -1$
D. $p < 1$ and $r < 1$
E. $p < 1$ and $r > 0$

The correct answer is C. At first glance, you might think that you don't have enough information to solve this problem. However, if you recognize that *pr* must be a positive fraction since it lies between 0 and 1, you can work your way through the answer choices and eliminate those that could be true.

> **Answer choice A:** If both *p* and *r* were less than 0, their product would be positive. It's possible for *pr* to be a positive fraction, because both *p* and *r* could be negative fractions, so eliminate answer choice A, because it could be true.
> **Answer choice B:** If *p* were −1 and *r* were also a negative number, their product would be positive. It's possible for *pr* to be a positive fraction, because *r* could be a negative fraction, so eliminate answer choice B, because it could be true.
> **Answer choice C:** If both *p* and *r* were less than −1, then *pr* would be greater than 1 (which violates the information given in the question), so this statement cannot be true, and answer choice C is correct.
> **Answer choice D:** If both *p* and *r* were less than 1, their product could be positive. It's possible for *pr* to be a positive fraction, because both *p* and *r* could be negative fractions, so eliminate answer choice D, because it could be true.
> **Answer choice E:** If *p* were less than 1, *p* could be a positive fraction. If *r* were greater than 0, it would be a positive number, and it's possible for *pr* to be a positive fraction; eliminate answer choice E, because it could be true.

Note: Once you arrive at the correct answer, it's not necessary to work through any remaining answer choices. We did it here just to show you that D and E are, in fact, incorrect.

TEST THE ANSWERS

Sometimes, the quickest way to answer an ACT mathematics question is to try the answer choices that they give you. The questions on the ACT Mathematics Test are often arranged in either ascending or descending order. It makes sense for most of these problems to "try" the middle value (choice C or choice H) first. If this middle value is too small, for example, you can then eliminate the other two smaller choices.

Additionally, if the question asks you for the greatest or smallest possible value, start with the middle value to determine if you are above or below the correct answer. Then work through the next smallest or largest remaining answer choices to verify that you have found the correct value. Remember that one of them is the correct choice. Consider the following example question:

If *x* is an integer and $y = 7x + 11$, what is the greatest value of *x* for which *y* is less than 50?
A. 7
B. 6
C. 5
D. 4
E. 3

The correct answer is C. Because the question asks for the greatest value of x, try answer choice C first, and substitute 5 for x:

Answer choice C: $y = 7(5) + 11 = 46$. This is less than 50, but you must be sure that it is the greatest possible value of x that works, so try the next largest answer.

Answer choice B: $y = 7(6) + 11 = 53$. This is not less than 50, so you can eliminate answer choice B and know that answer choice C is correct.

■ SUBSTITUTE NUMBERS FOR THE VARIABLES

You can sometimes simplify your work on a given problem by using actual numbers as "stand-ins" for variables. This strategy works when you have variables in the question and the same variables in the answer choices. You can simplify the answer choices by substituting actual numbers for the variables. Pick numbers that are easy to work with and that meet the parameters of the information given in the question. If you use this strategy, remember that numbers on the ACT Mathematics Test can be either positive or negative and are sometimes whole numbers and sometimes fractions. You should also be careful not to use 1 or 0 as your "stand-ins" because they can create "identities," which can lead to more than one seemingly correct answer choice.

In addition, it is sometimes necessary to try more than one number to see if the result always correctly responds to the question. If the numbers that you pick work for more than one answer choice, pick different numbers and try again.

Consider the following example questions:
Question 1:

If x and y are both positive even integers, which of the following must be even?

    I. x^y
   II. $(x + 1)^y$
  III. $x^{(y+1)}$

A. I only
B. II only
C. I and II only
D. I and III only
E. II and III only

The correct answer is D. The question states that both x and y are positive even integers. Therefore, you can pick any positive even integer and substitute that value for x and y in each of the Roman numeral choices, as follows:

Roman numeral I (x^y): $2^2 = 4$, which is even; $4^2 = 16$, which is also even. Any positive even integer raised to another positive even integer will result in an even number; therefore, Roman numeral I correctly answers the question. At this point, you could safely eliminate any answer choices that do not contain Roman numeral I.

Roman numeral II [$(x + 1)^y$]: $(2+1)^2 = 3^2 = 9$, which is odd; $(4+1)^2 = 5^2 = 25$, which is also odd. When you add 1 to a positive even integer and raise the sum to a positive even integer, the result will be odd; therefore, Roman numeral II does not correctly answer the question. At this point, you could safely eliminate any remaining answer choices that contain Roman numeral II.

Study Tip
When you pick numbers to substitute for the variables in a question, be sure to try both negative and positive numbers, unless the question indicates one or the other. For example, if the question states that $x < 5$, x could be a negative number.

Study Tip
Always take
each Roman
numeral as a
true/false
statement. As
you evaluate
the statements
to determine
whether they
are true or false
based on the
question,
eliminate
answer choices,
as we did in
the example
shown. This
process might
allow you to
arrive quickly
at the correct
answer without
looking at every
Roman
numeral
statement.

Roman numeral III ($x^{(y+1)}$): $2^{(2+1)} = 2^3 = 8$, which is even; $4^{(2+1)} = 4^3 = 64$, which is also even. Any positive even integer raised to an odd power will result in an even number; therefore, Roman numeral III correctly answers the question, and you can eliminate any remaining answer choices that do not contain Roman numeral III.

Question 2:

If a and b are positive consecutive odd integers, where $b > a$, which of the following is equal to $b^2 - a^2$?
F. $2a$
G. $4a$
H. $2a + 2$
J. $2a + 4$
K. $4a + 4$

The correct answer is K. You are given that both a and b are positive consecutive odd integers, and that b is greater than a. Pick two numbers that fit the criteria: $a = 3$ and $b = 5$. Now, substitute these numbers into $b^2 - a^2$: $5^2 = 25$ and $3^2 = 9$; therefore, $b^2 - a^2 = 16$. Now, plug the value that you selected for a into the answer choices until one of them yields 16, as follows:

$2(3) = 6$; eliminate answer choice F.
$4(3) = 12$; eliminate answer choice G.
$2(3) + 2 = 8$; eliminate answer choice H.
$2(3) + 4 = 10$; eliminate answer choice J.
$4(3) + 4 = 16$; answer choice K is correct.

READ THE QUESTIONS CAREFULLY

Read all of the questions carefully, so that you know exactly what operations you are being asked to perform. When attempting ratio problems, for example, note whether the question is giving a part-to-part ratio, or a part-to-whole ratio. The ratio of girls to boys in a class is a part-to-part ratio. The ratio of girls to students in a class is a part-to-whole ratio. Consider the following example question:

There are two types of candy in a bowl, chocolate and caramel. If the ratio of the number of pieces of chocolate candy to the number of pieces of caramel candy is 2:3, each of the following could be the total number of pieces of candy, EXCEPT:
A. 5
B. 12
C. 15
D. 20
E. 30

The correct answer is B. To solve this problem, you must realize that this is a part-to-part ratio of 2 pieces of chocolate candy to every 3 pieces of caramel candy. That means for every 5 pieces of candy, 2 are chocolate and 3 are caramel. In order for the ratio to be exactly 2:3, the total number of candies in the bowl must be a multiple of 5. All of the possible answer choices are multiples of 5 except answer choice B.

Note: This is a special kind of ACT problem, in that you are actually looking for the answer choice that is *not* true. Be especially cautious when answering these questions; don't just select the first "right" answer you see!

WHAT'S NEXT?

Chapter 4 reviews the content areas tested on the ACT Mathematics Test. If you need help with formulas and math terms, don't skip this chapter! Chapter 5 then gives you the opportunity to apply the strategies you just learned about and to continue building your math skills with dozens of practice questions and exercises.

PART II

ACT MATHEMATICS TEST CONTENT AREAS

CHAPTER 4

CONTENT AREAS TESTED

The ACT Mathematics Test questions are designed to measure your basic mathematical skills, as well as your ability to reason mathematically. You should be able to solve problems and apply relevant mathematics concepts in arithmetic, algebra, geometry, and data analysis.

This chapter provides a review of the mathematical concepts tested on the ACT Mathematics Test. Familiarize yourself with these basic mathematical concepts and be able to apply them to a variety of math problems.

- Pre-Algebra
- Elementary Algebra
- Intermediate Algebra
- Coordinate Geometry
- Plane Geometry
- Trigonometry

PRE-ALGEBRA

Pre-Algebra (7th-, or 8th-grade level) questions make up about 23 percent of the total number of questions on the ACT Mathematics Test. The questions test basic algebraic concepts such as:

1. Operations Using Whole Numbers, Fractions, and Decimals
2. Squares/Square Roots
3. Exponents
4. Scientific Notation
5. Mean, Median, and Mode
6. Ratios, Proportions, and Percent
7. Linear Equations with One Variable
8. Absolute Value
9. Simple Probability

Operations Using Whole Numbers, Decimals, and Fractions

The ACT Mathematics Test requires you to add, subtract, multiply, and divide whole numbers, fractions, and decimals. When performing these operations, be sure to keep track of negative signs and line up decimal points in order to eliminate careless mistakes.

These questions might involve basic arithmetic operations, operations involving decimals, factoring, percents, ratios, proportions, sequences, number sets, number lines, absolute value, and prime numbers.

The Properties of Integers

The following are properties of integers commonly tested on the ACT Mathematics Test:

- Integers include both positive and negative whole numbers.
- Zero is considered an integer.
- Consecutive integers follow one another and differ by 1. For example, 6, 7, 8, and 9 are consecutive integers. Likewise, 0, −1, −2, and −3 are consecutive integers.
- The value of a number does not change when multiplied by 1. For example, $13 \times 1 = 13$.

Real Numbers

The following are properties of real numbers commonly tested on the ACT Mathematics Test:

- All real numbers correspond to points on the number line, as shown below:

- All real numbers except zero are either positive or negative. On a number line, such as that shown above, numbers that correspond to points to the right of zero are positive, and numbers that correspond to points to the left of zero are negative.
- For any two numbers on the number line, the number to the left is always less than the number to the right.
- Ordering is the process of arranging numbers from smallest to greatest or from greatest to smallest. The symbol > is used to represent "greater than," and the symbol < is used to represent "less than." To represent "greater than or equal to," use the symbol ≥; to represent "less than or equal to," use the symbol ≤.
- If any number n lies between 0 and any positive number x on the number line, then $0 < n < x$; in other words, n is greater than 0 but less than x. If n is any number on the number line between 0 and any positive number x, including 0 and x, then $0 \leq n \leq x$, which means that n is greater than or equal to 0, or less than or equal to x.
- If any number n lies between 0 and any negative number x on the number line, then $-x < n < 0$; in other words, n is greater than $-x$ but less than 0. If n is any number on the number line between 0 and any negative number x, including 0 and $-x$, then $-x \leq n \leq 0$, which means that n is greater than or equal to $-x$, or less than or equal to 0.

Order of Operations (PEMDAS)

The acronym PEMDAS stands for Parentheses, Exponents, Multiplication, Division, Addition, Subtraction. It should help you to remember to do the operations in the correct order, as follows:

P—First, do the operations within the *parentheses*, if any.
E—Next, do the *exponents*, if any.
M/D—Next, do the *multiplication and/or division*, in order from left to right.
A/S—Next, do the *addition and/or subtraction*, in order from left to right.

For example, $\dfrac{2(4+1)^2 \times 3}{5} - 7$ would be solved in the following order:

$$= \dfrac{2(5)^2 \times 3}{5} - 7$$

$$= \dfrac{2(25) \times 3}{5} - 7$$

$$= \dfrac{50 \times 3}{5} - 7$$

$$= \dfrac{150}{5} - 7$$

$$= 30 - 7 = 23$$

Decimals

The following are properties of decimals that are commonly tested on the ACT Mathematics Test:

- Place value refers to the value of a digit in a number relative to its position. Starting from the left of the decimal point, the values of the digits are ones, tens, hundreds, and so on. Starting to the right of the decimal point, the values of the digits are tenths, hundredths, thousandths, and so on.
- When adding and subtracting decimals, be sure to line up the decimal points. For example: 236.78   78.90

$$\begin{array}{r} +113.21 \\ \hline 349.99 \end{array} \qquad \begin{array}{r} -23.42 \\ \hline 55.48 \end{array}$$

- When multiplying decimals, it is not necessary to line up the decimal points. Simply multiply the numbers, then count the total number of places to the right of the decimal points in the decimals being multiplied to determine placement of the decimal point in the product.
  For example:
  $$\begin{array}{r} 17.330 \\ \times .35 \\ \hline 6.06550 \end{array}$$
- When dividing decimals, first move the decimal point in the divisor to the right until the divisor becomes an integer. Then move the decimal point in the dividend the same number of places.

$$\overset{\text{dividend}}{\downarrow} \quad \overset{\text{divisor}}{\downarrow}$$

For example: $58.345 \div 3.21 = 5834.5 \div 321$. (The decimal point was moved two places to the right.)

You can then perform the long division with the decimal point in the correct place in the quotient, as shown below:

$$\begin{array}{r} 18.17 \\ 321{\overline{)\,5834.50}} \\ -321 \\ \hline 2624 \\ -2568 \\ \hline 565 \\ -321 \\ \hline 2440 \\ -2247 \\ \hline 193 \end{array}$$

and so on

Fractions

The following are properties of fractions and rational numbers that are commonly tested on the ACT Mathematics Test:

- The reciprocal of any number, n, is expressed as 1 over n, or $\frac{1}{n}$. The product of a number and its reciprocal is always 1. For example, the reciprocal of 3 is $\frac{1}{3}$, and $3 \times \frac{1}{3} = \frac{3}{3}$, which is equivalent to 1. By the same token, the reciprocal of $\frac{1}{3}$ is $\frac{3}{1}$, or 3.

- To change any fraction to a decimal, divide the numerator by the denominator. For example, $\frac{3}{4}$ is equivalent to $3 \div 4$, or 0.75.

- Multiplying and dividing both the numerator and the denominator of a fraction by the same non-zero number will result in an equivalent fraction. For example, $\frac{1}{4} \times \frac{3}{3} = \frac{3}{12}$, which can be reduced to $\frac{1}{4}$. This is true because whenever the numerator and the denominator are the same, the value of the fraction is 1; $\frac{3}{3} = 1$.

- When adding and subtracting like fractions, add or subtract the numerators and write the sum or difference over the denominator. So, $\frac{1}{8} + \frac{2}{8} = \frac{3}{8}$, and $\frac{4}{7} - \frac{2}{7} = \frac{2}{7}$.

- To simplify a fraction, find a common factor of both the numerator and the denominator. For example, $\frac{12}{15}$ can be simplified into $\frac{4}{5}$ by dividing both the numerator and the denominator by the common factor 3.

- To convert a mixed number to an improper fraction, multiply the whole number by the denominator in the fraction, add the result to the numerator, and place that value over the original denominator. For example, $3\frac{2}{5}$ is equivalent to $(3 \times 5) + 2$ over 5, or $\frac{17}{5}$.

- When multiplying fractions, multiply the numerators to get the numerator of the product, and multiply the denominators to get the denominator of the product. For example, $\frac{3}{5} \times \frac{7}{8} = \frac{21}{40}$.

- When dividing fractions, multiply the first fraction by the reciprocal of the second fraction. For example, $\frac{1}{3} \div \frac{1}{4} = \frac{1}{3} \times \frac{4}{1}$, which equals $\frac{4}{3}$, or $1\frac{1}{3}$.

Squares/Square Roots

The following are properties of squares and square roots that are commonly tested on the ACT Mathematics Test:

- Squaring a negative number yields a positive result. For example, $-2^2 = 4$.
- The square root of a number, n, is written as $\sqrt{n}$, or the non-negative value a that fulfills the expression $a^2 = n$. For example, "the square root of 5" is expressed as $\sqrt{5}$, and $\left(\sqrt{5}\right)^2 = 5$. A square root will always be a positive number.
- A number is considered a perfect square when the square root of that number is a whole number. The polynomial $a^2 \pm 2ab + b^2$ is also a perfect square because the solution set is $(a \pm b)^2$.

Exponents

The following are properties of exponents that are commonly tested on the ACT Mathematics Test:

- $a^m \times a^n = a^{(m+n)}$
  When multiplying the same base number raised to any power, add the exponents. For example: $3^2 \times 3^4 = 3^6$. Likewise, $3^6 = 3^2 \times 3^4$; $3^6 = 3^1 \times 3^5$; and $3^6 = 3^3 \times 3^3$.

- $(a^m)^n = a^{mn}$
  When raising an exponential expression to a power, multiply the exponent and power. For example: $(3^2)^4 = 3^8$. Likewise, $3^8 = (3^2)^4$; $3^8 = (3^4)^2$; $3^8 = (3^1)^8$; and $3^8 = (3^8)^1$.

- $(ab)^m = a^m \times b^m$
  When multiplying two different base numbers and raising the product to a power, the product is equivalent to raising each number to the power, and multiplying the exponential expressions. For example: $(3 \times 2)^2 = 3^2 \times 2^2$, which equals 9×4, or 36. Likewise, $3^2 \times 2^2 = (3 \times 2)^2$, or 6^2, which equals 36.

- $\left(\dfrac{a}{b}\right)^m = \dfrac{a^m}{b^m}$
  When dividing two different base numbers and raising the quotient to a power, the quotient is equivalent to raising each number to the power, and dividing the exponential expressions. For example: $\left(\dfrac{2}{3}\right)^2 = \dfrac{2^2}{3^2}$, or $\dfrac{4}{9}$.

- $a^0 = 1$, when $a \neq 0$
  When you raise any number to the power of 0, the result is always 1.

- $a^{-m} = \dfrac{1}{a^m}$, when $a \neq 0$
  When you raise a number to a negative power, the result is equivalent to 1 over the number raised to the same positive power. For example: $3^{-2} = \dfrac{1}{3^2}$, or $\dfrac{1}{9}$.

Scientific Notation

When numbers are very large or very small, scientific notation is used to shorten them. Scientific notation is expressed by setting a positive number, N, equal to a number less than 10, times 10 raised to an integer. To form the scientific notation of a number, the decimal point is moved until it is placed after the first nonzero digit from the left in the number.

For example, 568,000,000 written in scientific notation would be 5.68×10^8, because the decimal point was moved 8 places to the left. Likewise, 0.0000000354 written in scientific notation would be 3.54×10^{-8}, because the decimal point was moved 8 places to the right.

Mean, Median, and Mode

The following are properties of mean, median, and mode that are commonly tested on the ACT Mathematics Test:

- The arithmetic mean is equivalent to the average of a series of numbers. Calculate the average by dividing the sum of all of the numbers in the series by the total count of numbers in the series. For example: a student received scores of 80%, 85%, and 90% on 3 math tests. The average score received by the student on those tests is $80 + 85 + 90$ divided by 3, or $255 \div 3$, which is 85%.

- The median is the middle value of a series of numbers when those numbers are in either ascending or descending order. In the series (2, 4, 6, 8, 10) the median is 6. To find the median in a data set with an even number of items, find the average of the middle two numbers. In the series (3, 4, 5, 6) the median is 4.5.
- The mode is the number that appears most frequently in a series of numbers. In the series (2, 3, 4, 5, 6, 3, 7) the mode is 3, because 3 appears twice in the series and the other numbers each appear only once in the series.

Ratio, Proportion, and Percent

The following are properties of ratios, proportions, and percents that are commonly tested on the ACT Mathematics Test:

- A ratio expresses a mathematical comparison between two quantities. A ratio of 1 to 5, for example, is written as either $\frac{1}{5}$ or 1:5.
- When working with ratios, be sure to differentiate between part-to-part and part-to-whole ratios. In a part-to-part ratio, the elements being compared are parts of the whole. For example, if two components of a recipe are being compared to each other, it is a part-to-part ratio (2 cups of flour:1 cup of sugar). In a part-to-whole ratio, the elements being compared are one part of the whole to the whole itself. For example, if one group of students is being compared to the entire class, it is a part-to-whole ratio (13 girls:27 students).
- A proportion indicates that one ratio is equal to another ratio. For example, $\frac{1}{5} = \frac{x}{20}$ is a proportion, where $x = 4$.
- A percent is a fraction whose denominator is 100. The fraction $\frac{25}{100}$ is equal to 25%. To calculate the percent that one number is of another number, set up a ratio, as shown below:

> What percent of 40 is 5?
> 5 is to 40 as x is to 100
> $\frac{5}{40} = \frac{x}{100}$
> Cross-multiply and solve for x:
> $40x = 500$
> $x = \frac{500}{40} = 12.5$
> 5 is 12.5% of 40

Note: If a price is discounted by p percent, then the discounted price is $(100-p)$ percent of the original price. So, if a CD is on sale for 20% off the regular price, the sale price is equivalent to 80% of the original price.

Linear Equations with One Variable

The following are properties of linear equations with one variable that are commonly tested on the ACT Mathematics Test:

- In a linear equation with one variable, the variable cannot have an exponent or be in the denominator of a fraction. An example of a linear equation is $2x + 13 = 43$. The ACT Mathematics Test will most likely require you to solve for x in that equation. Do this by isolating x on the left side of the equation, as follows:

$$2x + 13 = 43$$
$$2x = 43 - 13$$
$$2x = 30$$
$$x = \frac{30}{2}, \text{ or } 15$$

- One common ACT example of a linear equation with one variable is in questions involving speed of travel. The basic formula to remember is Rate $\times$ Time = Distance. The question will generally give you two of these values and you will have to solve for the remaining value.

Absolute Value

The absolute value of a number is indicated by placing that number inside two vertical lines. For example, the absolute value of 10 is written as follows: $|10|$. Absolute value can be defined as the numerical value of a real number without regard to its sign. This means that the absolute value of 10, $|10|$, is the same as the absolute value of -10, $|-10|$, in that they both equal 10. Think of it as the distance from -10 to 0 on the number line, and the distance from 0 to 10 on the number line ... both distances equal 10 units.

Simple Probability

Following are properties of probability and outcomes that are commonly tested on the ACT Mathematics Test:

- Probability refers to the likelihood that an event will occur. For example, Jeff has three striped and four solid ties in his closet; therefore, he has a total of seven ties in his closet. He has three chances to grab a striped tie out of the seven total ties, because he has three striped ties. So, the likelihood of Jeff grabbing a striped tie is 3 out of 7, which can also be expressed as 3:7, or $\frac{3}{7}$.
- Two specific events are considered independent if the outcome of one event has no effect on the outcome of the other event. For example, if you toss a coin, there is a 1 in 2, or $\frac{1}{2}$ chance that it will land on either heads or tails. If you toss the coin again, the outcome will be the same. To find the probability of two or more independent events occurring together, multiply the outcomes of the individual events. For example, the probability that both coin-tosses will result in heads, is $\frac{1}{2} \times \frac{1}{2}$, or $\frac{1}{4}$.

The ACT Mathematics Test will assess your ability to calculate simple probabilities in everyday situations.

■ ELEMENTARY ALGEBRA

The Elementary Algebra (8th- or 9th-grade level) questions make up about 17 percent of the total number of questions on the ACT Mathematics Test. The questions test elementary algebraic concepts such as:

1. Functions
2. Polynomial Operations and Factoring Simple Quadratic Expressions
3. Linear Inequalities with One Variable

Functions

A function is a set of ordered pairs where no two of the ordered pairs has the same x-value. In a function, each input (x-value) has exactly one output (y-value). An example of this relationship would be $y = x^2$. Here, y is a function of x because for any value of x, there is exactly one value of y. However, x is not a function of y because for certain values of y, there is more than one value of x. (If $y = 4$, x could be either 2 or -2.) The *domain* of a function refers to the x-values, while the *range* of a function refers to the y-values. If the values in the domain correspond to more than one value in the range, the relation is not a function.

Consider the following example:

For the function $f(x) = x^2 - 3x$, what is the value of $f(5)$?

Solve this problem by substituting 5 for x wherever x appears in the function:

$$f(x) = x^2 - 3x$$
$$f(5) = (5)^2 - (3)(5)$$
$$f(5) = 25 - 15$$
$$f(5) = 10$$

Polynomial Operations and Factoring Simple Quadratic Expressions

Following are properties of polynomial operations and factoring simple quadratic expressions that are commonly tested on the ACT Mathematics Test:

- A polynomial is the sum or difference of expressions like $2x^2$ and $14x$. The most common polynomial takes the form of a simple quadratic expression, such as: $2x^2 + 14x + 8$, with the terms in decreasing order. The standard form of a simple quadratic expression is $ax^2 + bx + c$, where a, b, and c are whole numbers. When the terms include both a number and a variable, such as x, the number is called the *coefficient*. For example, in the expression $2x$, 2 is the coefficient of x.
- The ACT Mathematics Test will often require you to evaluate, or solve a polynomial, by substituting a given value for the variable, as follows:

For $x = -2$, $2x^2 + 14x + 8 = ?$

Substitute -2 for x and solve:

$$2(-2)^2 + 14(-2) + 8$$
$$= 2(4) + (-28) + 8$$
$$= 8 - 28 + 8 = -12$$

- You will also be required to add, subtract, multiply, and divide polynomials. To add or subtract polynomials, simply combine like terms, as in the following examples:

$$(2x^2 + 14x + 8) + (3x^2 + 5x + 32)$$
$$2x^2 + 3x^2 = 5x^2, \text{ and}$$
$$14x + 5x = 19x, \text{ and}$$
$$8 + 32 = 40, \text{ so}$$
$$5x^2 + 19x + 40$$

$$(8x^2 + 11x + 23) - (7x^2 + 3x + 13)$$
$$8x^2 - 7x^2 = x^2, \text{ and}$$
$$11x - 3x = 8x, \text{ and}$$
$$23 - 13 = 10, \text{ so}$$
$$x^2 + 8x = 10$$

To multiply polynomials, use the distributive property to multiply each term of one polynomial by each term of the other polynomial. Following are some examples:

$$(3x)(x^2 + 4x - 2)$$

Multiply each term in the second polynomial by $3x$.

$$(3x^3 + 12x^2 - 6x)$$

$$(2x^2 + 5x)(x - 3)$$

Remember the *FOIL* Method whenever you see this type of multiplication: multiply the *First* terms, then the *Outside* terms, then the *Inside* terms, then the *Last* terms.

$$(2x^2 + 5x)(x - 3)$$
First terms: $(2x^2)(x) = 2x^3$
Outside terms: $(2x^2)(-3) = -6x^2$
Inside terms: $(5x)(x) = 5x^2$
Last terms: $(5x)(-3) = -15x$

Now put the terms in decreasing order:

$$2x^3 + (-6x^2) + 5x^2 + (-15x)$$
$$= 2x^3 - 1x^2 - 15x$$

- You may also be asked to find the factors or solution sets of certain simple quadratic expressions. A factor or solution set takes the form, $(x \pm \text{ some number})$. Simple quadratic expressions will usually have 2 of these factors or solution sets. Remember that the standard form of a simple quadratic expression is $ax^2 + bx + c$. To factor the equation, find two numbers that, when multiplied together, will give you c, and when added together will give you b. The ACT Mathematics Test includes questions similar to the following:

What are the solution sets for $x^2 + 9x + 20 = 0$?
$$x^2 + 9x + 20 = 0$$
$$(x + \underline{\hspace{0.5cm}})(x + \underline{\hspace{0.5cm}}) = 0$$

5 and 4 are two numbers that, when multiplied together, give you 20, and when added together give you 9.

Therefore, $(x + 5)(x + 4)$ are the two solution sets for $x^2 + 9x + 20 = 0$.

Linear Inequalities with One Variable

Following are properties of linear inequalities with one variable that are commonly tested on the ACT Mathematics Test:

- Linear inequalities with one variable are solved in almost the same manner as linear equations with one variable: by isolating the variable on one side of the inequality (see previous examples).
- When an inequality is multiplied by a negative number, you must switch the sign.

  For example, follow these steps to solve for x in the inequality $-2x + 2 < 6$:

$$-2x + 2 < 6$$
$$-2x < 4$$
$$-x < 2$$
$$x > -2$$

▬▬ INTERMEDIATE ALGEBRA

The Intermediate Algebra (9th- or 10th-grade level) questions make up about 15 percent of the total number of questions on the ACT Mathematics Test. The questions test intermediate algebraic concepts such as:

1. Quadratic Formula
2. Radical and Rational Expressions
3. Inequalities and Absolute Value Equations
4. Sequences
5. Systems of Equations
6. Logarithms
7. Roots of Polynomials
8. Complex Numbers
9. Factorials

Quadratic Formula

The quadratic formula is not tested specifically on the ACT. However, you might find it useful when attempting questions that contain quadratic equations.

The quadratic formula is expressed as $x = \dfrac{-b \pm \sqrt{(b^2 - 4ac)}}{2a}$. This formula finds solutions to quadratic equations of the form $ax^2 + bx + c = 0$. It is the method that can be used in place of factoring for more complex polynomial expressions. The part of the formula $b^2 - 4ac$ is called the *discriminant* and can be used to quickly determine what kind of answer you should arrive at. If the discriminant is 0, then you will have only one solution. If the discriminant is positive, then you will have two real solutions. If the discriminant is negative, then you will have two complex solutions.

Radical and Rational Expressions

Following are properties of radical and rational expressions that are commonly tested on the ACT Mathematics Test:

- A radical is the root of a given quantity, indicated by the radical sign, $\sqrt{}$. For example, $\sqrt{9}$ is considered a radical, and 9 is the radicand. The following rules apply to radicals:

  - $\sqrt{a}$ means the "square root of a," $\sqrt[3]{a}$ means the "cube root of a," etc.
  - $\sqrt{a} \times \sqrt{b} = \sqrt{(ab)}$
  - $\sqrt[n]{a^n} = a$
  - $\sqrt[n]{\sqrt[m]{a}} = \sqrt[nm]{a}$

- A rational number is a number that can be expressed as a ratio of two integers. Fractions are rational numbers that represent a part of a whole number. To find the square root of a fraction, simply divide the square root of the numerator by the square root of the denominator. If the denominator is not a perfect square, rationalize the denominator by multiplying both the numerator and denominator by a number that would make the denominator a perfect square. For example:

$$\frac{\sqrt{1}}{\sqrt{3}}$$ can be rationalized in the following way:

$$= \frac{\sqrt{(1 \times 12)}}{\sqrt{(3 \times 12)}}$$

$$= \frac{\sqrt{(12)}}{\sqrt{(36)}}$$

$$= \frac{\sqrt{(4)(3)}}{6}$$

$$= \frac{2\sqrt{3}}{6} = \frac{\sqrt{3}}{3}$$

Inequalities and Absolute Value Equations

An inequality with an absolute value will be in the form of $|ax + b| > c$, or $|ax + b| < c$. To solve $|ax + b| > c$, first drop the absolute value and create two separate inequalities with the word *or* between them. To solve $|ax + b| < c$, first drop the absolute value and create two separate inequalities with the word *and* between them. The first inequality will look just like the original inequality without the absolute value. For the second inequality, you must switch the inequality sign and change the sign of c.

For example, to solve $|x + 3| > 5$, first drop the absolute value sign and create two separate inequalities with the word *or* between them:

$$x + 3 > 5 \ or \ x + 3 < -5$$

Solve for x:

$$x > 2 \ or \ x < -8$$

To solve $|x + 3| < 5$, first drop the absolute value sign and create two separate inequalities with the word *and* between them:

$x + 3 < 5$ *and* $x + 3 > -5$

Solve for x:

$x < 2$ *and* $x > -8$

Sequences

Following are properties of sequences that are commonly tested on the ACT Mathematics Test:

- An arithmetic sequence is one in which the difference between one term and the next is the same. To find the nth term, use the formula $a_n = a_1 + (n - 1)d$, where d is the common difference.
- A geometric sequence is one in which the ratio between two terms is constant. For example, $\frac{1}{2}$, 1, 2, 4, 8 ... is a geometric sequence where 2 is the constant ratio. To find the nth term, use the formula $a_n = a_1(r)^{n-1}$, where r is the constant ratio.

Systems of Equations

The ACT Mathematics Test commonly includes questions that contain two equations and two unknowns. To solve a system of equations like this, follow the steps below:

$4x + 5y = 21$
$5x + 10y = 30$

If you multiply the top equation by -2, you will get:

$-8x - 10y = -42$
$5x + 10y = 30$

Now, you can add the two equations together.

$-8x - 10y + 5x + 10y = -42 + 30$
$-3x = -12$

Notice that the two y-terms cancel each other out. Solving for x, you get $x = 4$. Now, choose one of the original two equations, substitute 4 for x, and solve for y:

$4(4) + 5y = 21$
$16 + 5y = 21$
$5y = 5$
$y = 1$

Logarithms

Logarithms are used to indicate exponents of certain numbers called *bases*, where $\log_a b = c$, if $a^c = b$. For example, $\log_2 16 = 4$ means the log to the base 2 of 16 is 4, because $2^4 = 16$.

Consider the following example:

What value of x satisfies $\log_x 9 = 2$?
$\log_x 9 = 2$ means the log to the base x of $9 = 2$.
So, x^2 must equal 9, and x must equal 3.

The ACT Mathematics Test might include one or two questions that require knowledge of the three most common logarithmic properties, shown next:

- $\log_b(xy) = \log_b x + \log_b y$

- $\log_b\left(\dfrac{x}{y}\right) = \log_b x - \log_b y$

- $\log_b(x^n) = n\log_b x$

Roots of Polynomials

When given a quadratic equation, $ax^2 + bx + c = 0$, you might be asked to find the roots of the equation. This means you need to find what value(s) of x make the equation true. You may either choose to factor the quadratic equation or to use the quadratic formula. For example, find the roots of $x^2 + 6x + 8 = 0$.

$x^2 + 6x + 8 = 0$
$(x + 4)(x + 2) = 0$; solve for x
$x + 4 = 0$ and $x + 2 = 0$, so $x = -4$ and $x = -2$.

The roots of $x^2 + 6x + 8 = 0$ are $x = -4$ and $x = -2$. Using the quadratic formula will yield the same solution.

Complex Numbers

Complex numbers are written in the form of $a + bi$, where i is an imaginary number equal to the square root of -1. Thus, $i = \sqrt{(-1)}$. It also follows that $i^2 = (i)(i) = \left(\sqrt{(-1)}\right)\left(\sqrt{(-1)}\right) = -1$, $i^3 = (i^2)(i) = (-1)i = -i$, and $i^4 = (i^2)(i^2) = (-1)(-1) = 1$.

Complex numbers can be added, subtracted, multiplied, and divided as shown below:

Simply combine like terms when adding. $(5 + 3i) + (7 + 2i) = 12 + 5i$
Simply combine like terms when subtracting. $(3 + 6i) - (4 + 3i) = -1 + 3i$
Use the *FOIL* Method when multiplying. $(2 + 3i)(4 - 2i)$
$= 8 - 4i + 12i - 6i^2$
$= 8 + 12i + 6 = 14 + 12i$ (Combine like terms, remembering that $i^2 = -1$.)

When dividing complex numbers, you must first eliminate all imaginary numbers from the denominator. Do this by multiplying the complex number in the denominator by its *conjugate*. The conjugate of $(a + bi)$ is simply $(a - bi)$:

$$\frac{(5 + 3i)}{(3 + 2i)}$$

First, multiply the numerator and denominator by $(3 - 2i)$; this will eliminate the imaginary number from the denominator.

$$= \frac{(5 + 3i)(3 - 2i)}{(3 + 2i)(3 - 2i)}$$

$$= \frac{15 - 10i + 9i - 6i^2}{9 - 6i + 6i - 4i^2}$$

$$= \frac{15 - i - 6(-1)}{9 - 4(-1)} = \frac{21 - i}{13}$$

Factorials

Factorials are represented by '!'. The factorial of any positive number (n) is equal to the product of all positive numbers less than or equal to n. For example, $5! = 1 \times 2 \times 3 \times 4 \times 5 = 120$. You may also see the expression $n!$, which means $1 \times 2 \times 3 \dots \times n$. Factorials are tested infrequently on the ACT Mathematics Test, so don't worry if you cannot remember these formulas.

When evaluating factorials, cancel out as many of the common terms as possible, as in the following example:

$$\frac{12!}{9!} = \frac{1 \times 2 \times 3 \dots \times 9 \times 10 \times 11 \times 12}{1 \times 2 \times 3 \dots \times 9}$$

The terms $1 \times 2 \times 3 \dots \times 9$ cancel out in the denominator, leaving you with an answer of $10 \times 11 \times 12 = 1{,}320$.

Additionally, it is valuable to remember that $0! = 1$, not 0.

▄▄▄ COORDINATE GEOMETRY

The Coordinate Geometry (Cartesian Coordinate Plane) questions make up about 15 percent of the total number of questions on the ACT Mathematics Test. The questions test coordinate geometry concepts such as:

1. Number Line Graphs
2. Equation of a Line
3. Slope
4. Parallel and Perpendicular Lines
5. Distance and Midpoint Formulas
6. Translation and Reflection

Number Line Graphs

The most basic type of graphing is graphing on a number line. For the most part, you will be asked to graph inequalities like those shown below:

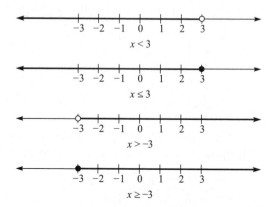

Equation of a Line

The standard form of an equation of a line is in the form $Ax + By = C$. This can be transformed into the slope-intercept (standard) form of the equation of a line, $y = mx + b$, where m is the slope of the line and b is the y-intercept (that is, the point at which the graph of the line crosses the y-axis). The ACT Mathematics Test will often require you to put the equation of a line into the slope-intercept form to determine either the slope or the y-intercept, as follows:

$$3x + 4y - 16 = 0$$

Put the equation in the slope-intercept form by isolating y on the left side:

$$4y = -3x + 16$$
$$y = -\frac{3}{4}x + 4$$

The slope of the line is $-\frac{3}{4}$, and the y-intercept is 4.

Slope

Following are properties of slope that are commonly tested on the ACT Mathematics Test:

- The slope of a line is calculated by taking the change in y-coordinates divided by the change in x-coordinates from two given points on a line. The formula for slope is $m = \frac{(y_2 - y_1)}{(x_2 - x_1)}$ where (x_1, y_1) and (x_2, y_2) are the two given points. For example, the slope of a line that contains the points $(3, 6)$ and $(2, 5)$ is equivalent to $\frac{(6 - 5)}{(3 - 2)}$, or $\frac{1}{1}$, which equals 1.
- A positive slope means the graph of the line goes up and to the right. A negative slope means the graph of the line goes down and to the right. A horizontal line has a slope of 0, while a vertical line has an undefined slope, because it never crosses the y-axis. See the figure below for a visual representation of different slopes of a line.

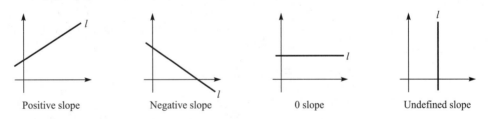

| Positive slope | Negative slope | 0 slope | Undefined slope |

Parallel and Perpendicular Lines

Following are properties of parallel and perpendicular lines that are commonly tested on the ACT Mathematics Test:

- Two lines are parallel if and only if they have the same slope. For example, the two lines with equations $2y = 6x + 7$ and $y = 3x - 14$ have the same slope (3).
- Two lines are perpendicular if and only if the slope of one of the lines is the negative reciprocal of the slope of the other line. In other words, if line a has a slope of 2, and line b has a slope of $-\frac{1}{2}$, the two lines are perpendicular.

Distance and Midpoint Formulas

Following are properties of distance and midpoint formulas that are commonly tested on the ACT Mathematics Test:

- To find the distance between two points in the (x, y) coordinate plane, use the Distance Formula $\sqrt{([x_2 - x_1]^2 + [y_2 - y_1]^2)}$, where (x_1, y_1) and (x_2, y_2) are the two given points. For example, if you are given the points $(2, 3)$ and $(4, 5)$, you would set up the following equation to determine the distance between the two points:

$$= \sqrt{(4 - 2)^2 + (5 - 3)^2}$$
$$= \sqrt{(2)^2 + (2)^2}$$
$$= \sqrt{4 + 4}$$
$$= \sqrt{8} = 2\sqrt{2}$$

- To find the midpoint of a line given two points on the line, use the Midpoint Formula $\left(\frac{[x_1 + x_2]}{2}, \frac{[y_1 + y_2]}{2}\right)$. For example, you would set up the following equation to determine the midpoint of the line between the two points $(2, 3)$ and $(4, 5)$:

$$\frac{(2 + 4)}{2} = \frac{6}{2} = 3; \text{ the } x\text{-value of the midpoint is 3.}$$
$$\frac{(3 + 5)}{2} = \frac{8}{2} = 4; \text{ the } y\text{-value of the midpoint is 4.}$$

Therefore, the midpoint of the line between the points $(2, 3)$ and $(4, 5)$ is $(3, 4)$.

Translation and Reflection

Following are properties of translation and reflection that are commonly tested on the ACT Mathematics Test:

- A translation slides an object in the coordinate plane to the left or right or up or down. The object retains its shape and size and faces in the same direction as the original object. In the translation shown below, the triangle in the first graph is translated x units down in the second graph.

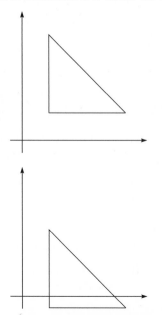

- A reflection flips an object in the coordinate plane over either the *x*-axis or the *y*-axis. When a reflection occurs across the *x*-axis, the *x*-coordinate remains the same, but the *y*-coordinate is transformed into its opposite. When a reflection occurs across the *y*-axis, the *y*-coordinate remains the same, but the *x*-coordinate is transformed into its opposite. The object retains its shape and size. The figure below shows a triangle that has been reflected across the *y*-axis.

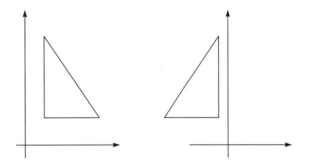

PLANE GEOMETRY

Plane Geometry questions make up about 23 percent of the total number of questions on the ACT Mathematics Test. The questions test plane geometry concepts such as:

1. Properties and Relations of Plane Figures
2. Angles, Parallel Lines, and Perpendicular Lines
3. Simple 3-Dimensional Geometry

Properties and Relations of Plane Figures

The ACT Mathematics Test requires you to apply your knowledge of plane figures such as triangles, quadrilaterals, other polygons, and circles. This section includes a description of many of the formulas that will help you to more quickly answer geometry questions.

Triangles

A triangle is a polygon with three sides and three angles. The following are properties of triangles that are commonly tested on the ACT Mathematics Test:

- In an equilateral triangle, all three sides have the same length, and each interior angle measures 60°, as shown below.

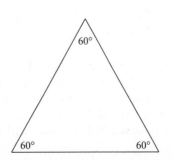

- In an isosceles triangle, two sides have the same length, and the angles opposite those sides are congruent, or equal, as shown below.

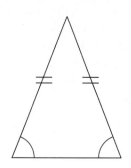

- In a right triangle, one of the angles measures 90°. The side opposite the right angle is the hypotenuse, and it is always the longest side, as shown below.

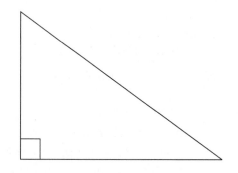

- The sum of the interior angles in any triangle is always 180°.
- The perimeter (P) of a triangle is the sum of the lengths of the sides.
- The area (A) of a triangle is equivalent to $\frac{1}{2}$(base)(height). The height is equal to the perpendicular distance from an angle to a side, as shown below.

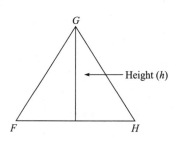

- In triangle *FGH* above, the height is the perpendicular line drawn from *G* to the midpoint of side *FH*. The height is *not* the distance from *F* to *G* or from *G* to *H*.
- The Pythagorean Theorem states that $a^2 + b^2 = c^2$, where c is the hypotenuse (the side opposite the right angle) of a right triangle and a and b are the two other sides of the triangle.
- In Special Right Triangles, the side lengths have direct relationships, as shown below. You will not be tested directly on these relationships, but

they will help you to more quickly answer some ACT Mathematics Test questions.

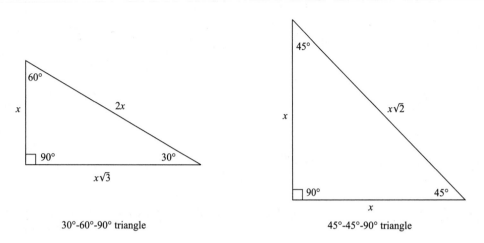

30°-60°-90° triangle   45°-45°-90° triangle

- The sides of a 3-4-5 Special Right Triangle have the ratio 3:4:5.

Quadrilaterals

A quadrilateral is any four-sided object. The following are properties of quadrilaterals that are commonly tested on the ACT Mathematics Test:

Parallelogram

- In a parallelogram, the opposite sides are of equal length, and the opposite angles are equal, as shown below.

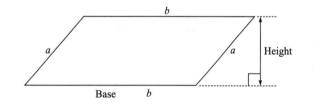

- The area (A) of a parallelogram is equivalent to (base)(height). The height is equal to the perpendicular distance from an angle to a side.
- The sum of the interior angles of a parallelogram is 360°.

Rectangle

- A rectangle has four sides (two sets of congruent, or equal sides) and four right angles, as shown below. All rectangles are parallelograms.

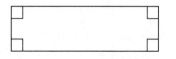

- The sum of the angles in a rectangle is always 360° because a rectangle contains four 90° angles.
- The perimeter (P) of both a parallelogram and a rectangle is equivalent to $2l + 2w$, where l is the length and w is the width.
- The area (A) of a rectangle is equivalent to $(l)(w)$.

- The lengths of the diagonals of a rectangle are congruent, or equal in length. A diagonal is a straight line between opposite angles, as shown below.

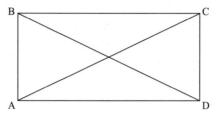

Square

- A square is a special rectangle where all four sides are of equal length. All squares are rectangles.
- The length of each diagonal of a square is equivalent to the length of one side times $\sqrt{2}$. So, for example, a square with a side length of x would have diagonals equal to $x\sqrt{2}$, as shown below.

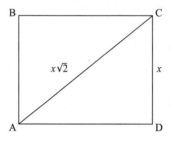

- The area (A) of a square is equivalent to one side squared (s^2).

Trapezoid

- A trapezoid is a polygon with four sides and four angles, as shown below.

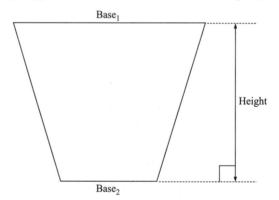

- The bases of the trapezoids (top and bottom) are never the same length.
- The sides of the trapezoid can be the same length (isosceles trapezoid) or they may not be.
- The perimeter (P) of the trapezoid is the sum of the lengths of the sides and bases.
- The area (A) of a trapezoid is $A = \frac{1}{2}(\text{base}_1 + \text{base}_2)(\text{height})$. Height is the distance between the bases.
- The diagonals of a trapezoid have a unique feature. When the diagonals of a trapezoid intersect, the ratio of the top of the diagonals to the bottom of the diagonals is the same as the ratio of the top base to the bottom base.

Other Polygons

The following are properties of other polygons (multisided objects) that are commonly tested on the ACT Mathematics Test:

- The sum of the interior angles of any polygon can be calculated using the formula $(n - 2)(180°)$, where n is the number of sides.
- A pentagon is a five-sided figure, as shown below.

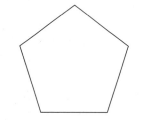

- The sum of the interior angles of a pentagon is $(5 - 2)(180°)$, or $540°$.
- A hexagon is a six-sided figure, as shown below.

- The sum of the interior angles of a hexagon is $(6 - 2)(180°)$, or $720°$.
- An octagon is an eight-sided figure, as shown below.

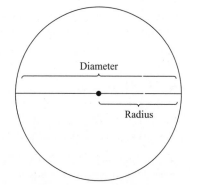

- The sum of the interior angles of an octagon is $(8 - 2)(180°)$, or $1,080°$.

Circles

The following are properties of circles that are commonly tested on the ACT Mathematics Test:

- The radius (r) of a circle is the distance from the center of the circle to any point on the circle.
- The diameter (d) of a circle is twice the radius, as shown below.

Diameter

Radius

- The area (A) of a circle is equivalent to πr^2. So, the area of a circle with a radius of 3 is $3^2\pi$, or 9π.
- The circumference (C) of a circle is equivalent to $2\pi r$ or πd. So, the circumference of a circle with a radius of 3 is $2(3)\pi$, or 6π.
- The equation of a circle centered at the point (h, k) is $(x-h)^2+(y-k)^2 = r^2$, where r is the radius of the circle.
- The complete arc of a circle has 360°.
- A tangent to a circle is a line that touches the circle at exactly one point.

Angles, Parallel Lines, and Perpendicular Lines

The following are properties of angles, parallel lines, and perpendicular lines that are commonly tested on the ACT Mathematics Test:

- A line is generally understood as a straight line.
- A line segment is the part of a line that lies between two points on the line.
- Two distinct lines are said to be parallel if they lie in the same plane and do not intersect.
- Two distinct lines are said to be perpendicular if their intersection creates right angles.
- When two parallel lines are cut by a transversal, each parallel line has four angles surrounding the intersection that are matched in measure and position with a counterpart at the other parallel line. The vertical (opposite) angles are congruent, and the adjacent angles are supplementary (they total 180°).

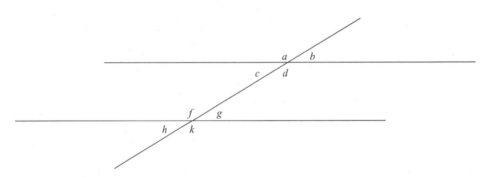

- ○ Vertical angles: $a = d = f = k$
- ○ Vertical angles: $b = c = g = h$
- ○ Supplementary angles: $a + b = 180°$
- ○ Supplementary angles: $c + d = 180°$
- ○ Supplementary angles: $f + g = 180°$
- ○ Supplementary angles: $h + k = 180°$

- An acute angle is any angle that is smaller than 90°.
- An obtuse angle is any angle that is greater than 90° and less than 180°.
- A right angle is an angle that measures exactly 90°.

Simple Three-Dimensional Geometry

The following are properties of three-dimensional figures that are commonly tested on the ACT Mathematics Test:

- The formula for the volume (V) of a rectangular solid is $V = lwh$, where l = length, w = width, and h = height.

- The surface area of a rectangular solid is the sum of the area ($l \times w$) of the six faces of the solid. Think of each face as a square or a rectangle.
- The formula for the surface area of a rectangular solid is $A = 2(wl + lh + wh)$, where l = length, w = width, and h = height.

TRIGONOMETRY

The Trigonometry questions make up about 7 percent of the total number of questions on the ACT Mathematics Test. The questions test basic trigonometric concepts (which apply only to right triangles as shown below).

Basic Trigonometric Concepts

Trigonometry deals with the measures of the angles in a right triangle. The ACT Mathematics Test will generally only ask you about the sine, cosine, and tangent of those angles. Following are some basic trigonometric concepts that will help you to correctly answer the 4 or 5 trigonometry questions that will appear on your actual ACT Mathematics Test.

- The sine (sin) of each of the two smaller angles can be determined by the ratio of the length of the side opposite the given angle to the length of the hypotenuse: opposite/hypotenuse.
- The cosine (cos) can be determined by the ratio of the length of the side adjacent to the given angle to the length of the hypotenuse: adjacent/hypotenuse.
- The tangent (tan) can be determined by the ratio of the length of the side opposite to the given angle to the length of the side adjacent to the given angle: opposite/adjacent.
- The mnemonic device "SOHCAHTOA" can be used to help you remember these ratios.

(SOH)SIN = **O**PPOSITE/**H**YPOTENUSE
(CAH)COS = **A**DJACENT/**H**YPOTENUSE
(TOA)TAN = **O**PPOSITE/**A**DJACENT

Consider the triangle below.

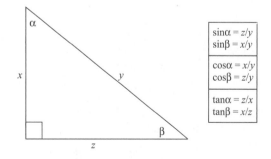

Advanced Trigonometric Concepts

You may find one or two questions on your ACT Mathematics Test that deal with more advanced trigonometric concepts, such as secant, cosecant, and cotangent. The secant, cosecant, and cotangent can be found as follows:

- SEC (secant) = 1/COS
- CSC (cosecant) = 1/SIN
- COT (cotangent) = 1/TAN

Radians

One or two of the many released ACT exams we have evaluated contain a question about radians. We have included the following information to help you correctly answer any questions involving radians that might appear on your actual ACT Mathematics Test.

- To change from degrees to radians, multiply the angle measure by $\frac{\pi}{180}$. For example, 120 degrees $120\left(\frac{\pi}{180}\right) = \frac{120\pi}{180} = \frac{2\pi}{3}$ radians. Conversely, to change from radians to degrees, take the number of radians, multiply by 180 and drop the π.

▭ WHAT'S NEXT?

Chapter 5, "Applying Strategies, Building Skills," includes practice questions in format, divided by content area and difficulty level. Work through the questions, focusing on the areas that give you the most trouble. Then, read the detailed explanations and refer back to Chapters 3 and 4 as needed.

CHAPTER 5

APPLYING STRATEGIES, BUILDING SKILLS

This chapter contains exercises designed to help you focus on the concepts generally tested on the ACT Mathematics Test: Pre-Algebra, Elementary Algebra, Intermediate Algebra, Coordinate Geometry, Plane Geometry, and Trigonometry. The questions in this chapter, although in ACT format, are presented differently from those you will see on your ACT exam. They are separated first into broad content areas and then assigned one of three difficulty levels: easy, medium, or hard. We did this to allow you an additional opportunity to practice working with and recognizing specific math concepts at varying levels of difficulty. Keep in mind that you will likely see many different questions on your actual ACT, and that this and subsequent chapters represent a sample of question types that have appeared on previous tests.

Chapters 6, 7, 8, and 9 contain four simulated ACT Mathematics Tests. These additional tests will allow you to become more familiar with the types of questions you will see on your actual ACT exam.

PRE-ALGEBRA

These questions will test your knowledge of operations using whole numbers, fractions, and decimals; square roots; scientific notation; linear inequalities with one variable; ratio, proportion, and percent; absolute value; simple probability; data interpretation; and very basic statistics. Pre-Algebra questions make up approximately 23 percent of the ACT Mathematics Test.

Difficulty Level: Easy

1. The odometer on Jordan's car read 23,273 miles when he left on a trip and 23,650 miles when he returned. Jordan drove his car 6.5 hours on the trip. Based on the odometer readings, what was his average driving speed on the trip, in miles per hour?
   A. 53
   B. 58
   C. 60
   D. 65
   E. 67

2. For integers x and y such that $xy = 8$, which of the following is NOT a possible value of x ?
   F. -8
   G. -6
   H. -4
   J. 1
   K. 2

3. For the campers attending College Prep Camp this summer, the ratio of male campers to female campers is 3:5. Which of the following statements about the campers is(are) true?
   I. For every 5 females, there are 3 males.
   II. There are more males than females.
   III. Males comprise $\dfrac{3}{5}$ of the campers.
   A. I only
   B. II only
   C. III only
   D. II and III only
   E. I, II, and III

4. Al needs $12\dfrac{1}{4}$ feet of lumber to complete a project. He has $8\dfrac{1}{2}$ feet of lumber. How many more feet of lumber does he need?
   F. $3\dfrac{1}{2}$ feet
   G. $3\dfrac{1}{3}$ feet
   H. $3\dfrac{3}{4}$ feet
   J. 4 feet
   K. $4\dfrac{1}{3}$ feet

5. What is the solution to the equation $5b - (-b + 3) = 21$?
   A. -4
   B. 4
   C. 6
   D. 7
   E. 13

6. What is the median of the data given below?

   8, 13, 9, 8, 15, 14, 10

   F. 8
   G. 8.5
   H. 10
   J. 11
   K. 15

7. What is the value of $|4 - x|$ if $x = 7$?
  A. -3
  B. 3
  C. 4
  D. 11
  E. 28

8. Mike has 2 more baseball cards than Jen. Then he bought 3 baseball cards from Jen. Now how many more baseball cards does Mike have than Jen?
  F. 12
  G. 8
  H. 6
  J. 2
  K. -4

Difficulty Level: Medium

9. The cost for a company to produce c computers in 1 year is $200c +$ $300,000. How many computers can the company produce in 1 year at a cost of $700,000?
  A. 2,000
  B. 2,667
  C. 3,500
  D. 5,000
  E. 5,333

10. $\left(\dfrac{1}{2}\right)^2 + \left(\dfrac{1}{3}\right)^2 + \left(\dfrac{1}{4}\right)^2 =$?
  F. $\dfrac{1}{29}$

  G. $\dfrac{3}{29}$

  H. $\dfrac{61}{144}$

  J. $\dfrac{15}{32}$

  K. 9

11. If you add up 6 consecutive even integers that are each greater than 25, what is the smallest possible sum?
  A. 150
  B. 165
  C. 174
  D. 186
  E. 210

12. About what percent of $\dfrac{3}{5}$ is $\dfrac{1}{5}$?
  F. 20%
  G. 33%
  H. 50%
  J. 67%
  K. 300%

13. According to a recent survey of children about their favorite color, 20% of the children preferred red, 40% of the children preferred blue, 20% of the children preferred purple, and the remaining children preferred green. If each child preferred only 1 color and 30 children preferred green, how many children were surveyed?

    A. 60
    B. 90
    C. 120
    D. 150
    E. 180

14. The ratio of the side of square X to the length of rectangle Y is 4:5. The ratio of a side of square X to the width of rectangle Y is 4:3. What is the ratio of the area of square X to the area of rectangle Y?

    F. 12:15
    G. 16:15
    H. 18:15
    J. 10:16
    K. 12:16

Difficulty Level: Hard

15. For all nonzero a and b, $\dfrac{(a \times 0.01)(b \times 10^3)}{(a \times 10^{-2})(b \times 1,000)} = ?$

    A. 1
    B. 10
    C. 10^5
    D. $\dfrac{a}{b}$
    E. $\dfrac{b^2}{a}$

16. Let $a \blacklozenge b = (a - b)^3$ for all integers a and b. Which of the following is the value of $3 \blacklozenge (-2)$?

    F. 1
    G. 19
    H. 35
    J. 125
    K. 216

17. For any real number n, the equation $|x - n| = 8$ can be thought of as meaning "the distance on the real number line from x to n is 8 units." How far apart are the 2 solutions for n?

    A. n
    B. $2n$
    C. $8 + n$
    D. $\sqrt{8^2 + n^2}$
    E. 16

18. What is the 211th digit after the decimal point in the repeating decimal $0.\overline{84392}$?

    F. 9
    G. 8
    H. 4
    J. 2
    K. 0

ELEMENTARY ALGEBRA

These questions will test your knowledge of operations involving functions; factoring simple quadratic equations; evaluating algebraic expressions using substitution; and properties of integer exponents. Elementary Algebra questions make up approximately 17 percent of the ACT Mathematics Test.

Difficulty Level: Easy

1. For all a and b, $(2a - b)(a^2 + b) = ?$
   A. $2a^2 - b^2$
   B. $2a^3 - b^2$
   C. $2a^3 + ab - b^2$
   D. $2a^3 + 2ab - a^2b^2$
   E. $2a^3 - a^2b + 2ab - b^2$

2. The expression $x^2 - x - 42$ can be written as the product of 2 binomials with integer coefficients. One of the binomials is $(x - 7)$. Which of the following is the other binomial?
   F. $x^2 - 6$
   G. $x^2 + 6$
   H. $x - 6$
   J. $x + 6$
   K. $x + 7$

3. On a recent test, some questions were worth 3 points each and the rest were worth 2 points each. Bailey answered correctly the same number of 3-point questions as 2-point questions and earned a score of 80. How many 2-point questions did she answer correctly?
   A. 10
   B. 13
   C. 15
   D. 16
   E. 18

4. Which of the following is equivalent to $10^{\frac{1}{2}}$?
   F. 5
   G. $\dfrac{1^2}{10}$
   H. $\sqrt{10}$
   J. $\sqrt[5]{10}$
   K. -1×10^2

5. What is the value of $4 \times 2^{a+b}$ when $a = -2$ and $b = 3$?
   A. -8
   B. 8
   C. 12
   D. 16
   E. 24

Difficulty Level: Medium

6. If x is a real number and $5^x = 625$, then $3 \times 3^x = ?$
   F. 5
   G. 9
   H. 45
   J. 125
   K. 243

7. Given $f(x) = 2x^2 - 3x + 6$, what is the value of $f(-4)$?
   A. 26
   B. 50
   C. 58
   D. 76
   E. 82

8. $(2a - 3b)^2$ is equivalent to:
   F. $4a^2 - 12ab + 9b^2$
   G. $4a^2 - 10ab + 9b^2$
   H. $4a^2 - 9b^2$
   J. $4a^2 + 9b^2$
   K. $4a - 6b$

Difficulty Level: Hard

9. If $h(x) = g(x) - f(x)$, where $g(x) = 5x^2 + 15x - 25$ and $f(x) = 5x^2 - 6x - 11$, then $h(x)$ is *always* divisible by which of the following?
   A. 17
   B. 9
   C. 7
   D. 5
   E. 3

10. Given $f(x) = \dfrac{x^3 + \dfrac{5}{8}}{x + 1/4}$, what is $f\left(\dfrac{1}{2}\right)$?
   F. $\dfrac{7}{2}$

   G. $\dfrac{20}{8}$

   H. $\dfrac{36}{24}$

   J. 1

   K. $\dfrac{30}{32}$

▬▬ INTERMEDIATE ALGEBRA

These questions will test your knowledge of operations involving the quadratic formula; radical and rational expressions; inequalities and absolute-value equations; algebraic and geometric sequences; systems of equations; logarithms; roots of polynomials; and complex numbers. Intermediate Algebra questions make up approximately 15 percent of the ACT Mathematics Test.

Difficulty Level: Easy

1. The geometric mean of 2 positive numbers is the square root of the product of the 2 numbers. What is the geometric mean of 4 and 49?
   A. 9
   B. 14
   C. 26
   D. 98
   E. 196

2. If x is a real number such that $x^3 = 729$, then $x^2 + \sqrt{x} = $?
   F. 9
   G. 27
   H. 30
   J. 84
   K. 90

3. What two numbers should be placed in the blanks below so that the difference between the consecutive numbers is the same?

   13, ___, ___, 34
   A. 19, 28
   B. 20, 27
   C. 21, 26
   D. 23, 24
   E. 24, 29

4. The first 5 terms of a geometric sequence are 0.75, −3, 12, −48, and 192. What is the 6th term?
   F. −768
   G. −144
   H. −75
   J. 132
   K. 255.75

Difficulty Level: Medium

5. What is the solution set of $|2a - 1| \geq 5$?
   A. $\{a: a \leq -4 \text{ or } a \geq 6\}$
   B. $\{a: a \leq -3 \text{ or } a \geq 3\}$
   C. $\{a: a \leq -2 \text{ or } a \geq 3\}$
   D. $\{a: a \geq 3\}$
   E. { } (the empty set)

6. If the following system of equations has a solution, what is the x-coordinate of the solution?
   $$x + 6y = 24$$
   $$3x + 6y = 52$$
   F. 0
   G. 6
   H. 14
   J. 19
   K. The system has no solution.

7. For a single production run, when x items are made and sold, a company's profit, D dollars, can be modeled by $D = x^2 - 300x - 100,000$. What is the smallest number of items that must be made and sold in order for the company not to lose money on the production run?
   A. 150
   B. 200
   C. 300
   D. 350
   E. 500

Difficulty Level: Hard

8. If $-4 \leq a \leq -3$, and $2 \leq b \leq 5$, what is the maximum value of $|a - 2b|$?
   F. 7
   G. 8
   H. 13
   J. 14
   K. 20

9. For all positive integers n, which of the following is a correct ordering of the terms n^n, $(n!)^n$, and $(n!)^{n!}$?
   A. $(n!)^{n!} \geq n^n \geq (n!)^n$
   B. $(n!)^{n!} \geq (n!)^n \geq n^n$
   C. $n^n \geq (n!)^n \geq (n!)^{n!}$
   D. $(n!)^n \geq (n!)^{n!} \geq n^n$
   E. $(n!)^n \geq n^n \geq (n!)^{n!}$

10. Whenever a, b, and c are positive real numbers, which of the following expressions is equivalent to $2\log_3 a + \dfrac{1}{2}\log_6 b - \log_3 c$?

   F. $2\log_3(a - c) + \log_6\left(\dfrac{b}{2}\right)$

   G. $\log_3(a - c) + \log_6(\sqrt{b})$

   H. $\log_3\left(\dfrac{c}{a^2}\right) + \log_6\left(\dfrac{b}{2}\right)$

   J. $\log_3\left(\dfrac{a^2}{c}\right) + \log_6(\sqrt{b})$

   K. $\log_3\left(\dfrac{a^2 b}{c}\right)$

▬▬ COORDINATE GEOMETRY

These questions will test your knowledge of operations involving number line graphs; the equation of a line; slope; and the distance and midpoint formulas. Coordinate Geometry questions make up approximately 15 percent of the ACT Mathematics Test.

Difficulty Level: Easy

1. Which of the following inequalities represents the graph shown below on the real number line?

A. $-4 \leq x < 3$

B. $-4 \leq x < 2$

C. $0 \leq x < 3$

D. $4 \leq x \leq 4$

E. $3 < x \leq -4$

2. As shown below, the diagonals of rectangle *RSTU* intersect at the point (1, 4) in the standard (x, y) coordinate plane. Point *R* is at $(-3, 2)$. Which of the following are the coordinates of point *T*?

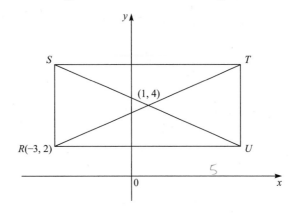

F. $(-3, 6)$

G. $(4, 5)$

H. $(5, 5)$

J. $(5, 6)$

K. $(7, 6)$

3. What is the slope of any line parallel to the line $2x - 3y = 7$?

A. -3

B. $-\dfrac{2}{3}$

C. $\dfrac{2}{3}$

D. 2

E. 3

4. If two lines in the standard (x, y) coordinate plane are perpendicular and the slope of one of the lines is -5, what is the slope of the other line?

F. -5

G. -1

H. $-\dfrac{1}{5}$

J. $\dfrac{1}{5}$

K. 5

Difficulty Level: Medium

5. What is the distance, in coordinate units, between the points (3, 5) and (−4, 1) in the standard (x, y) coordinate plane?
- **A.** $\sqrt{27}$
- **B.** $4\sqrt{2}$
- **C.** 8
- **D.** $8\sqrt{2}$
- **E.** $\sqrt{65}$

6. Which of the following is an equation of the line that passes through the points (−3, 11) and (1, 5) in the standard (x, y) coordinate plane?
- **F.** $3x + 2y = 13$
- **G.** $2x + 3y = 21$
- **H.** $2x + 2y = 16$
- **J.** $x + 3y = 16$
- **K.** $x + y = 6$

7. The graph of the line with the equation $−5y = 25$ does NOT have points in what quadrant(s) on the standard (x, y) coordinate plane below?

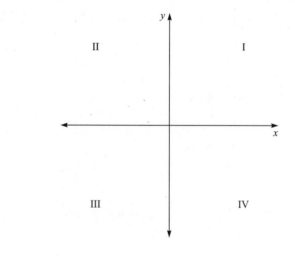

- **A.** Quadrant I only
- **B.** Quadrant II only
- **C.** Quadrant III only
- **D.** Quadrants I and II only
- **E.** Quadrants II and III only

Difficulty Level: Hard

8. An angle in the standard position in the standard (x, y) coordinate plane has its vertex at the origin and its initial side on the positive x-axis. If the measure of the angle in the standard position is 2,585°, it has the same terminal side as an angle of each of the following measures EXCEPT:
- **F.** −1,375°
- **G.** −295°
- **H.** 65°
- **J.** 435°
- **K.** 785°

9. In the standard (x, y) coordinate plane, $\left(4, \dfrac{5}{3}\right)$ is halfway between $(a, a + 3)$ and $(2a, a - 5)$. What is the value of a?

 A. $\dfrac{4}{3}$

 B. $\dfrac{8}{3}$

 C. 4

 D. $\dfrac{9}{2}$

 E. 6

10. What is the perimeter of quadrilateral $QRST$ if it has vertices with (x, y) coordinates $Q(0,0)$, $R(1,3)$, $S(4,4)$, and $T(3,1)$?

 F. 100

 G. 40

 H. $6\sqrt{2} + 2\sqrt{10}$

 J. $4\sqrt{10}$

 K. $2\sqrt{10}$

▬ PLANE GEOMETRY

These questions will test your knowledge of operations involving plane figures such as circles, triangles, rectangles, parallelograms, and trapezoids; angles, parallel lines, and perpendicular lines; perimeter, area, and volume; and simple three-dimensional figures. Plane Geometry questions make up a considerable portion of the more difficult math tested on the ACT Mathematics Test. Approximately 23 percent of the questions will fall under this category.

Difficulty Level: Easy

1. What is the volume, in cubic inches, of a cube whose edges each measure 3 inches in length?

 A. 9

 B. 12

 C. 18

 D. 27

 E. 81

2. In the figure below, M, N, and O are colinear, the measure of angle MNP is $3x°$, and the measure of angle ONP is $6x°$. What is the measure of angle MNP ?

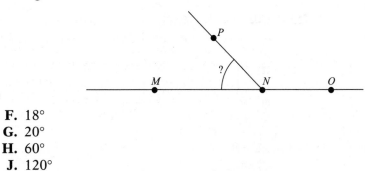

 F. 18°

 G. 20°

 H. 60°

 J. 120°

 K. 162°

3. For the polygon below, the lengths of 2 sides are not given. Each angle between adjacent sides measures 90°. What is the polygon's perimeter, in centimeters?

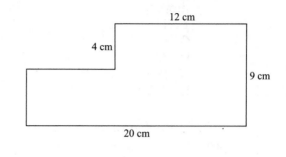

A. 45
B. 58
C. 87
D. 90
E. 180

4. The area of △ABC below is 40 square inches. If $\overline{AC}$ is 10 inches long, how long is the altitude $\overline{BD}$, in inches?

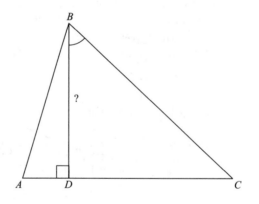

F. 4
G. 6
H. 8
J. 10
K. 12

5. What is the area, in square inches, of a trapezoid with a height of 6 inches and parallel bases of 9 inches and 7 inches, respectively?
A. 24
B. 32
C. 48
D. 96
E. 378

Difficulty Level: Medium

6. The area of a wheel is 78.5 inches. About how many revolutions does one of these wheels make traveling 100 feet (1,200 inches) without slipping?
   F. 12
   G. 15
   H. 38
   J. 100
   K. 942

7. In the figure below, if $a = 140$, what is the value of $b + c$?

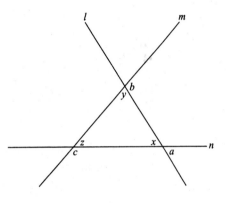

   A. 320°
   B. 220°
   C. 180°
   D. 140°
   E. 50°

8. Triangles WXY and ZXY, shown below, are isosceles with base $\overline{XY}$. Segments $\overline{XZ}$ and $\overline{YZ}$ bisect $\angle WXY$ and $\angle WYX$, respectively. Which of the following angle congruences is necessarily true?

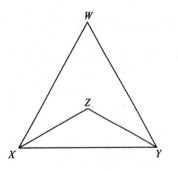

   F. $\angle WXY \cong \angle WYZ$
   G. $\angle WXZ \cong \angle WYX$
   H. $\angle WXZ \cong \angle XYZ$
   J. $\angle WYZ \cong \angle XWY$
   K. $\angle XYZ \cong \angle XWY$

9. Mandy plans to carpet the entire floor of her bedroom. The floor is flat and all adjacent sides meet at right angles, as shown below. Mandy can purchase 8-foot × 12-foot pieces of carpet on sale. What is the minimum number of pieces of carpet that she must purchase in order to carpet her bedroom floor?

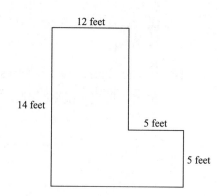

A. 1
B. 2
C. 3
D. 4
E. 5

10. Triangle *ABC* is similar to triangle *XYZ*. $\overline{AB}$ is 5 inches long, $\overline{BC}$ is 8 inches long, and $\overline{AC}$ is 3 inches long. If the longest side of △*XYZ* is 20 inches long, what is the perimeter, in inches, of △*XYZ* ?
F. 16
G. 28
H. 40
J. 64
K. 88

Difficulty Level: Hard

11. The noncommon rays of 2 adjacent angles form a straight angle. The measure of one angle is 3 times the measure of the other angle. What is the measure of the smaller angle?
A. 40°
B. 45°
C. 50°
D. 55°
E. 60°

12. A square has sides that are the same length as the radius of a circle. If the circle has a circumference of 64π square units, how many units long is the perimeter of the square?
F. 8
G. 16
H. 32
J. 128
K. 256

13. In a certain rectangle, *PQRS*, angle *QPS* and angle *PSR* are right angles. If the length of line $\overline{PR}$ is 34 units and the length of line $\overline{PS}$ is 30 units, what is the length of line $\overline{RS}$?
   A. $\sqrt{30}$
   B. 16
   C. $\sqrt{34}$
   D. $2\sqrt{514}$
   E. 14

14. In the figure below, lines *a* and *b* are parallel and angle measures are as marked. If it can be determined, what is the value of *x* ?

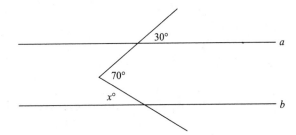

   F. 30°
   G. 40°
   H. 55°
   J. 70°
   K. Cannot be determined from the given information.

15. Which of the following degree measures is equivalent to 3.75π radians?
   A. 2,700°
   B. 1,350°
   C. 675°
   D. 337.5°
   E. 225°

16. The radius of a circle is $\dfrac{32}{\pi}$ centimeters. What is the area of the circle?
   F. 64
   G. 32π
   H. $\dfrac{1,024}{\pi}$
   J. 1,024
   K. $1,024\pi$

▇▇ TRIGONOMETRY

These questions will test your knowledge of operations involving trigonometry, including the relationships in right angles; the definitions of trigonometric functions; graphing trigonometric functions; using trigonometric identities; and solving trigonometric equations. Since trigonometry is seen by the ACT as "higher math," these practice questions are categorized as either medium or hard only; they make up a very small percentage (about 7 percent) of the ACT Mathematics Test, and will usually only appear in the latter half of the questions on your ACT Mathematics Test.

Difficulty Level: Medium

1. The sides of a right triangle measure 5 in, 12 in, and 13 in. What is the cosine of the acute angle adjacent to the side that measures 12 in ?

    A. $\dfrac{5}{12}$

    B. $\dfrac{5}{13}$

    C. $\dfrac{12}{13}$

    D. $\dfrac{13}{12}$

    E. $\dfrac{12}{5}$

2. In the right triangle pictured below, r, s, and t are the lengths of its sides. What is the value of $\tan \alpha$?

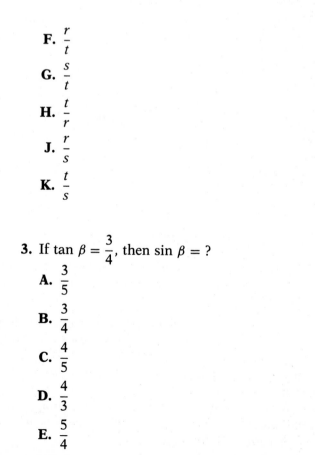

    F. $\dfrac{r}{t}$

    G. $\dfrac{s}{t}$

    H. $\dfrac{t}{r}$

    J. $\dfrac{r}{s}$

    K. $\dfrac{t}{s}$

3. If $\tan \beta = \dfrac{3}{4}$, then $\sin \beta = $?

    A. $\dfrac{3}{5}$

    B. $\dfrac{3}{4}$

    C. $\dfrac{4}{5}$

    D. $\dfrac{4}{3}$

    E. $\dfrac{5}{4}$

4. In the right triangle shown below, cos ∠A = ?

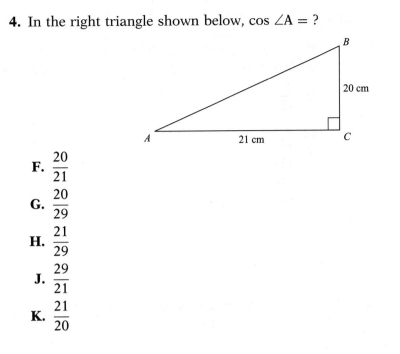

F. $\dfrac{20}{21}$

G. $\dfrac{20}{29}$

H. $\dfrac{21}{29}$

J. $\dfrac{29}{21}$

K. $\dfrac{21}{20}$

Difficulty Level: Hard

5. For values of x where $\sin x$, $\cos x$, and $\tan x$ are all defined, $\dfrac{(\cos x)}{(\tan x \sin x)} = ?$

A. $\dfrac{\cos^2 x}{\sin^2 x}$

B. $\tan^2 x$

C. 1

D. $\sin^2 x$

E. $\sec x$

6. As shown in the figure below, a ramp leading from a loading dock is 35 feet long and forms a 15° angle with level ground.

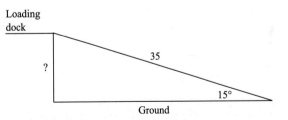

Given the trigonometric approximations in the table below, what is the height above ground of the loading dock, to the nearest 0.1 foot?

cos 15°	0.966
tan 15°	0.268
sin 15°	0.259

F. 9.4

G. 9.1

H. 7.7

J. 7.4

K. 2.8

7. Whenever $\dfrac{\tan \alpha}{\sin \alpha}$ is defined, it is equivalent to:

A. $\cos \alpha$

B. $\dfrac{1}{\cos \alpha}$

C. $\dfrac{1}{\sin \alpha}$

D. $\dfrac{1}{\sin^2 \alpha}$

E. $\dfrac{\cos \alpha}{\sin \alpha}$

ANSWERS AND EXPLANATIONS

PRE-ALGEBRA—DIFFICULTY LEVEL: EASY

1. **The correct answer is B.** Average speed is found by dividing the total distance traveled by the time it took to travel that distance. Since Jordan's odometer began at 23,273 and read 23,650 at the end of the trip, the total distance can be found by subtracting 23,273 from 23,650. This distance, 377 miles can than be divided by 6.5 (the total time) to find an average speed of 58 miles per hour.

2. **The correct answer is G.** Since integers are positive and negative whole numbers, any two integers that are multiplied together, as in the case of xy, to equal some other number, must both be factors of that other number. In other words, both x and y must divide evenly into 8. Since the question is asking which of the following is NOT a possible value of x, you need to find the number that leaves a remainder when divided into eight; negative six leaves a remainder of one-third, while the other numbers all divide cleanly into eight.

3. **The correct answer is A.** The ratio in this question is a part-to-part ratio. This means that it is comparing one part of the group, males, to another part of the group, females. In part-to-part ratios, the top of the ratio has comparatively that many of the whole to the bottom of the ratio (3 males for every 5 females out of the total number of campers). A part-to-whole ratio is found by adding the two parts of the ratio together ($3 + 5 = 8$, so the ratio of male campers to total campers is 3:8). The only statement that is true, then, is Roman numeral I—that for every 5 females there are 3 males. Roman numeral II is untrue as there are clearly more females (5) than males (3) and Roman numeral III is untrue since males comprise $\frac{3}{8}$ of the campers, not $\frac{3}{5}$. Once you determined that Roman numeral I was a true statement, you could have eliminated answer choices B, C, and D, because they do not include Roman numeral I.

4. **The correct answer is H.** This problem requires you to subtract fractions, so the fractions must have the same denominator. The first step is to convert the mixed numbers to improper fractions. This can be accomplished by multiplying 12 by 4 (the denominator) and adding 1 (the numerator), to get $\frac{49}{4}$. Next, multiply 8 by 4 (twice the denominator) and add 2 (twice the numerator), to get $\frac{34}{4}$. Subtracting $\frac{34}{4}$ from $\frac{49}{4}$ leaves $\frac{15}{4}$, which reduces to 3 and $\frac{3}{4}$ feet.

5. **The correct answer is B.** To quickly solve this problem, first multiply the quantity $(-b + 3)$ by -1, to result in $5b + b - 3 = 21$. Simplifying this results in $6b = 24$. Dividing 24 by 6 leaves $b = 4$.

6. **The correct answer is H.** The median is the middle value in an ordered set of values. Therefore, the first step is to put the numbers in order, as follows:

   8, 8, 9, 10, 13, 14, 15

   As you can see, 10 is the middle value.

7. **The correct answer is B.** The absolute value of a number is indicated by placing that number inside two vertical lines. For example, the absolute value of 10 is written as follows: $|10|$. Absolute value can be defined as the numerical value of a real number without regard to its sign. This means that the absolute value of 10, $|10|$, is the same as the absolute value of -10, $|-10|$, in that they both equal 10. Think of it as the distance from -10 to 0 on the number line, and the distance from 0 to 10 on the number line … both distances equal 10 units. In order to solve this problem, you must first substitute the number 7 for the x to get $|4 - 7|$. Then, perform the operation within the vertical lines, so that you get $|-3|$. Since you must disregard the negative sign in order to determine absolute value, the absolute value of -3 is 3.

8. **The correct answer is G.** Mike currently has 2 more baseball cards than Jen. If he buys 3 baseball cards from Jen, he will have at least 5 more baseball cards than Jen has. You can now eliminate answer choices J and K. The mathematical solution is as follows:

   $M = J + 2$ (original number of Mike's baseball cards)

   $M = J + 2 + 3$, or $J + 5$ (number of Mike's baseball cards after he buys 3 from Jen)

   $J = M - 3$ (Number of Jen's baseball cards after she sold 3 to Mike)

   Since Jen now has 3 *fewer* baseball cards than she had before (because Mike bought them), Mike has $5 + 3$, or 8 more baseball cards than Jen now has.

PRE-ALGEBRA—DIFFICULTY LEVEL: MEDIUM

9. **The correct answer is A.** The easiest way to solve this problem is to create an equation where cost is a function of the price per unit plus a fixed cost. Cost = 200c + 300,000. Substituting 700,000 for cost yields 700,000 = 200c + 300,000. This can

be simplified to $400,000 = 200c$, making c (the number of computers) $= 2,000$.

10. **The correct answer is H.** To solve this problem, first square each fraction: $\left(\frac{1}{2}\right)^2 + \left(\frac{1}{3}\right)^2 + \left(\frac{1}{4}\right)^2 = \frac{1}{4} + \frac{1}{9} + \frac{1}{16}$. Remember that to be added, fractions must have a common denominator. In this case, since 4 is a factor of 16, the lowest common denominator is $(9)(16) = 144$. To convert fractions into different denominators, you must multiply the top and bottom of a fraction by the *same* number. If $\frac{1}{4}$ is multiplied by $\frac{36}{36}$, the result is $\frac{36}{144}$. Likewise, multiplying $\frac{1}{9}$ by $\frac{16}{16}$ yields $\frac{16}{144}$, and multiplying $\frac{1}{16}$ by $\frac{9}{9}$ yields $\frac{9}{144}$. Therefore $\frac{1}{4} + \frac{1}{9} + \frac{1}{16} = \frac{36}{144} + \frac{16}{144} + \frac{9}{144} = \frac{(36 + 16 + 9)}{144}$, or $\frac{61}{144}$.

11. **The correct answer is D.** Since you are asked for the smallest possible sum of six consecutive even integers greater than 25, add together the *next* six even numbers following 25. The smallest possible sum is then $26 + 28 + 30 + 32 + 34 + 36 = 186$.

12. **The correct answer is G.** In order to find what percentage one number is of another number, divide the part by the whole. In this case, divide $\frac{1}{5}$ by $\frac{3}{5}$ to get $\frac{1}{3}$. Another way to look at this problem would be to view $\frac{3}{5}$ as 60 and $\frac{1}{5}$ as 20 (translating the fractions into percentages themselves). This way, it is easy to tell that 20 is $\frac{1}{3}$ or 33% of 60.

13. **The correct answer is D.** Since the question gives you a number of students who preferred green, and it is asking for the total number of students surveyed, the first task is to determine what percentage of the total are the students who preferred green. The question states that 40% preferred one color, and 20% preferred each of two other colors; $40 + 20 + 20 = 80$. This leaves another 20% who prefer green. If the 30 students who prefer green make up 20% of the total, this can be turned into a ratio of 30:20 as x:100. Cross-multiply to get $20x = 3,000$, and $x = 150$.

14. **The correct answer is G.** To solve this problem, imagine a square with sides of length 4. The area of the square is $4 \times 4 = 16$. Next imagine that the rectangle has length 5 and width 3. The area of the rectangle is $5 \times 3 = 15$. The ratio of the area of square X to the area of rectangle Y is 16:15.

PRE-ALGEBRA—DIFFICULTY LEVEL: HARD

15. **The correct answer is A.** To solve this problem, recall that $10^{-2} = 0.01$ $\left(10^{-2} = \frac{1}{10^2} = \frac{1}{100} = 0.01\right)$ and $10^3 = 1,000$. Substituting those numbers into the problem results in a fraction that has the same numerator and denominator, which has a value of 1, as shown below:

$$\frac{(a \times 0.01)(b \times 1,000)}{(a \times 0.01)(b \times 1,000)} = 1$$

16. **The correct answer is J.** Given that $a \blacklozenge b = (a-b)^3$ for all integers a and b, when $a = 3$ and $b = -2$, $a \blacklozenge b = (3 - (-2))^3$.

    Subtracting a negative number is the same as adding: $(3 - (-2))^3 = (3 + 2)^3$

    Complete operations within parentheses first. $(3 + 2)^3 = 5^3 = 125$

17. **The correct answer is E.** Because the equation $|x - n| = 8$ can be thought of as meaning "the distance on the real number line from x to n," there are two possible solutions for n: one that comes before x and one that comes after x. If you know that the distance between x and n is 8, the distance between the two possible values of n on a number line must be twice that, or 16.

18. **The correct answer is G.** Notice that there are 5 digits in the repeating decimal (only count the digits after the decimal point). The fifth digit is the number 2, so every place that is a multiple of 5 will be the number 2. For example: .84392843928439284392 and so on. Since 210 is a multiple of 5, the 210th digit will be 2; likewise, since the number 8 always follows the number 2 in this repeating decimal, the 211th digit will be 8.

ELEMENTARY ALGEBRA—DIFFICULTY LEVEL: EASY

1. **The correct answer is E.** In this question, you are given the factored form and must find the equation. Use the *FOIL* method to find the equation. The *FOIL* method refers to the order in which to multiply the elements of the factors. You must multiply the quantity $(2a - b)$ by the quantity $(a^2 + b)$ in the following order:

    First terms $\rightarrow 2a \times a^2 = 2a^3$
    Outside terms $\rightarrow 2a \times b = 2ab$
    Inside terms $\rightarrow -b \times a^2 = -ba^2$
    Last terms $\rightarrow -b \times b = -b^2$.

    Then, add the results of these multiplications together:

    $2a^3 + 2ab + (-ba^2) + (-b^2)$, or $2a^3 + 2ab - ba^2 - b^2$.

Finally, simplify and put the terms in descending order:

$$2a^3 - a^2b + 2ab - b^2.$$

2. **The correct answer is J.** This problem asks you to factor $x^2 - x - 42$. You are given one factor, $(x - 7)$; therefore, you must ask the question "what multiplied by $(x - 7)$ yields $x^2 - x - 42$?" It makes sense that the other factor is either $(x - 6)$ or $(x + 6)$, because $7 \times 6 = 42$. Checking these two possibilities leaves $(x + 6)$ as the correct answer.

3. **The correct answer is D.** Since you don't know how many 2 or 3-point questions Bailey answered correctly, you can represent that number with a variable, q. The same variable can be used to represent the number of 2-point questions answered correctly and the number of 3-point questions answered correctly because Bailey answered the same number of each type correctly. Bailey correctly answered the same number of 3-point questions as 2-point questions and earned a score of 80, which can be written mathematically as the equation $3q + 2q = 80$. Now, solve for q:

$$3q + 2q = 80$$
$$5q = 80$$
$$q = 16$$

4. **The correct answer is H.** To solve this problem, remember that any number taken to the $\frac{1}{2}$ power is the same as taking the square root of that number. Therefore $10^{\frac{1}{2}} = \sqrt{10}$.

5. **The correct answer is B.** To solve this problem, substitute the given values for a and b, as follows:

$$4 \times 2^{a+b}, a = -2 \text{ and } b = 3$$
$$4 \times 2^{-2+3}$$
$$4 \times 2^1 = 4 \times 2 = 8; \text{ remember that an exponent of 1 doesn't change the base.}$$

ELEMENTARY ALGEBRA—DIFFICULTY LEVEL: MEDIUM

6. **The correct answer is K.** To solve this problem, first find the value of x in $5^x = 625$. One way to do this is to try exponents until you reach the correct value:

$$5^2 = 25$$
$$5^3 = 125$$
$$5^4 = 625$$

Therefore $x = 4$. To solve 3×3^x, simply substitute 4 for x:

$$3 \times 3^4$$
$$3 \times 81 = 243$$

7. **The correct answer is B.** To find the value of $f(-4)$ when $f(x) = 2x^2 - 3x + 6$, substitute -4 for x:

$$2x^2 - 3x + 6$$
$$= 2(-4)^2 - 3(-4) + 6$$
$$= 2(16) - (-12) + 6$$
$$= 32 + 12 + 6 = 50$$

8. **The correct answer is F.** To solve this problem, first expand $(2a - 3b)^2$, as follows:

$$(2a - 3b)^2 = (2a - 3b)(2a - 3b)$$

Next, perform the multiplication, and combine like terms:

FOIL: $4a^2 - 6ab - 6ab + 9b^2$
Combine like terms: $4a^2 - 12ab + 9b^2$

ELEMENTARY ALGEBRA—DIFFICULTY LEVEL: HARD

9. **The correct answer is C.** To solve this problem, simplify $h(x)$. Given $h(x) = g(x) - f(x)$, where $g(x) = 5x^2 + 15x - 25$ and $f(x) = 5x^2 - 6x - 11$:

$$h(x) = (5x^2 + 15x - 25) - (5x^2 - 6x - 11)$$
$$= 5x^2 + 15x - 25 - 5x^2 + 6x + 11$$
Rearrange like terms: $h(x) = 5x^2 - 5x^2 + 15x + 6x - 25 + 11$
Simplify: $h(x) = 21x - 14$

Because 21 and 14 are both divisible by 7, $h(x)$ will always be divisible by 7.

10. **The correct answer is J.** To solve this problem, substitute $\frac{1}{2}$ for x in the equation and simplify, as shown next.

$$f(x) = \frac{x^3 + \frac{5}{8}}{x + \frac{1}{4}}, x = \frac{1}{2}$$

$$= \frac{\left(\frac{1}{2}\right)^3 + \frac{5}{8}}{\frac{1}{2} + \frac{1}{4}}$$

$$= \frac{\frac{1}{8} + \frac{5}{8}}{\frac{2}{4} + \frac{1}{4}}$$

$$= \frac{\frac{6}{8}}{\frac{3}{4}}$$

(Recall that dividing by a fraction is the same as multiplying by the reciprocal)

$$= \frac{6}{8} \times \frac{4}{3} = \frac{24}{24} = 1$$

INTERMEDIATE ALGEBRA—DIFFICULTY LEVEL: EASY

1. **The correct answer is B.** Given that the geometric mean of 2 positive numbers is the square root of the product of the 2 numbers, the geometric mean of 4 and 49 is $\sqrt{(4 \times 49)} = \sqrt{196} = 14$.

2. **The correct answer is J.** To calculate the value of $x^2 + \sqrt{x}$, first solve $x^3 = 729$ for x. The solution is the cube root of 729, which is 9. Substitute 9 into the original expression, arriving at $9^2 + \sqrt{9}$. This expression simplifies to $81 + 3$, or 84.

3. **The correct answer is B.** To solve this problem, it is important to realize that the question is about an arithmetic sequence, a sequence in which each pair of successive terms differs by the same number. To find the difference, define d as that difference, 13 as the first term, and 34 as the fourth term. By definition, the second term is $13 + d$, and the third term is $13 + d + d$. The fourth term, 34, can also be written as $(13 + d + d) + d$. Using that expression, obtain the equation $34 = 13 + d + d + d$, or $34 = 13 + 3d$. After subtracting 13 from both sides, divide by 3, which results in $7 = d$. The difference is 7. Thus the second term is $13 + 7$, or 20, and the third term is $20 + 7$, or 27.

4. **The correct answer is F.** To find the 6th term in the sequence, first recognize the pattern that relates each term to the next. Recall that a geometric sequence is a sequence of numbers where each term after the first is found by multiplying the previous one by a *common ratio*. Given the first five terms 0.75, −3, 12, −48, and 192, the common ratio can be found by finding the ratio between any term and the one that precedes it. For instance:

$$\frac{192}{-48} = -4$$

$$-\frac{48}{12} = -4$$

$$\frac{12}{-3} = -4$$

It is apparent that the common ratio is −4. The 6th term can then be found by multiplying the 5th term, 192, by −4 to get $192(-4) = -768$.

INTERMEDIATE ALGEBRA—DIFFICULTY LEVEL: MEDIUM

5. **The correct answer is C.** To solve $|2a - 1| \geq 5$, recall that you must "split" this into two separate inequalities and then solve:

$2a - 1 \geq 5$	or	$2a - 1 \leq -5$
$2a \geq 6$	Add 1 to both sides	$2a \leq -4$
$a \geq 3$	Divide by 2	$a \leq -2$

We now have two inequalities that describe the solution set $\{a: a \leq -2 \text{ or } a \geq 3\}$.

6. **The correct answer is H.** This system is a prime target for the use of elimination as a solution strategy. Elimination involves subtracting one entire equation from another. This is possible because we can think of an equation as a balanced scale. Adding equal amounts to a balanced scale will not disturb the current balance.

$$x + 6y = 24$$
$$3x + 6y = 52$$

Subtract the bottom equation from the top equation:

$$x + 6y = 24$$
$$\underline{-(3x + 6y = 52)}$$
$$-2x + 0 = -28$$

Solve for x:

$$x = 14$$

7. **The correct answer is E.** Given that profit is modeled by $D = x^2 - 300x - 100,000$, the minimum number of items that must be produced for the company not to lose money will result in a profit of 0. To find the number of items, set the equation $D = x^2 - 300x - 100,000$ equal to 0 and solve for x by factoring (think of two numbers that multiply to get −100,000 and add to get −300):

$$0 = x^2 - 300x - 100,000$$
$$0 = (x - 500)(x + 200)$$

Therefore $x = 500$ or $x = -200$. Since it does not make sense to produce a negative quantity of items, the correct answer is 500. Also, note that −200 is not among the answer choices.

INTERMEDIATE ALGEBRA—DIFFICULTY LEVEL: HARD

8. **The correct answer is J.** To find the maximum values of $|a - 2b|$ given that $-4 \leq a \leq -3$, and $2 \leq b \leq 5$, start by using the extreme values for each variable. For a, we'll use −4 and −3. For b we'll use 2 and 5. Now substitute different configurations of these extreme values into $|a - 2b|$ to find the maximum value:

$a = -4, b = 2$	$\|-4 - 2(2)\| = \|-4 - 4\|$
	$= \|-8\| = 8$
$a = -4, b = 5$	$\|-4 - 2(5)\| = \|-4 - 10\|$
	$= \|-14\| = 14$
$a = -3, b = 2$	$\|-3 - 2(2)\| = \|-3 - 4\|$
	$= \|-7\| = 7$
$a = -3, b = 5$	$\|-3 - 2(5)\| = \|-3 - 10\|$
	$= \|-13\| = 13$

The maximum value is 14.

9. **The correct answer is B.** Recall that $n!$ is the factorial of n. The factorial of a positive integer, n, is the product of that number, n, and all the positive integers less than n: $n(n-1)(n-2)\dots$ and so on. This means that for all positive integers, n, the following inequality holds: $n! \geq n$. Therefore $(n!)^n \geq n^n$ and $(n!)^{n!} \geq (n!)^n$. Note that you do not have to do any actual calculations to solve this problem; you just have to understand the relationship between various operations. The correct answer is $(n!)^{n!} \geq (n!)^n \geq n^n$.

10. **The correct answer is J.** To solve this problem, you must make use of several rules of simplifying logarithms. First, an exponent on everything inside of a log can be moved out front as a multiplier, and vice versa ($log_b(m^n) = n \times log_b(m)$). The expression $2 \log_3 a + \frac{1}{2} \log_6 b - \log_3 c$ is equivalent to $\log_3 a^2 + \log_6 b^{\frac{1}{2}} - \log_3 c$. Next, as long as two logarithmic expressions have the same base, division inside the log can be turned into subtraction outside the log, and vice versa ($log_b\left(\frac{m}{n}\right) = log_b(m) - log_b(n)$). Therefore, $\log_3 a^2 + \log_6 b^{\frac{1}{2}} - \log_3 c$ is equivalent to $\log_3\left(\frac{a^2}{c}\right) + \log_6(b^{\frac{1}{2}})$. Finally, recall that taking a number to the $\frac{1}{2}$ power is the same as taking the square root. Therefore, the final answer is $\log_3\left(\frac{a^2}{c}\right) + \log_6(\sqrt{b})$.

COORDINATE GEOMETRY—DIFFICULTY LEVEL: EASY

1. **The correct answer is A.** The number line graph shows a "closed circle" at -4 because x is "greater than or equal to" -4. Additionally, the number line graph shows an open circle at 3 because x is strictly "less than (but not equal to)" 3. The inequality $-4 \leq x < 3$ is correct because the first half of that combined inequality is merely $x \geq -4$ with the elements reversed.

2. **The correct answer is J.** Point $(1, 4)$ serves as the midpoint of the segment RT. To find the coordinates of point T, find the difference between point $R(-3, 2)$ and the point at $(1, 4)$.

$$x = (-1 - 3) = 4$$
$$y = (4 - 2) = 2$$

To find point T, simply add the distance from point R to the midpoint: $T(1 + 4, 4 + 2) = T(5, 6)$.

3. **The correct answer is C.** To solve this problem, recall that parallel lines always have the same slope. To find the slope of the line, convert the equation

$2x - 3y = 7$ into slope-intercept form ($y = mx + b$, where m is the slope):

$$2x - 3y = 7$$
$$-3y = -2x + 7$$
$$y = \frac{2}{3}x - \frac{7}{3}$$

Thus the slope of this line, and any line parallel to it, is $\frac{2}{3}$.

4. **The correct answer is J.** Perpendicular lines have slopes that are the "opposite reciprocal" of each other. That means that if one line has slope m, a line perpendicular to it must have slope $-\frac{1}{m}$. Given that the slope of the line is -5, the slope of a line perpendicular to it is $\frac{1}{5}$.

COORDINATE GEOMETRY—DIFFICULTY LEVEL: MEDIUM

5. **The correct answer is E.** The distance between the points $(3, 5)$ and $(-4, 1)$ can be found using the distance formula, which states that for two points (x_1, y_1) and (x_2, y_2), the distance between them is $d = \sqrt{[(x_1 - x_2)^2 + (y_1 - y_2)^2]}$. To solve, substitute the given points into the distance formula:

$$d = \sqrt{[(3 - (-4))^2 + (5 - 1)^2}$$
$$d = \sqrt{[7^2 + 4^2]} = \sqrt{[49 + 16]} = \sqrt{65}.$$

6. **The correct answer is F.** To find the equation of a line, you need a point and a slope. To solve, first find the slope between the points $(-3, 11)$ and $(1, 5)$. The slope formula is $m = \frac{(y_2 - y_1)}{(x_2 - x_1)}$. For these points $m = \frac{(5 - 11)}{(1 - (-3))} = -\frac{6}{4} = -\frac{3}{2}$. Given the slope-intercept form of an equation, $y = mx + b$, where m is the slope and b is the y-intercept, substitute a point $(1, 5)$ and $m\left(-\frac{3}{2}\right)$ and then solve for b:

$$y = mx + b$$
$$5 = \left(-\frac{3}{2}\right)(1) + b$$

Convert 5 to $\frac{10}{2}$ and add $\frac{3}{2}$ to both sides.

$$\frac{13}{2} = b$$

Therefore, the equation is $y = \left(-\frac{3}{2}\right)x + \frac{13}{2}$.

Convert to standard form: $\left(\frac{3}{2}\right)x + y = \frac{13}{2}$.

Multiply the entire equation by 2 to get rid of the fraction: $3x + 2y = 13$.

7. **The correct answer is D.** To solve this problem, first simplify and graph the equation $-5y = 25$: $y = -5$. This line, shown below, has a slope of 0, and crosses two quadrants.

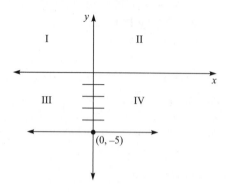

Since the question asks in which quadrants the line does NOT have points, the answer is only Quadrants I and II, answer choice D.

COORDINATE GEOMETRY—DIFFICULTY LEVEL: HARD

8. **The correct answer is J.** Angles that have the same terminal side are called "coterminal." Coterminal angles are found by adding or subtracting whole-number multiples of $360°$. To find coterminal angles of $2,585°$, consider the expression $2,585° + n360°$, where n is an integer. You can generate a table of coterminal angles by varying the value of n:

$$2,585° + n360°$$

Value of n	−11	−10	−9	−8	−7	−6	−5	−4	−3	−2	−1	0
angle °	−1,375	−1,015	−655	−295	65	425	785	1,145	1,505	1,865	2,225	2,585

Evaluate the chart to determine that $435°$ cannot be the measure of the angle.

9. **The correct answer is B.** One way to find the value of a is to avoid the fractions and just look at the x-coordinates. The x-coordinate of the midpoint is found by averaging the values of the x-coordinates. Therefore, the average of a and $2a$ is 4. Set up the following equation and solve for a:

$$\frac{(a + 2a)}{2} = 4$$
$$a + 2a = 8$$
$$3a = 8$$
$$a = \frac{8}{3}$$

10. **The correct answer is J.** This question requires repeated use of the distance formula, which states that for two points (x_1, y_1) and (x_2, y_2), the distance between them is $d = \sqrt{[(x_1 - x_2)^2 + (y_1 - y_2)^2]}$. Given that quadrilateral $QRST$ has vertices $Q(0,0)$, $R(1,3)$, $S(4,4)$, and $T(3,1)$, the perimeter can be found by taking the sum of $\overline{QR} + \overline{RS} + \overline{ST} + \overline{TQ}$.

$Q(0,0)$, $R(1,3)$: $QR = \sqrt{[(0 - 1)^2 + (0 - 3)^2]} = \sqrt{[1 + 9]} = \sqrt{10}$

$R(1,3)$, $S(4,4)$: $RS = \sqrt{[(1 - 4)^2 + (3 - 4)^2]} = \sqrt{[9 + 1]} = \sqrt{10}$

$S(4,4)$, $T(3,1)$: $ST = \sqrt{[(4 - 3)^2 + (4 - 1)^2]} = \sqrt{[1 + 9]} = \sqrt{10}$

$T(3,1)$, $Q(0,0)$: $TQ = \sqrt{[(0 - 1)^2 + (0 - 3)^2]} = \sqrt{[1 + 9]} = \sqrt{10}$

The perimeter is therefore $\sqrt{10} + \sqrt{10} + \sqrt{10} + \sqrt{10} = 4\sqrt{10}$.

PLANE GEOMETRY—DIFFICULTY LEVEL: EASY

1. **The correct answer is D.** The volume of a rectangular prism is $l \times w \times h$. A cube is a special case in which the length, width, and height are all equal. The volume of a cube with edges of length 3 is $3 \times 3 \times 3 = 3^3 = 27$.

2. **The correct answer is H.** Because points M, N, and O are colinear, angle MNO has a measure of $180°$. When split into two component angles, the sum of those component angles must equal $180°$. Therefore the measure of angle MNP plus the measure of angle ONP equals $180°$. Since the measure of angle MNP is $3x°$, and the measure of angle ONP is $6x°$, it follows that $3x + 6x = 180$:

$$3x + 6x = 180$$
$$9x = 180$$
$$x = 20$$

The measure of angle MNP is $3x° = 3(20)° = 60°$

3. **The correct answer is B.** Because all of the angles are known to be right angles, you can conclude that the length of all the right-facing sides must equal the length of all the left-facing sides. Since the length of the right-facing side is 9, the missing left-facing side will have length 5. Similarly, the length of all up-facing sides must equal the length of all down-facing sides, making the length of the missing up-facing side 8. The perimeter (beginning with the left-facing side and moving clockwise) is $5 + 8 + 4 + 12 + 9 + 20 = 58$ cm.

4. The correct answer is H. The area of a triangle is $\frac{1}{2}bh$, where b is the length of the base and h is the height of the triangle. In this case, $\overline{AC}$ is the base of the triangle and $\overline{BD}$ is the height. Substitute the given values into the formula and solve:

$$40 = \frac{1}{2}(10)h$$
$$40 = 5h$$
$$8 = h; \overline{BD} \text{ has length } 8.$$

5. The correct answer is C. To solve this problem, recall that the area of a trapezoid is found by multiplying the average of the parallel bases by the height. Since the parallel bases have length 9 and 7, the average is $\frac{(9+7)}{2} = \frac{16}{2} = 8$. The area is the average of the bases multiplied by the height, or $8 \times 6 = 48$ square inches.

PLANE GEOMETRY—DIFFICULTY LEVEL: MEDIUM

6. The correct answer is H. When a wheel makes one revolution, it goes completely around one time. The distance one time around a wheel is equal to the wheel's circumference. A wheel is a circle, so the formula for the circumference of a wheel is $C = 2\pi r$. You are given that the area of the wheel is 78.5 inches. The formula for the area of a circle $A = \pi r^2$, so $78.5 = \pi r^2$. Solve for r, the radius, as follows:

$$78.5 = \pi r^2$$
$$78.5 = 3.14(r^2)$$
$$25 = r^2$$
$$5 = r$$

Now calculate the circumference, C, of the wheel, as follows:

$$C = 2\pi(5)$$
$$C = 2(3.14)(5) = 31.4$$

Because the circumference of the wheel is 31.4, one revolution of the wheel is equal to 31.4 inches. Divide the total number of inches traveled (1,200) by 31.4 to find the number of revolutions the wheel makes:

$1,200 \div 31.4 = 38.2$; the wheel makes about 38 revolutions.

7. The correct answer is A. To solve this problem, use the fact that supplementary angles add up to 180°. In the figure shown, x, y, and z form relationships with a, b, and c, respectively. Because a and x are vertical angles, they have the same measure.

Angles b and y are supplementary, so they add up to 180, making $y = 180 - b$. Likewise, $z = 180 - c$. Therefore, the sum of the angles within the triangle is $180 = x + y + z$, which is equivalent to $a + (180 - b) + (180 - c)$. You are given that $a = 140$, so substitute 140 for a, as follows:

$$180 = 140 + (180 - b) + (180 - c)$$
$$180 = 140 + 180 + 180 - b - c$$
$$180 = 500 - b - c$$
$$-320 = -b - c$$
$$320 = b + c$$

8. The correct answer is H. Because you are given that segments $\overline{XZ}$ and $\overline{YZ}$ bisect $\angle WXY$ and $\angle WYX$, respectively, you can conclude the following:

$$\angle WXZ \cong \angle YXZ$$
$$\angle WYZ \cong \angle XYZ$$

Furthermore, because you know that these two triangles are isosceles, you know that the base angles are congruent. Because of this congruence, you can conclude that the four angles written above are all congruent: $\angle WXZ \cong \angle YXZ \cong \angle WYZ \cong \angle XYZ$. Therefore, through transitivity, you can conclude that $\angle WXZ \cong \angle XYZ$.

9. The correct answer is C. Since Mandy's room is an L-shape comprised of a 14-foot × 7-foot rectangle and a 5-foot × 5-foot square, the area of her room is $(14 \times 12) + (5 \times 5) = 168 + 25$, or 193 square feet. An 8-foot × 12-foot piece of carpet covers 96 square feet ($8 \times 12 = 96$), so the area of 193 square feet is slightly larger than what 1 piece of carpet will cover. Therefore, Mandy will need at least 3 pieces of carpet.

10. The correct answer is H. When $\overline{AB}$ is 5 inches long, $\overline{BC}$ is 8 inches long, and $\overline{AC}$ is 3 inches long, $\triangle ABC$ has a perimeter of $5 + 8 + 3 = 16$. To find the perimeter of $\triangle XYZ$ when its longest side is 20, set up proportions to find the lengths of the sides. The sides of similar triangles are in proportion to each other. In this case, you can take the proportion of the longest sides, 20:8 $\left(\frac{20}{8}\right)$, and apply it to the perimeter, p, as follows:

$$\frac{20}{8} = \frac{p}{16}$$
$$p = \frac{(20 \times 16)}{8} = 40$$

PLANE GEOMETRY—DIFFICULTY LEVEL: HARD

11. The correct answer is B. To solve this problem, remember that the noncommon rays of two adjacent angles are the sides of the angles that are *not* shared. As shown in the figure below, these rays form a straight angle, or straight line, which you know contains 180°.

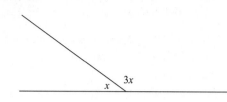

To find the measure of either angle, set up an equation: x (the measure of the smaller angle) $+ 3x$ (the measure of the larger angle) $= 180°$. Solve for x:

$$4x = 180°$$
$$x = 45°$$

12. **The correct answer is J.** The circumference of a circle is given by $2\pi r$, where r is the radius. If a circle has a circumference of 64π square units, then $64\pi = 2\pi r$. Dividing both sides by 2π yields $r = 32$. Since the square has sides that are the same length as the radius of the circle, 32, the perimeter of that square is $4(32) = 128$.

13. **The correct answer is B.** You are given that angle *QPR* and angle *PRS* are right angles; you are also given the lengths of diagonal $\overline{PR}$ (34), and side $\overline{PS}$ (30). It may help to write the lengths of the various line segments on a diagram as shown below:

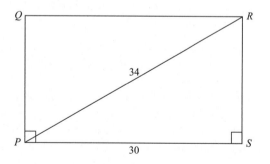

You should now see that you have the length of one side of the right triangle *PRS* (30), and the length of the hypotenuse (34). Use the Pythagorean theorem to calculate the length of the remaining side:

$$a^2 + b^2 = c^2$$
$$30^2 + b^2 = 34^2$$
$$900 + b^2 = 1,156$$
$$b^2 = 256$$
$$b = 16$$

The length of $\overline{RS}$ is 16.

14. **The correct answer is G.** To solve this problem, it is helpful to extend the lines of the angle given in the diagram as shown below:

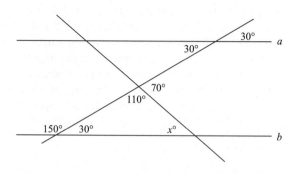

Make use of the properties of angles made by transversals that cross the parallel lines a and b. Also note the newly created triangle, which angle x is a part of. Given that opposite angles are congruent, one angle of that triangle is equal to 30°. Additionally, the supplement of the 70° is 110°. Knowing that two angles of a triangle are 110° and 30°, $x° + 140° = 180°$, and $x = 40°$.

15. **The correct answer is C.** To solve this problem, use the fact that π radians is equal to 180°. Given a radian measure, to convert to degrees simply divide by π and multiply by 180:

$$\frac{3.75\pi}{\pi} = 3.75$$
$$3.75 \times 180 = 675°$$

16. **The correct answer is H.** The area of a circle is given by πr^2, where r is the radius. If the radius is $\dfrac{32}{\pi}$, then the area is $\pi \left(\dfrac{32}{\pi}\right)^2 = \dfrac{1,024\pi}{\pi^2} = \dfrac{1,024}{\pi}$.

TRIGONOMETRY—DIFFICULTY LEVEL: MEDIUM

1. **The correct answer is C.** The cosine of an angle in a right triangle is the ratio of the side adjacent to that angle divided by the hypotenuse of the triangle. Since the side adjacent measures 12 and the hypotenuse is 13 (always the longest side in a right triangle), the cosine of the angle is $\dfrac{12}{13}$.

2. **The correct answer is J.** Tangent is the ratio of the side opposite an angle in a right triangle divided by the side adjacent to that angle. According to the figure, the side opposite α is r and the side adjacent is s. Therefore $\tan \alpha = \dfrac{r}{s}$.

3. **The correct answer is A.** To solve this problem, recall that tangent is the ratio of the side opposite an angle in a right triangle divided by the side adjacent to that angle. If $\tan \beta = \dfrac{3}{4}$, then you can think of this triangle as having legs of 3 and 4. The side opposite β is 3 and the side adjacent to β is 4. Now use the Pythagorean theorem to find the length of the hypotenuse ($c^2 = a^2 + b^2$, where c is the hypotenuse and a and b are the legs in a right triangle). The hypotenuse in this case is 5. The sine of an angle in a right triangle is the ratio of the side opposite to that angle divided by the hypotenuse of the triangle, making $\sin \beta = \dfrac{3}{5}$.

4. **The correct answer is H.** The cosine of any angle is calculated by dividing the length of the side adjacent to the acute angle by the hypotenuse $\left(\cos = \dfrac{\text{adj}}{\text{hyp}}\right)$, so the $\cos \angle A = \dfrac{21}{x}$.
To find the length of the hypotenuse, use the Pythagorean theorem, $a^2 + b^2 = c^2$:

$21^2 + 20^2 = c^2$

$441 + 400 = 841 = c^2$

$\sqrt{841} = \sqrt{c^2}$, so $c = 29$

The cos of $\angle A = \dfrac{21}{29}$.

TRIGONOMETRY—DIFFICULTY LEVEL: HARD

5. **The correct answer is A.** By definition, the tangent of any angle is the sin/cos of that angle.
Therefore, $\dfrac{(\cos x)}{(\tan x \sin x)}$ is equal to $\dfrac{\cos x}{\dfrac{(\sin x)}{(\cos x)}(\sin x)}$.
Multiply both the numerator and denominator by $\cos x$ to get $\dfrac{\cos^2 x}{\sin^2 x}$.

6. **The correct answer is G.** The unknown side, x, is the side opposite the 15° angle. Recall that the sine of an angle in a right triangle is the ratio of the side opposite to that angle divided by the hypotenuse of the triangle. $\sin 15° = \dfrac{x}{35}$.

Substitute the approximated value for sin 15°:

$0.259 = \dfrac{x}{35}$

$35(0.259) = x$

$9.065 = x$, which is approximately 9.1

7. **The correct answer is B.** The ratio $\tan \alpha$ is defined as $\dfrac{\sin \alpha}{\cos \alpha}$. The ratio $\dfrac{\tan \alpha}{\sin \alpha}$ can be written as:

$\dfrac{\sin \alpha}{\cos \alpha} \times \dfrac{1}{\sin \alpha}$

This simplifies to $\dfrac{1}{\cos \alpha}$.

███ WHAT'S NEXT?

Part III contains four simulated ACT Mathematics Practice tests in format. Apply the strategies and techniques you learned in the previous chapters to correctly answer as many of these questions as possible. Review the explanations for the questions that you miss.

PART III

PRACTICE QUESTIONS

CHAPTER 6

PRACTICE TEST 1 WITH EXPLANATIONS

 **ANSWER SHEET**

ACT MATHEMATICS TEST 1
Answer Sheet

MATHEMATICS

1 Ⓐ Ⓑ Ⓒ Ⓓ Ⓔ	16 Ⓕ Ⓖ Ⓗ Ⓙ Ⓚ	31 Ⓐ Ⓑ Ⓒ Ⓓ Ⓔ	46 Ⓕ Ⓖ Ⓗ Ⓙ Ⓚ
2 Ⓕ Ⓖ Ⓗ Ⓙ Ⓚ	17 Ⓐ Ⓑ Ⓒ Ⓓ Ⓔ	32 Ⓕ Ⓖ Ⓗ Ⓙ Ⓚ	47 Ⓐ Ⓑ Ⓒ Ⓓ Ⓔ
3 Ⓐ Ⓑ Ⓒ Ⓓ Ⓔ	18 Ⓕ Ⓖ Ⓗ Ⓙ Ⓚ	33 Ⓐ Ⓑ Ⓒ Ⓓ Ⓔ	48 Ⓕ Ⓖ Ⓗ Ⓙ Ⓚ
4 Ⓕ Ⓖ Ⓗ Ⓙ Ⓚ	19 Ⓐ Ⓑ Ⓒ Ⓓ Ⓔ	34 Ⓕ Ⓖ Ⓗ Ⓙ Ⓚ	49 Ⓐ Ⓑ Ⓒ Ⓓ Ⓔ
5 Ⓐ Ⓑ Ⓒ Ⓓ Ⓔ	20 Ⓕ Ⓖ Ⓗ Ⓙ Ⓚ	35 Ⓐ Ⓑ Ⓒ Ⓓ Ⓔ	50 Ⓕ Ⓖ Ⓗ Ⓙ Ⓚ
6 Ⓕ Ⓖ Ⓗ Ⓙ Ⓚ	21 Ⓐ Ⓑ Ⓒ Ⓓ Ⓔ	36 Ⓕ Ⓖ Ⓗ Ⓙ Ⓚ	51 Ⓐ Ⓑ Ⓒ Ⓓ Ⓔ
7 Ⓐ Ⓑ Ⓒ Ⓓ Ⓔ	22 Ⓕ Ⓖ Ⓗ Ⓙ Ⓚ	37 Ⓐ Ⓑ Ⓒ Ⓓ Ⓔ	52 Ⓕ Ⓖ Ⓗ Ⓙ Ⓚ
8 Ⓕ Ⓖ Ⓗ Ⓙ Ⓚ	23 Ⓐ Ⓑ Ⓒ Ⓓ Ⓔ	38 Ⓕ Ⓖ Ⓗ Ⓙ Ⓚ	53 Ⓐ Ⓑ Ⓒ Ⓓ Ⓔ
9 Ⓐ Ⓑ Ⓒ Ⓓ Ⓔ	24 Ⓕ Ⓖ Ⓗ Ⓙ Ⓚ	39 Ⓐ Ⓑ Ⓒ Ⓓ Ⓔ	54 Ⓕ Ⓖ Ⓗ Ⓙ Ⓚ
10 Ⓕ Ⓖ Ⓗ Ⓙ Ⓚ	25 Ⓐ Ⓑ Ⓒ Ⓓ Ⓔ	40 Ⓕ Ⓖ Ⓗ Ⓙ Ⓚ	55 Ⓐ Ⓑ Ⓒ Ⓓ Ⓔ
11 Ⓐ Ⓑ Ⓒ Ⓓ Ⓔ	26 Ⓕ Ⓖ Ⓗ Ⓙ Ⓚ	41 Ⓐ Ⓑ Ⓒ Ⓓ Ⓔ	56 Ⓕ Ⓖ Ⓗ Ⓙ Ⓚ
12 Ⓕ Ⓖ Ⓗ Ⓙ Ⓚ	27 Ⓐ Ⓑ Ⓒ Ⓓ Ⓔ	42 Ⓕ Ⓖ Ⓗ Ⓙ Ⓚ	57 Ⓐ Ⓑ Ⓒ Ⓓ Ⓔ
13 Ⓐ Ⓑ Ⓒ Ⓓ Ⓔ	28 Ⓕ Ⓖ Ⓗ Ⓙ Ⓚ	43 Ⓐ Ⓑ Ⓒ Ⓓ Ⓔ	58 Ⓕ Ⓖ Ⓗ Ⓙ Ⓚ
14 Ⓕ Ⓖ Ⓗ Ⓙ Ⓚ	29 Ⓐ Ⓑ Ⓒ Ⓓ Ⓔ	44 Ⓕ Ⓖ Ⓗ Ⓙ Ⓚ	59 Ⓐ Ⓑ Ⓒ Ⓓ Ⓔ
15 Ⓐ Ⓑ Ⓒ Ⓓ Ⓔ	30 Ⓕ Ⓖ Ⓗ Ⓙ Ⓚ	45 Ⓐ Ⓑ Ⓒ Ⓓ Ⓔ	60 Ⓕ Ⓖ Ⓗ Ⓙ Ⓚ

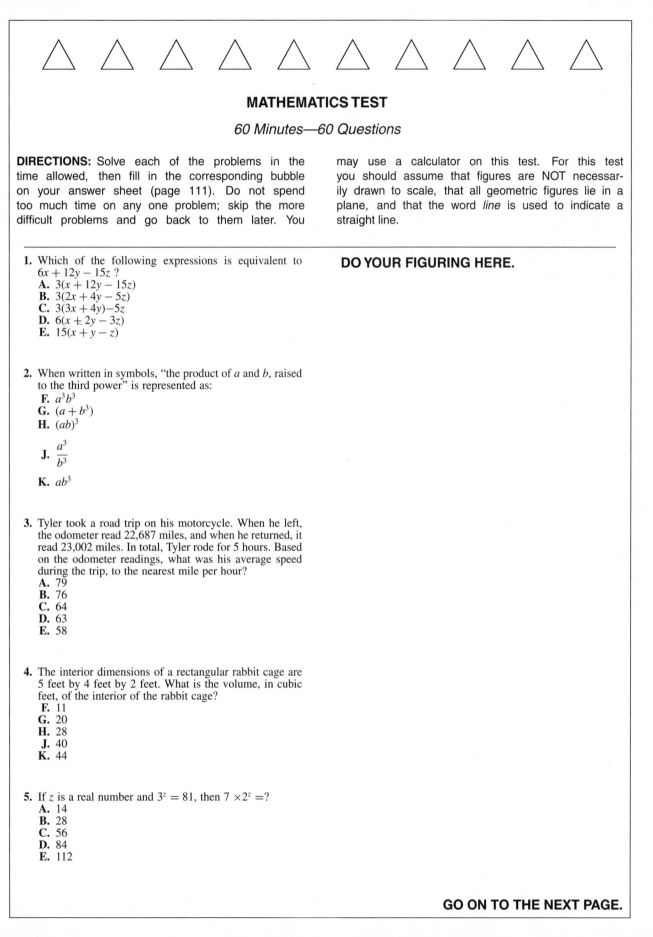

MATHEMATICS TEST

60 Minutes—60 Questions

DIRECTIONS: Solve each of the problems in the time allowed, then fill in the corresponding bubble on your answer sheet (page 111). Do not spend too much time on any one problem; skip the more difficult problems and go back to them later. You may use a calculator on this test. For this test you should assume that figures are NOT necessarily drawn to scale, that all geometric figures lie in a plane, and that the word *line* is used to indicate a straight line.

DO YOUR FIGURING HERE.

1. Which of the following expressions is equivalent to $6x + 12y - 15z$?
   A. $3(x + 12y - 15z)$
   B. $3(2x + 4y - 5z)$
   C. $3(3x + 4y) - 5z$
   D. $6(x + 2y - 3z)$
   E. $15(x + y - z)$

2. When written in symbols, "the product of a and b, raised to the third power" is represented as:
   F. $a^3 b^3$
   G. $(a + b^3)$
   H. $(ab)^3$
   J. $\dfrac{a^3}{b^3}$
   K. ab^3

3. Tyler took a road trip on his motorcycle. When he left, the odometer read 22,687 miles, and when he returned, it read 23,002 miles. In total, Tyler rode for 5 hours. Based on the odometer readings, what was his average speed during the trip, to the nearest mile per hour?
   A. 79
   B. 76
   C. 64
   D. 63
   E. 58

4. The interior dimensions of a rectangular rabbit cage are 5 feet by 4 feet by 2 feet. What is the volume, in cubic feet, of the interior of the rabbit cage?
   F. 11
   G. 20
   H. 28
   J. 40
   K. 44

5. If z is a real number and $3^z = 81$, then $7 \times 2^z = ?$
   A. 14
   B. 28
   C. 56
   D. 84
   E. 112

GO ON TO THE NEXT PAGE.

DO YOUR FIGURING HERE.

6. For the students at Bayside College, the ratio of professors to students is 2:43. There are currently 9,030 students enrolled. Which of the following statements is (are) true?
   I. There are 420 professors.
   II. Each professor has 43 students in his or her course.
   III. Professors comprise $\dfrac{2}{43}$ of the Bayside population.

   F. I only
   G. II only
   H. III only
   J. I and III only
   K. I, II, and III

7. If the probability that a specific event will occur is 0.09, what is the probability that the event will NOT occur?
   A. 0.00
   B. 0.11
   C. 0.70
   D. 0.91
   E. 1.00

8. As shown below, the diagonals of rectangle $ABCD$ intersect at the point $(-4, 2)$ in the standard (x, y) coordinate plane. Point D is at $(1, -1)$. Which of the following are the coordinates of point B?

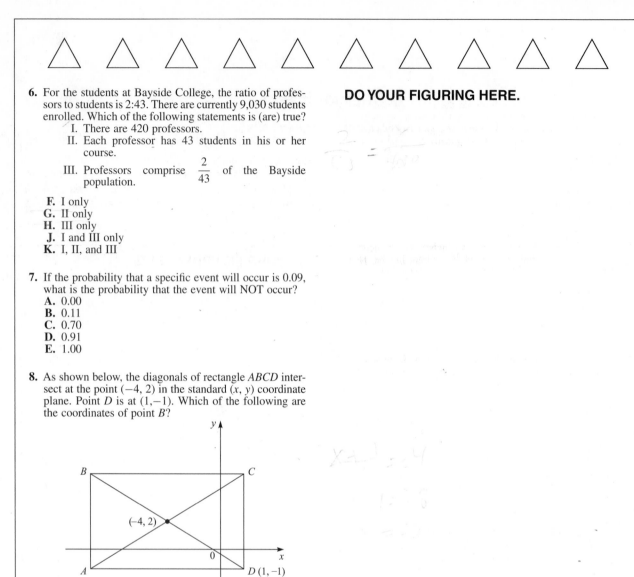

   F. $(1, 5)$
   G. $(-6, 4)$
   H. $(-9, -1)$
   J. $(-9, 5)$
   K. $(-11, 6)$

9. Which of the following expressions is equivalent to $\dfrac{16s + 48}{8}$?

   A. $48s$
   B. $8s$
   C. $2s + 6$
   D. $2s + 48$
   E. $s + 6$

10. The expression $5m(-3m + 6n) - 9mn$ is equivalent to:
    F. $30mn - 8m$
    G. $21mn - 15m^2$
    H. $15mn - 9m^2$
    J. $6mn$
    K. $-15m^2$

GO ON TO THE NEXT PAGE.

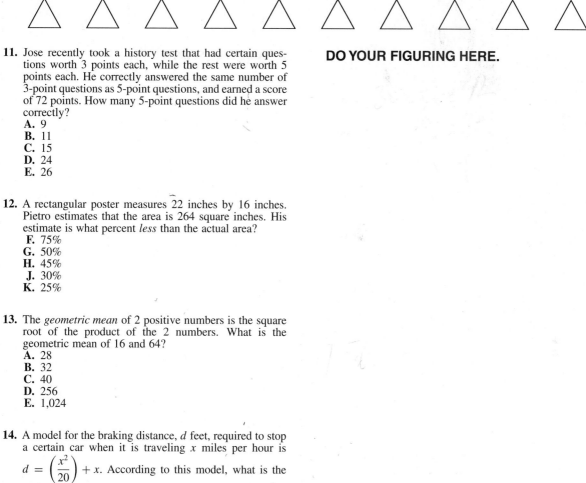

11. Jose recently took a history test that had certain questions worth 3 points each, while the rest were worth 5 points each. He correctly answered the same number of 3-point questions as 5-point questions, and earned a score of 72 points. How many 5-point questions did he answer correctly?
    A. 9
    B. 11
    C. 15
    D. 24
    E. 26

12. A rectangular poster measures 22 inches by 16 inches. Pietro estimates that the area is 264 square inches. His estimate is what percent *less* than the actual area?
    F. 75%
    G. 50%
    H. 45%
    J. 30%
    K. 25%

13. The *geometric mean* of 2 positive numbers is the square root of the product of the 2 numbers. What is the geometric mean of 16 and 64?
    A. 28
    B. 32
    C. 40
    D. 256
    E. 1,024

14. A model for the braking distance, d feet, required to stop a certain car when it is traveling x miles per hour is $d = \left(\dfrac{x^2}{20} \right) + x$. According to this model, what is the braking distance, in feet, required to stop this car when it is traveling at 30 miles per hour?
    F. 30
    G. 52
    H. 75
    J. 90
    K. 102

15. The expression $2x^2 + 10x - 28$ can be written as the product of 2 binomials with integer coefficients. One of the binomials is $(x + 7)$. Which of the following is the other binomial?
    A. $2x^2 - 4$
    B. $2x^2 + 4$
    C. $2x - 6$
    D. $2x - 4$
    E. $x + 4$

16. The cost for a business to produce x television commercials in 1 year is $225x + \$17,000$. How many commercials can the company produce in 1 year at a cost of $35,000?
    F. 75
    G. 80
    H. 100
    J. 155
    K. 231

DO YOUR FIGURING HERE.

GO ON TO THE NEXT PAGE.

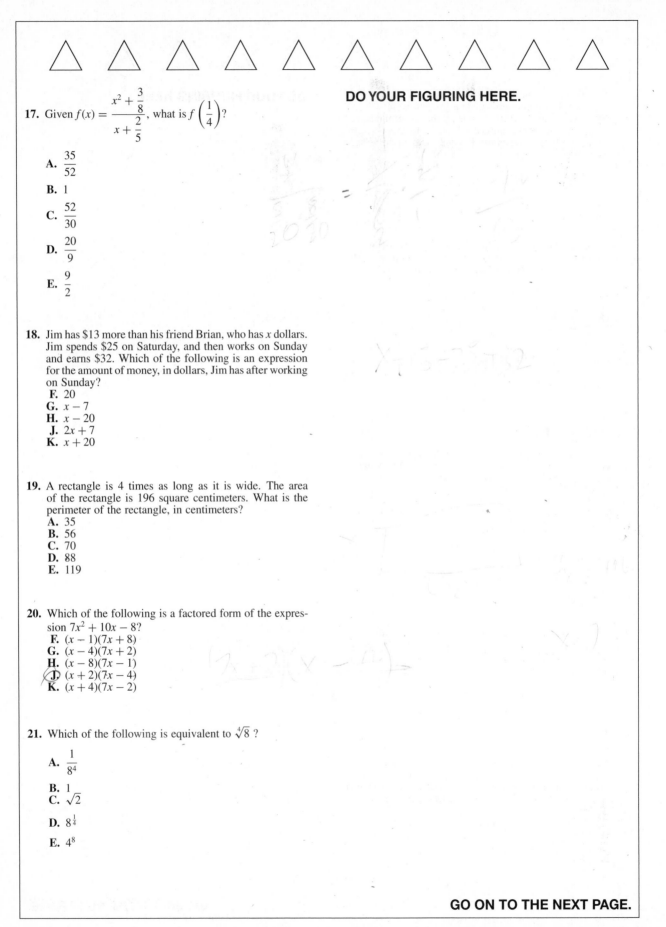

DO YOUR FIGURING HERE.

17. Given $f(x) = \dfrac{x^2 + \frac{3}{8}}{x + \frac{2}{5}}$, what is $f\left(\dfrac{1}{4}\right)$?

   A. $\dfrac{35}{52}$

   B. 1

   C. $\dfrac{52}{30}$

   D. $\dfrac{20}{9}$

   E. $\dfrac{9}{2}$

18. Jim has \$13 more than his friend Brian, who has x dollars. Jim spends \$25 on Saturday, and then works on Sunday and earns \$32. Which of the following is an expression for the amount of money, in dollars, Jim has after working on Sunday?
   F. 20
   G. $x - 7$
   H. $x - 20$
   J. $2x + 7$
   K. $x + 20$

19. A rectangle is 4 times as long as it is wide. The area of the rectangle is 196 square centimeters. What is the perimeter of the rectangle, in centimeters?
   A. 35
   B. 56
   C. 70
   D. 88
   E. 119

20. Which of the following is a factored form of the expression $7x^2 + 10x - 8$?
   F. $(x - 1)(7x + 8)$
   G. $(x - 4)(7x + 2)$
   H. $(x - 8)(7x - 1)$
   J. $(x + 2)(7x - 4)$
   K. $(x + 4)(7x - 2)$

21. Which of the following is equivalent to $\sqrt[4]{8}$?

   A. $\dfrac{1}{8^4}$

   B. 1
   C. $\sqrt{2}$

   D. $8^{\frac{1}{4}}$

   E. 4^8

GO ON TO THE NEXT PAGE.

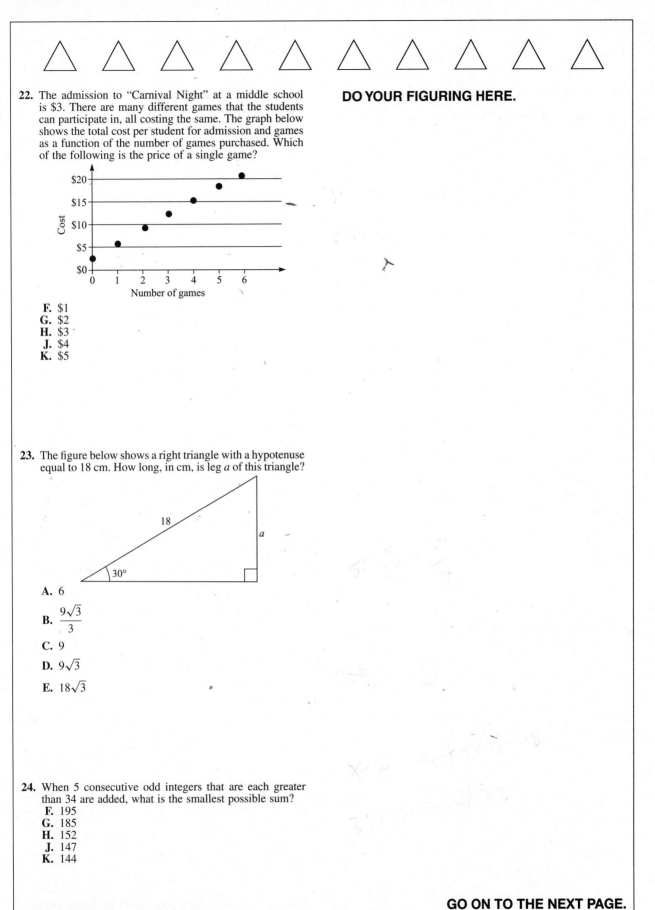

22. The admission to "Carnival Night" at a middle school is $3. There are many different games that the students can participate in, all costing the same. The graph below shows the total cost per student for admission and games as a function of the number of games purchased. Which of the following is the price of a single game?

DO YOUR FIGURING HERE.

F. $1
G. $2
H. $3
J. $4
K. $5

23. The figure below shows a right triangle with a hypotenuse equal to 18 cm. How long, in cm, is leg *a* of this triangle?

A. 6

B. $\dfrac{9\sqrt{3}}{3}$

C. 9

D. $9\sqrt{3}$

E. $18\sqrt{3}$

24. When 5 consecutive odd integers that are each greater than 34 are added, what is the smallest possible sum?
F. 195
G. 185
H. 152
J. 147
K. 144

GO ON TO THE NEXT PAGE.

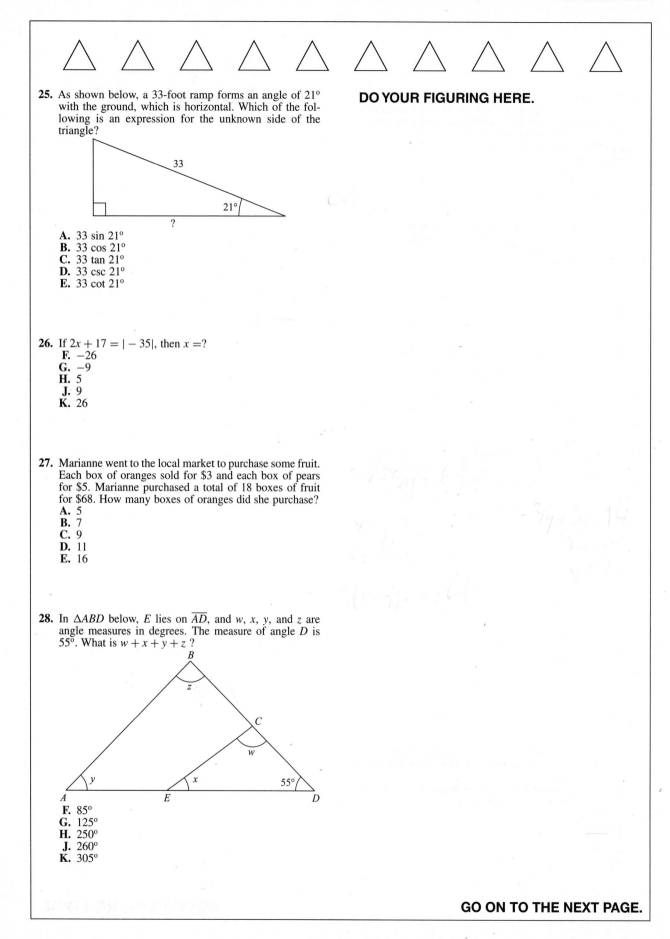

25. As shown below, a 33-foot ramp forms an angle of 21° with the ground, which is horizontal. Which of the following is an expression for the unknown side of the triangle?

DO YOUR FIGURING HERE.

- **A.** 33 sin 21°
- **B.** 33 cos 21°
- **C.** 33 tan 21°
- **D.** 33 csc 21°
- **E.** 33 cot 21°

26. If $2x + 17 = |-35|$, then $x =$?
- **F.** −26
- **G.** −9
- **H.** 5
- **J.** 9
- **K.** 26

27. Marianne went to the local market to purchase some fruit. Each box of oranges sold for $3 and each box of pears for $5. Marianne purchased a total of 18 boxes of fruit for $68. How many boxes of oranges did she purchase?
- **A.** 5
- **B.** 7
- **C.** 9
- **D.** 11
- **E.** 16

28. In $\triangle ABD$ below, E lies on $\overline{AD}$, and w, x, y, and z are angle measures in degrees. The measure of angle D is 55°. What is $w + x + y + z$?

- **F.** 85°
- **G.** 125°
- **H.** 250°
- **J.** 260°
- **K.** 305°

GO ON TO THE NEXT PAGE.

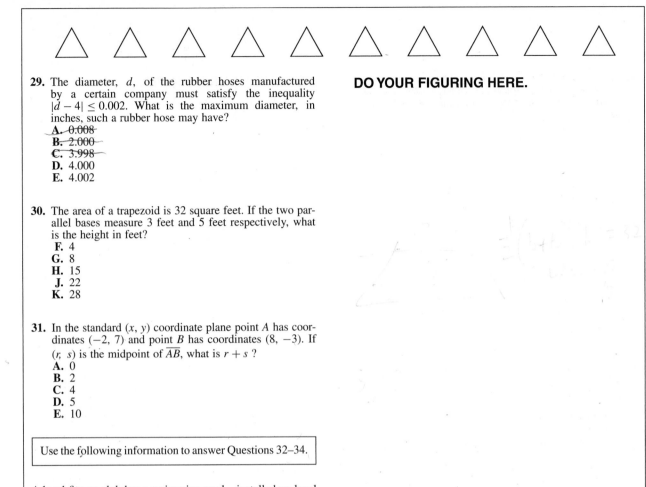

DO YOUR FIGURING HERE.

29. The diameter, d, of the rubber hoses manufactured by a certain company must satisfy the inequality $|d - 4| \leq 0.002$. What is the maximum diameter, in inches, such a rubber hose may have?
    A. 0.008
    B. 2.000
    C. 3.998
    D. 4.000
    E. 4.002

30. The area of a trapezoid is 32 square feet. If the two parallel bases measure 3 feet and 5 feet respectively, what is the height in feet?
    F. 4
    G. 8
    H. 15
    J. 22
    K. 28

31. In the standard (x, y) coordinate plane point A has coordinates $(-2, 7)$ and point B has coordinates $(8, -3)$. If (r, s) is the midpoint of $\overline{AB}$, what is $r + s$?
    A. 0
    B. 2
    C. 4
    D. 5
    E. 10

Use the following information to answer Questions 32–34.

A local fitness club has a swimming pool—installed on level ground—that is a right cylinder with a diameter of 20 feet and a height of 5 feet. A diagram of the pool and its entry ladder is shown below.

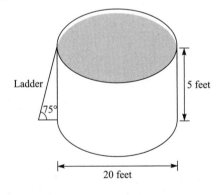

Ladder

75°

5 feet

20 feet

32. To the nearest cubic foot, what is the volume of water that will be in the pool when it is filled with water to a depth of 4 feet?
    (Note: The volume of a cylinder is given by $\pi r^2 h$, where r is the radius and h is the height.)
    F. 5,024
    G. 1,882
    H. 1,256
    J. 251
    K. 126

GO ON TO THE NEXT PAGE.

33. A solar cover is made for the pool. The cover will rest on the top of the pool and will include a wedge-shaped flap that forms a 30° angle at the center of the cover, as shown in the figure below. A zipper will be sewn along 1 side of the wedge-shaped flap and around the arc. Which of the following is closest to the length, in feet, of the zipper?

DO YOUR FIGURING HERE.

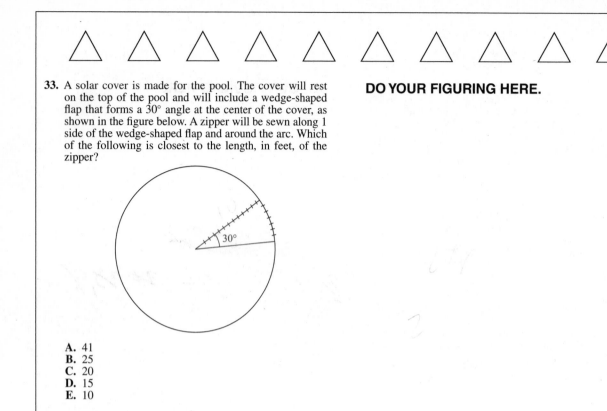

- **A.** 41
- **B.** 25
- **C.** 20
- **D.** 15
- **E.** 10

34. A hose connected to a hydraulic pump was used to fill the pool. The pump had been on the medium setting for 10 hours and had filled the pool to the 3-foot mark when someone realized that the pump could be set to a higher setting that increased the flow by 33%. The pool was then filled to the 4-foot mark at the greater flow rate. Which of the following graphs shows the relationship between the time spent filling the pool and the height of the water in the pool?

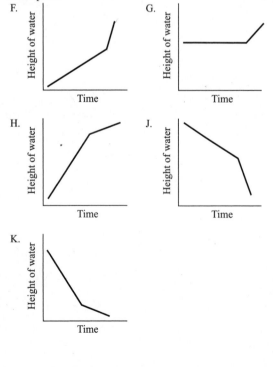

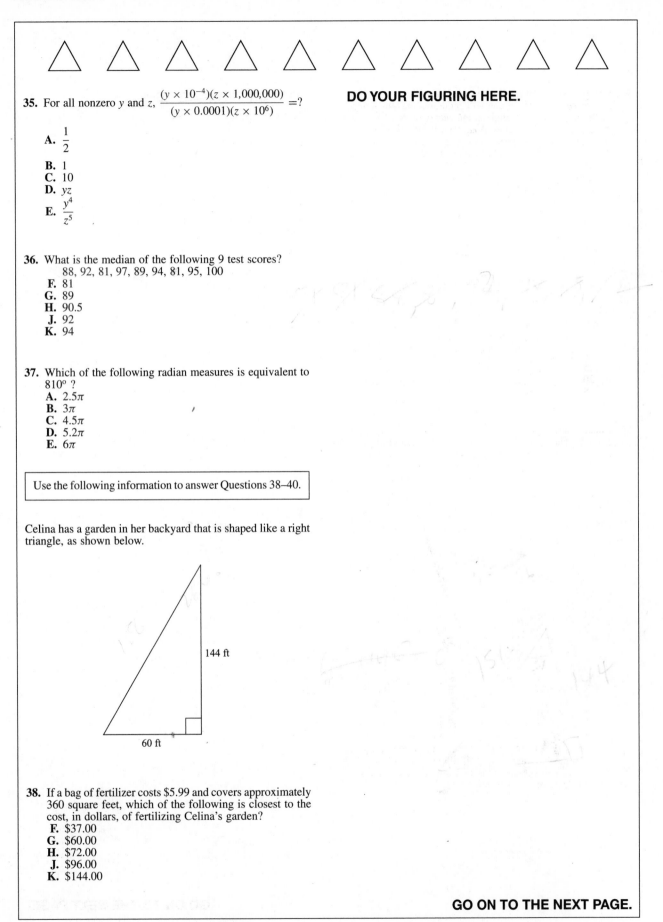

DO YOUR FIGURING HERE.

35. For all nonzero y and z, $\dfrac{(y \times 10^{-4})(z \times 1{,}000{,}000)}{(y \times 0.0001)(z \times 10^6)} = ?$

  A. $\dfrac{1}{2}$

  B. 1
  C. 10
  D. yz

  E. $\dfrac{y^4}{z^5}$

36. What is the median of the following 9 test scores?
    88, 92, 81, 97, 89, 94, 81, 95, 100
  F. 81
  G. 89
  H. 90.5
  J. 92
  K. 94

37. Which of the following radian measures is equivalent to 810° ?
  A. 2.5π
  B. 3π
  C. 4.5π
  D. 5.2π
  E. 6π

Use the following information to answer Questions 38–40.

Celina has a garden in her backyard that is shaped like a right triangle, as shown below.

144 ft

60 ft

38. If a bag of fertilizer costs $5.99 and covers approximately 360 square feet, which of the following is closest to the cost, in dollars, of fertilizing Celina's garden?
  F. $37.00
  G. $60.00
  H. $72.00
  J. $96.00
  K. $144.00

GO ON TO THE NEXT PAGE.

39. Celina wants to put a fence around her garden to protect it from animals. Before she buys the fencing, she calculates the perimeter of the garden. What is its perimeter, in feet?

A. 204
B. 216
C. 300
D. 360
E. 408

DO YOUR FIGURING HERE.

40. The angle opposite the 60-foot side of the garden measures approximately 26.4°. Celina wants to change the shape of her garden. It will still be a right triangle with the 144-foot side as one leg, but she is going to extend the 60-foot side until the angle opposite that side is about 37°. By approximately how many feet would Celina need to extend the 60-foot side?
(Note: sin 37° = 0.60, cos 37° = 0.80, tan 37° = 0.75)

F. 26
G. 48
H. 55
J. 60
K. 108

41. What is the point in the standard (x, y) coordinate plane that is the center of a circle with the equation $(x + 6)^2 + (y - 9)^2 = 25$?

A. $(-9, 6)$
B. $(-6, 9)$
C. $(0, 5)$
D. $(6, -9)$
E. $(-9, 6)$

42. Brendan's average score after 4 math quizzes was 78. His score on the 5th quiz was 93. If all 5 of the quizzes are weighted equally, which of the following is closest to his average score after 5 quizzes?

F. 93
G. 90
H. 87
J. 81
K. 78

GO ON TO THE NEXT PAGE.

43. Ratings for a particular 2-hour television program reveal that the greatest number of viewers tuned in right at the start of the program and a majority of them remained tuned in for the 1st half-hour of the program. For the next hour, the number of viewers steadily declined, until it jumped back up for the last half-hour. Among the following graphs, which one best represents the relationship between the rating of the program, in thousands of viewers, and the time, in minutes, from the start to the finish of the program?

DO YOUR FIGURING HERE.

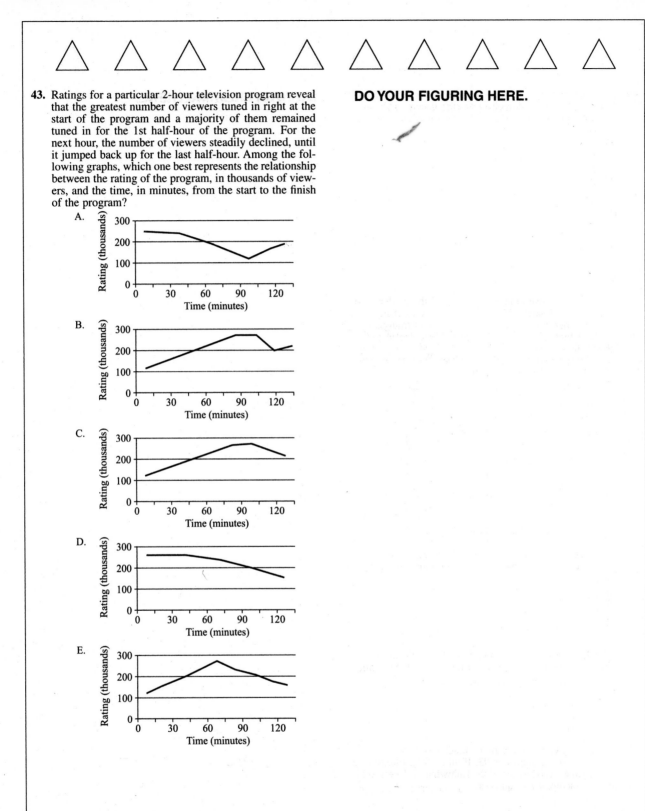

44. The sides of a right triangle measure 20 cm, 21 cm, and 29 cm. What is the sine of the angle adjacent to the side that measures 20 cm?

F. $\dfrac{20}{29}$

G. $\dfrac{21}{29}$

H. $\dfrac{20}{21}$

J. $\dfrac{29}{21}$

K. $\dfrac{29}{20}$

DO YOUR FIGURING HERE.

45. In the figure below, a square is circumscribed about a circle with a diameter of 20 cm. Points Q, R, S, and T are the midpoints of the square's sides. What is the total area, in cm^2, of the shaded regions?

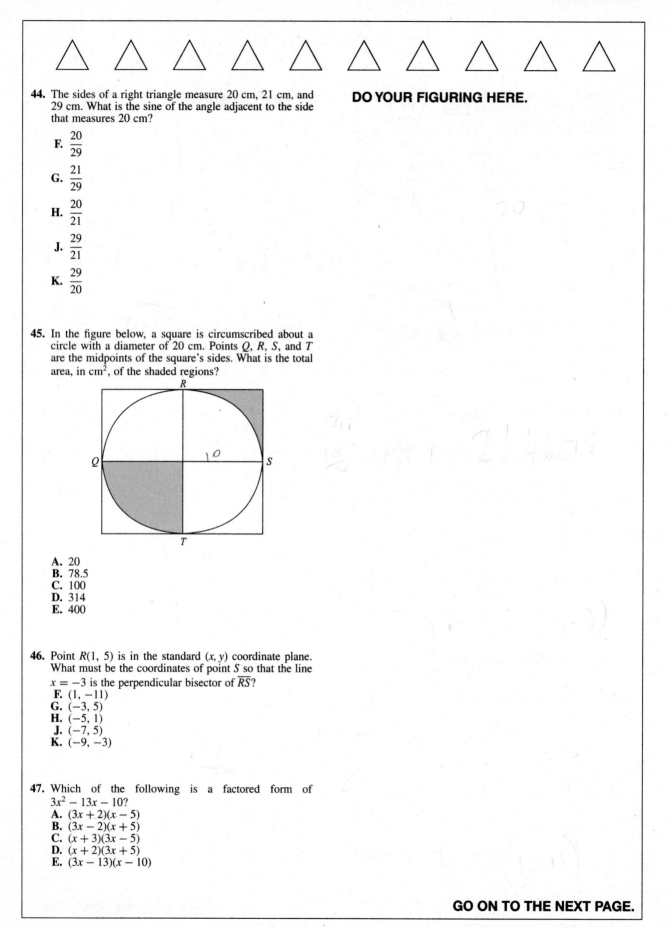

A. 20
B. 78.5
C. 100
D. 314
E. 400

46. Point $R(1, 5)$ is in the standard (x, y) coordinate plane. What must be the coordinates of point S so that the line $x = -3$ is the perpendicular bisector of $\overline{RS}$?
F. $(1, -11)$
G. $(-3, 5)$
H. $(-5, 1)$
J. $(-7, 5)$
K. $(-9, -3)$

47. Which of the following is a factored form of $3x^2 - 13x - 10$?
A. $(3x + 2)(x - 5)$
B. $(3x - 2)(x + 5)$
C. $(x + 3)(3x - 5)$
D. $(x + 2)(3x + 5)$
E. $(3x - 13)(x - 10)$

GO ON TO THE NEXT PAGE.

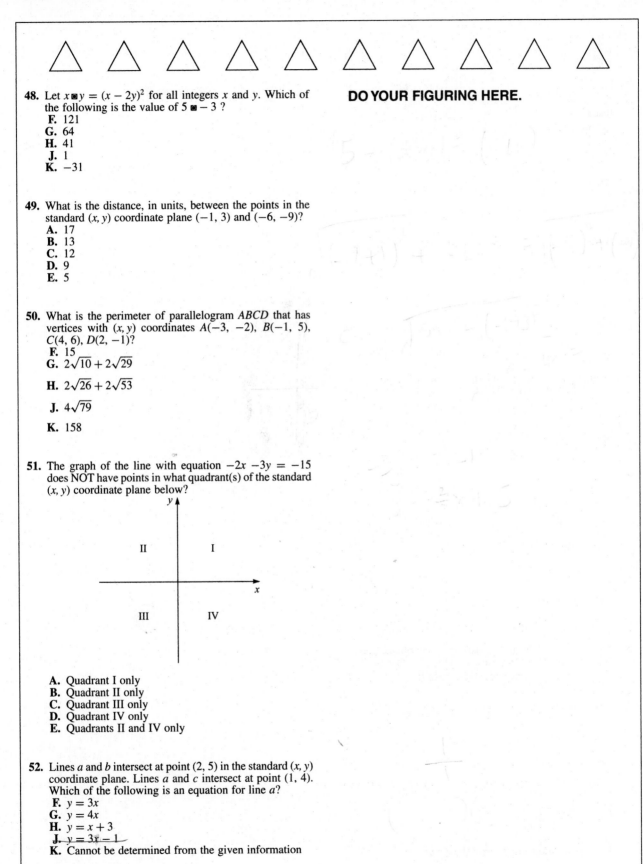

48. Let $x ■ y = (x - 2y)^2$ for all integers x and y. Which of the following is the value of $5 ■ - 3$?
    F. 121
    G. 64
    H. 41
    J. 1
    K. −31

49. What is the distance, in units, between the points in the standard (x, y) coordinate plane $(-1, 3)$ and $(-6, -9)$?
    A. 17
    B. 13
    C. 12
    D. 9
    E. 5

50. What is the perimeter of parallelogram $ABCD$ that has vertices with (x, y) coordinates $A(-3, -2)$, $B(-1, 5)$, $C(4, 6)$, $D(2, -1)$?
    F. 15
    G. $2\sqrt{10} + 2\sqrt{29}$
    H. $2\sqrt{26} + 2\sqrt{53}$
    J. $4\sqrt{79}$
    K. 158

51. The graph of the line with equation $-2x - 3y = -15$ does NOT have points in what quadrant(s) of the standard (x, y) coordinate plane below?

    A. Quadrant I only
    B. Quadrant II only
    C. Quadrant III only
    D. Quadrant IV only
    E. Quadrants II and IV only

52. Lines a and b intersect at point $(2, 5)$ in the standard (x, y) coordinate plane. Lines a and c intersect at point $(1, 4)$. Which of the following is an equation for line a?
    F. $y = 3x$
    G. $y = 4x$
    H. $y = x + 3$
    J. $y = 3x - 1$
    K. Cannot be determined from the given information

DO YOUR FIGURING HERE.

GO ON TO THE NEXT PAGE.

53. $3^0 + 3^2 + 3^{-2} = ?$

   A. 0

   B. $\dfrac{1}{9}$

   C. 9

   D. $10\dfrac{1}{9}$

   E. 19

DO YOUR FIGURING HERE.

54. The circumference of a circle is 10π inches. What is the area, in square inches, of the circle?

   F. 5

   G. $\dfrac{25}{\pi}$

   H. 10

   J. 5π

   K. 25π

55. In the (x, y) coordinate plane, what is the radius of the circle with a diameter having endpoints $(-2, 8)$ and $(1, 4)$?

   A. 2.5

   B. 5

   C. 9

   D. 16.5

   E. 25

56. The graph of the function $f(x) = \dfrac{x^3 - 4}{x^2 + 3x - 10}$ is shown in the standard (x, y) coordinate plane below. Which of the following, if any, is a list of each of the *vertical* asymptotes of $f(x)$?

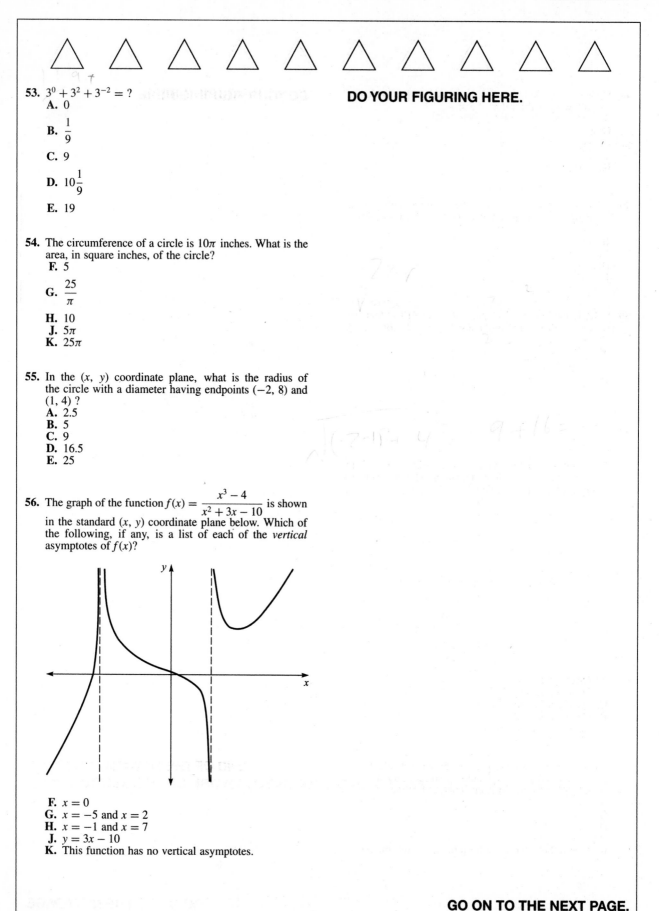

   F. $x = 0$

   G. $x = -5$ and $x = 2$

   H. $x = -1$ and $x = 7$

   J. $y = 3x - 10$

   K. This function has no vertical asymptotes.

GO ON TO THE NEXT PAGE.

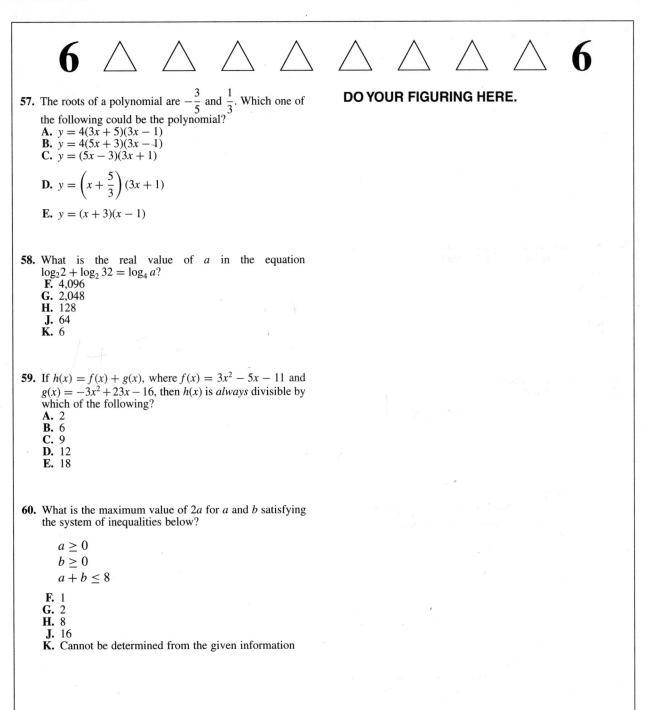

6 △ △ △ △ △ △ △ △ **6**

57. The roots of a polynomial are $-\dfrac{3}{5}$ and $\dfrac{1}{3}$. Which one of the following could be the polynomial?

A. $y = 4(3x + 5)(3x - 1)$
B. $y = 4(5x + 3)(3x - 1)$
C. $y = (5x - 3)(3x + 1)$

D. $y = \left(x + \dfrac{5}{3}\right)(3x + 1)$

E. $y = (x + 3)(x - 1)$

58. What is the real value of a in the equation $\log_2 2 + \log_2 32 = \log_4 a$?

　F. 4,096
　G. 2,048
　H. 128
　J. 64
　K. 6

59. If $h(x) = f(x) + g(x)$, where $f(x) = 3x^2 - 5x - 11$ and $g(x) = -3x^2 + 23x - 16$, then $h(x)$ is *always* divisible by which of the following?

　A. 2
　B. 6
　C. 9
　D. 12
　E. 18

60. What is the maximum value of $2a$ for a and b satisfying the system of inequalities below?

$$a \geq 0$$
$$b \geq 0$$
$$a + b \leq 8$$

　F. 1
　G. 2
　H. 8
　J. 16
　K. Cannot be determined from the given information

END OF THE MATHEMATICS TEST
STOP! IF YOU HAVE TIME LEFT OVER, CHECK YOUR WORK ON THIS SECTION ONLY.

ANSWER KEY

Mathematics Test

1. B	16. G	31. D	46. J
2. H	17. A	32. H	47. A
3. D	18. K	33. D	48. F
4. J	19. C	34. F	49. B
5. E	20. J	35. B	50. H
6. F	21. D	36. J	51. C
7. D	22. H	37. C	52. H
8. J	23. C	38. H	53. D
9. C	24. F	39. D	54. K
10. G	25. B	40. G	55. A
11. A	26. J	41. B	56. G
12. K	27. D	42. J	57. B
13. B	28. H	43. A	58. F
14. H	29. E	44. G	59. C
15. D	30. G	45. C	60. J

SCORING WORKSHEET

On each ACT multiple-choice test (English, Mathematics, Reading, and Science Reasoning) you will receive a SCALED SCORE on a scale of 1 to 36. Use the following guidelines to determine your approximate SCALED SCORE on the ACT Mathematics Diagnostic Test that you just completed.

Step 1 Determine your RAW SCORE.

Your RAW SCORE is the number of questions that you answered correctly. Because there are 60 questions on the ACT Mathematics Test, the highest possible RAW SCORE is 60.

Step 2 Determine your SCALED SCORE using the following Scoring Worksheet.

Mathematics _____ × **36** = _____ ÷ **60** = _____

           RAW SCORE

                                                                        + 1 (*correction factor)

                                                                         SCALED SCORE

---

*The correction factor is an approximation based on the average from several recent ACT tests. It is most valid for scores in the middle 50% (approximately 16–24 scaled composite score) of the scoring range. The scores are all approximate. Actual ACT scoring scales vary from one administration to the next based upon several factors.

ANSWERS AND EXPLANATIONS

1. **The correct answer is B.** To solve this problem, factor out 3, as it is the greatest common factor of the three monomials ($3 \times 2 = 6$, $3 \times 4 = 12$, $3 \times -5 = -15$). Use these values to simplify the expression:

$$6x + 12y - 15z$$
$$= 3(2x + 4y - 5z)$$

Once you determined that 3 was the greatest common factor, you could eliminate answer choices D and E.

2. **The correct answer is H.** The product of two numbers is found by multiplying them ($a \times b$ in this case). Raising the product of a and b to the third power is represented by $(ab)^3$, since you are raising the entire product to the third power, not just one of the variables (as shown in answer choice K).

3. **The correct answer is D.** Before calculating Tyler's average speed, you must find out how far he traveled. If his odometer read 22,687 when he left, and 23,002 when he returned, he traveled 315 miles ($23,002 - 22,687$). You are given that he drove for 5 hours, so you can use the formula Distance = Rate $\times$ Time to find his average speed:

$$315 = R(5)$$
$$R = 63$$

His average speed was 63 miles per hour.

4. **The correct answer is J.** The volume of a rectangle is given by Length $\times$ Height $\times$ Width. For the rabbit cage, the volume would be $(5 \times 4 \times 2) = 40$ cubic feet.

5. **The correct answer is E.** The first step in solving this problem is to determine the value of z. You are given that 3 raised to the power of z equals 81. Therefore, z must equal 4 ($3^4 = 81$). Use this value to solve 7×2^z:

$$7 \times 2^4 = 7 \times 16 = 112$$

6. **The correct answer is F.** You are given the ratio of professors to students (2:43) and the number of students (9,030). You can use this information to set up a proportion to determine the number of professors:

$$\frac{2}{43} = \frac{x}{9,030}$$

$$18,060 = 43x$$
$$x = 420$$

There are 420 professors at Bayside, so Roman numeral I is true. Eliminate answer choices G and H because they do not include Roman numeral I. Roman numeral II is not supported by any of the

given information (you don't know the total number of courses), therefore it is not true. There is not enough information given for Roman numeral III (i.e. other employees of the school) so it also is not true. Since only Roman numeral I is true, answer choice F is correct.

7. **The correct answer is D.** In simple probability, the probability that an event will occur plus the probability that that event will not occur must equal 1. Therefore, if the probability that a specific event will occur is 0.09, then the probability that it will not occur is $1.00 - 0.09 = 0.91$, answer choice D.

8. **The correct answer is J.** To find the value of B, you can use the midpoint formula. Since the diagonals of the rectangle intersect at point $(-4, 2)$, this is the midpoint of segments $\overline{BD}$ and $\overline{AC}$. The formula for determining the midpoint of a segment with endpoints (x_1, y_1) and (x_2, y_2) is $\left(\dfrac{x_1 + x_2}{2}, \dfrac{y_1 + y_2}{2} \right)$. You already have the coordinates of the midpoint and point D, so you can use these to determine the coordinates of point B:

x-coordinate:

$$-4 = 1 + \frac{x_2}{2}$$
$$-8 = 1 + x_2$$
$$-9 = x_2$$

y-coordinate:

$$2 = -1 + \frac{y_2}{2}$$
$$4 = -1 + y_2$$
$$5 = y_2$$

The coordinates of point B are $(-9, 5)$.

9. **The correct answer is C.** To solve this problem, first try to simplify the expression $16s + 48$. You can see that 16 and 48 have a greatest common factor of 16, so you can factor out 16:

$$\frac{16(s + 3)}{8}$$

Simplify the fraction by dividing both the numerator and the denominator by 8:

$$2(s + 3)$$
$$= 2s + 6$$

10. **The correct answer is G.** To solve this problem, distribute $5m$ as shown next:

$$5m(-3m + 6n) - 9mn$$
$$= -15m^2 + 30mn - 9mn$$
$$= -15m^2 + 21mn$$
$$= 21mn - 15m^2$$

11. The correct answer is A. Since Jose answered the same number of 3-point questions correctly as he did 5-point questions, you can set up an equation:

$5x + 3x = 72$ (5 points times the number of 5-point questions answered correctly, plus 3 points times the number of 3-point questions answered correctly, equals 72.)

$8x = 72$
$x = 9$

Jose answered nine 5-point questions and nine 3-point questions, correctly.

12. The correct answer is K. First, you need to find the actual area of the poster, which is $22 \times 16 = 352$ square inches. Next, find the percentage of the actual area that is represented by Pietro's estimate $\left(\dfrac{264}{352} = 0.75\right)$. Pietro's estimate of the area is 75% of the actual area; therefore his estimate is 25% less than the actual area.

13. The correct answer is B. You are told that the geometric mean is the square root of the product of two numbers. To find the geometric mean of 16 and 64, first find the product of the two numbers ($16 \times 64 = 1,024$). Now, take the square root of this number ($\sqrt{1,024} = 32$). The geometric mean of 16 and 64 is 32.

14. The correct answer is H. To solve this problem, insert 30 into the equation wherever there is an instance of x:

$d = (30^2 \div 20) + 30$
$d = (900 \div 20) + 30$
$d = 45 + 30$
$d = 75$

When traveling 30 miles per hour, the braking distance for this car would be 75 feet.

15. The correct answer is D. To solve this problem, you can test the answer choices to see which one, when multiplied by the given binomial, $(x + 7)$, equals $2x^2 + 10x - 28$ (remember to use the FOIL method):

Answer choice A: $(2x^2 - 4)(x+7) = 2x^3 + 14x^2 - 4x - 28$. Eliminate answer choice A.

Answer choice B: $(2x^2 + 4)(x+7) = 2x^3 + 14x^2 + 4x + 28$. Eliminate answer choice B.

Answer choice C: $(2x - 6)(x+7) = 2x^2 + 14x - 6x - 42 = 2x^2 + 8x - 42$. Eliminate answer choice C.

Answer choice D: $(2x - 4)(x + 7) = 2x^2 + 14x - 4x - 28 = 2x^2 + 10x - 28$

Answer choice D is correct, so there is no need to test answer choice E.

16. The correct answer is G. To solve this problem, take the given information and set up an equation to solve for x:

$35,000 = 225x + 17,000$
$18,000 = 225x$
$x = 80$

The business can produce 80 commercials during the year at a cost of $35,000.

17. The correct answer is A. To solve this problem, substitute $\dfrac{1}{4}$ for every instance of x in the equation:

$$f(x) = \frac{\left(\dfrac{1}{4}\right)^2 + \dfrac{3}{8}}{\dfrac{1}{4} + \dfrac{2}{5}}$$

$$f(x) = \frac{\dfrac{1}{16} + \dfrac{3}{8}}{\dfrac{1}{4} + \dfrac{2}{5}}$$

Find the least common denominators, and add the fractions in the numerator and the denominator:

$$f(x) = \frac{\dfrac{1}{16} + \dfrac{6}{16}}{\dfrac{5}{20} + \dfrac{8}{20}}$$

$$f(x) = \frac{\dfrac{7}{16}}{\dfrac{13}{20}}$$

Dividing by a fraction is equivalent to multiplying by the reciprocal of the fraction:

$$f(x) = \frac{7}{16} \times \frac{20}{13} = \frac{140}{208},$$ which reduces to $\dfrac{35}{52}$.

18. The correct answer is K. Jim has $13 more than Brian, who has x dollars, so the amount of money that Jim has can be expressed as $x + 13$. If Jim spends $25, then his total can be expressed as $x + 13 - 25$, which equals $x - 12$. The next day Jim earns $32, so the amount of money that he now has can be expressed as $x - 12 + 32 = x + 20$.

19. The correct answer is C. The rectangle is 4 times as long as it is wide, so its length can be expressed as $4W$. You are given that the area is 196 square centimeters, so you can use this to set up a formula to solve for the width:

$$A = L \times W$$
$$196 = 4W \times W$$
$$196 = 4W^2$$
$$49 = W^2$$
$$W = 7$$

Since you know that the width is 7, the length must be (4×7) or 28. Now that you have both measurements, you can solve for the perimeter:

$$P = 2L + 2W$$
$$P = 2(28) + 2(7)$$
$$P = 56 + 14$$
$$P = 70$$

The perimeter of the rectangle is 70 centimeters.

20. **The correct answer is J.** To solve this problem, test each of the answer choices until you find the correct factored form (use the FOIL method):

Answer choice F: $(x - 1)(7x + 8) = 7x^2 + 8x - 7x - 8 = 7x^2 + x - 8$. Eliminate answer choice F.

Answer choice G: $(x - 4)(7x + 2) = 7x^2 + 2x - 28x - 8 = 7x^2 - 26x - 8$. Eliminate answer choice G.

Answer choice H: $(x - 8)(7x - 1) = 7x^2 - x - 56x + 8 = 7x^2 - 57x + 8$. Eliminate answer choice H.

Answer choice J: $(x + 2)(7x - 4) = 7x^2 - 4x + 14x - 8 = 7x^2 + 10x - 8$.

Answer choice J is the correct factored form of the expression, so there is no need to test answer choice K.

21. **The correct answer is D.** This problem tests your knowledge of roots and exponents. The expression $\sqrt[4]{8}$ means the fourth root of 8, and represents the number that when raised to the fourth power equals 8. This can also be written as $8^{\frac{1}{4}}$, answer choice D.

22. **The correct answer is H.** To answer this question, notice that a student will always have to pay the cost of admission, $3. Therefore, when a student plays 0 games, that student will pay a total of $3. The graph shows that, for one game played, the total cost is around $6, and for two games played, the cost is around $9. This trend continues along the graph, so it is clear that each game costs $3.

23. **The correct answer is C.** For this triangle, you are given a 90° angle and a 30° angle. This means that the missing angle must be 60° ($30 + 60 + 90 = 180$).

In a 30-60-90 triangle, the ratio of the sides is equivalent to x, $x\sqrt{3}$, and $2x$, as shown below:

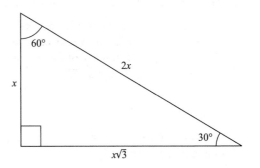

You are given that the side opposite the 90° angle measures 18, so the side opposite the 30° (leg a) must measure 9, and the side opposite the 60° angle must measure $9\sqrt{3}$.

24. **The correct answer is F.** To find the smallest possible sum, take the 5 consecutive odd integers that are the closest to 34 (remember, they all must be greater than 34). These numbers would be: 35, 37, 39, 41, and 43. Add them together: $35 + 37 + 39 + 41 + 43 = 195$.

25. **The correct answer is B.** For this triangle, you are given the value of the hypotenuse, and are asked to find the value of the side that is adjacent to the 21° angle. The trigonometric function dealing with the hypotenuse and the adjacent side is cosine $\left(\cos = \dfrac{\text{adj}}{\text{hyp}}\right)$. Use this to solve for the unknown side:

$$\cos 21° = \frac{x}{33}$$
$$33 \cos 21° = x$$

The missing side of the triangle can be expressed by $33 \cos 21°$.

26. **The correct answer is J.** The absolute value of a number is its numerical value without regard to its sign. Start by finding the absolute value in the equation ($|-35| = 35$). Now solve for x:

$$2x + 17 = 35$$
$$2x = 18$$
$$x = 9$$

27. **The correct answer is D.** To solve this problem, set up two different equations:

$$x + y = 18$$

x is the number of boxes of oranges and y is the number of boxes of pears; a total of 18 boxes was purchased.

$$3x + 5y = 68$$

3 times the number of boxes of oranges, plus 5 times the number of boxes of pears, equals 68 total dollars spent.

Now, solve the first equation for y in terms of x:

$$y = 18 - x$$

Take this value for y and substitute it into the second equation to solve for x:

$$3x + 5(18 - x) = 68$$
$$3x + 90 - 5x = 68$$
$$-2x + 90 = 68$$
$$-2x = -22$$
$$x = 11$$

Marianne purchased 11 boxes of oranges.

28. **The correct answer is H.** The three angles of a triangle must always add up to 180°. As you can see in the figure, there is a smaller triangle within triangle $\triangle ABD$ ($\triangle DCE$). Since you are given that the measure of angle D is 55°, the measures of angles x and w must add up to 125° ($125 + 55 = 180$). This goes for angles y and z as well. If $x + w = 125$, and $y + z = 125$, then $w + x + y + z = 250$.

29. **The correct answer is E.** The first step in solving this problem is clearing the absolute value according to the pattern:

$$|d - 4| \leq 0.002$$
$$-0.002 \leq d - 4 \leq 0.002$$

This is the pattern for "less than." Now, solve for d:

$$3.998 \leq d \leq 4.002$$

Since d is less than or equal to 4.002, the maximum value of the diameter is 4.002 inches. Watch out for answer choice C, which is the smallest possible diameter.

30. **The correct answer is G.** The area of a trapezoid is given by the sum of the bases, times the height, divided by 2: $\left(\dfrac{h(\text{base}_1 + \text{base}_2)}{2}\right)$. In this problem, you are given the area and the measurements of the two bases. Use these values in the equation for area to determine the height:

$$32 = \frac{h(3 + 5)}{2}$$
$$64 = h(3 + 5)$$
$$64 = 3h + 5h$$
$$64 = 8h$$
$$h = 8$$

The height of the trapezoid is 8 feet.

31. **The correct answer is D.** To solve this problem, find the midpoint of the segment between points $(-2, 7)$ and $(8, -3)$ by taking the average of the

x-coordinates and the average of the y-coordinates. The midpoint is $\left[\dfrac{(-2 + 8)}{2}, \dfrac{(7 + -3)}{2}\right] = (3, 2)$. Therefore the quantity $x + y$ is $3 + 2 = 5$.

32. **The correct answer is H.** The volume of a cylinder is given by $\pi r^2 h$, where r is the radius and h is the height. In this case the radius is 10 because it is half the diameter, which is 20. The height, h, is 4 since the pool was filled to that depth. Therefore the volume of water in the pool is $\pi(10)^2(4) = 3.14(100)(4) = 1,256$ ft^3.

33. **The correct answer is D.** The length of the zipper includes the radius, 10, and the length of the arc formed by the 30° angle. Eliminate answer choice E, because you know the length must be greater than 10. Calculate this measurement by finding the circumference of the circle, given by πd, where d is the diameter, and then multiplying by the ratio $\dfrac{30}{360}$, since the arc only occupies 30 of the 360 degrees in an entire circle. The circumference is $\pi(20) = 62.8$. The arc length is $62.8 \times \left(\dfrac{30}{360}\right)$, which is equivalent to $62.8 \div 12$, or approximately 5. The total length of the zipper, then, is approximately $10 + 5 = 15$ feet.

34. **The correct answer is F.** Since the pool is filling at a constant rate for the first 10 hours, the graph should show a straight line that increases (rises) from left to right. At some point the slope of that line should increase (become steeper) because the flow increases. Only the graph in answer choice F reflects this description of the rate of flow.

35. **The correct answer is B.** To solve this problem, write out the numbers that are given in scientific notation:

$$(y \times 10^{-4}) = y \times 0.0001$$
$$\left(\text{Remember, } 10^{-4} = \frac{1}{10^4} = \frac{1}{10,000} = 0.0001\right)$$
$$(z \times 10^6) = z \times 1,000,000$$

Now, rewrite the expression with these numbers:

$$\frac{(y \times 0.0001)(z \times 1,000,000)}{(y \times 0.0001)(z \times 1,000,000)}$$

As you can see, the numerator is the same as the denominator; therefore, when dividing the two, the answer will be 1.

36. **The correct answer is J.** To find the median of the 9 test scores, write them out in order, from smallest to greatest: 81, 81, 88, 89, 92, 94, 95, 97, 100. The median is the number in the middle. Since there are an odd number of scores, the median is 92 (four

spaces from the lowest score, and four spaces from the highest score). If there were an even number of scores, you would find the median by taking the average of the two scores in the middle.

37. **The correct answer is C.** To find the measure of an angle in radians, take the angle measure and divide it by 180π:

$$\frac{810}{180}\pi = 4.5\pi$$

38. **The correct answer is H.** To solve this problem, you must first find the area of her garden. Since the garden is in the shape of a triangle, use the formula for area of a triangle $\left(A = \frac{1}{2}hb\right)$:

$$A = \frac{1}{2}(144)(60)$$

$$A = 4,320 \text{ square feet}$$

If one bag of fertilizer covers 360 square feet, then Celina will need 12 bags of fertilizer $\left(\frac{4,320}{360}\right)$. You are given that one bag costs \$5.99, so the total cost of fertilizing the garden would be $5.99 \times 12 = 71.88$ (round up to \$72.00).

39. **The correct answer is D.** To find the perimeter of the garden, you must first find the missing side length. Use the Pythagorean theorem to solve:

$$a^2 + b^2 = c^2$$
$$60^2 + 144^2 = c^2$$
$$3,600 + 20,736 = c^2$$
$$24,336 = c^2$$
$$c = 156$$

The perimeter of the garden is $60 + 144 + 156 = 360$ feet.

40. **The correct answer is G.** To solve this problem, it is a good idea to draw a picture of the new shape of the garden, as shown below:

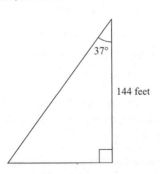

The only information that you have now is the length of the side adjacent to the 37° angle (144), and you need to find the value of the length opposite

to the 37° angle. The trigonometric function that uses the adjacent side and the opposite side is tangent (tan = opp/adj). For the missing side, this can be expressed as:

$$\tan 37° = \frac{x}{144}$$
$$144 \tan 37° = x$$
$$144(0.75) = x$$
$$x = 108$$

If the side opposite the 37° angle is going to be 108 feet, which means that it will need to be extended by 48 feet $(108 - 60)$.

41. **The correct answer is B.** The equation of a circle is given by $(x - h)^2 + (y - k)^2 = r^2$, where (h, k) are the coordinates of the center of the circle, and r is the radius. For this circle, h is -6, and k is 9, so the center of the circle is $(-6, 9)$.

42. **The correct answer is J.** If Brendan's average score after 4 quizzes was 78, then his total score on all 4 quizzes is $4 \times 78 = 312$. He scored 93 on the 5th quiz, so he now has a total of 405 $(312 + 93)$. His average after taking the 5th quiz will be 81 $\left(\frac{405}{5}\right)$.

43. **The correct answer is A.** The correct representation of the program's ratings on a graph would show the highest number at the start, with a slight decline during the first 30 minutes. For the next 60 minutes (from 30 to 90 on the graph), there should be a steady downward slope. During the last 30 minutes (from 90 to 120), the graph should go back up. The only graph that correctly displays this information is answer choice A.

44. **The correct answer is G.** It is a good idea to draw the triangle for this problem, as shown below.

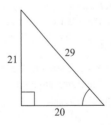

You are asked to find the sine of the angle adjacent to the 20 cm side. The sine of an angle is given by $\frac{\text{opposite}}{\text{hypotenuse}}$. For this angle, the sine would be $\frac{21}{29}$.

45. **The correct answer is C.** Since the square is circumscribed about the circle with diameter 20cm, the length of each of the sides of the square is also 20cm. Therefore, the area of the entire square is $(20)^2 = 400\text{cm}^2$. However, the question

asks for the area, in square centimeters, of the shaded regions. Based on the figure, it is apparent that the shaded regions occupy a total of one quarter of the entire square. Therefore, the area of the shaded region is $\dfrac{400}{4} = 100 \text{cm}^2$.

46. The correct answer is J. The line $x = -3$ is a vertical line that intersects the x-axis at -3. Since it is the perpendicular bisector of $\overline{RS}$, the segment $\overline{RS}$ must be horizontal. Every point on a horizontal segment has the same y-coordinate. Therefore the y-coordinate of S must be the same as the y-coordinate of R, which is 5. Eliminate answer choices F, H, and K. Furthermore, since the segment is bisected by the vertical line, it must be bisected at $(-3, 5)$. The points R and S are equidistant from the point of bisection. Therefore, the only possible answer is the point $(-7, 5)$ as it and $(1, 5)$ are equidistant from $(-3, 5)$. Watch out for answer choice G, which is a partial answer.

47. The correct answer is A. To solve, FOIL each of the answer choices to find the choice that results in the polynomial given in the question, $3x^2 - 13x - 10$. The expression $(3x + 2)(x - 5)$ distributes to $3x^2 - 15x + 2x - 10 = 3x^2 - 13x - 10$.

48. The correct answer is F. This question describes a new operation. You are given that $x \boxdot y = (x - 2y)^2$, and are asked to solve $5 \boxdot (-3)$. To do this, simply replace x with 5, and y with -3:

$$x \boxdot y = (x - 2y)^2$$
$$5 \boxdot (-3) = (5 - 2(-3))^2$$
$$5 \boxdot (-3) = (5 - (-6))^2$$
$$5 \boxdot (-3) = (5 + 6)^2$$
$$5 \boxdot (-3) = (11)^2$$
$$5 \boxdot (-3) = 121$$

49. The correct answer is B. To solve this problem, use the distance formula $(d = \sqrt{(x_2 - x_1)^2 + (y_2 - y_1)^2})$ to find the distance between the points $(-1, 3)$ and $(-6, -9)$.

$$d = \sqrt{(-1 - (-6))^2 + (3 - (-9))^2}$$
$$d = \sqrt{(-1 + 6)^2 + (3 + 9)^2}$$
$$d = \sqrt{(5)^2 + (12)^2}$$
$$d = \sqrt{25 + 144}$$
$$d = \sqrt{169} = 13$$

50. The correct answer is H. The perimeter of parallelogram ABCD is equal to the sum of the sides. The measure of each side is the distance between corresponding points. To solve this problem, use the distance formula $(d = \sqrt{(x_2 - x_1)^2 + (y_2 - y_1)^2})$ to find the distance between A and B:

$$d = \sqrt{(-1) - (-3))^2 + (5 - (-2))^2}$$
$$d = \sqrt{(-1 + 3)^2 + (5 + 2)^2}$$

$$d = \sqrt{(2)^2 + (7)^2}$$
$$d = \sqrt{4 + 49}$$
$$d = \sqrt{53}$$

Now, use the same formula to find the distance between A and D:

$$d = \sqrt{(2 - (-3))^2 + (-1 - (-2))^2}$$
$$d = \sqrt{(2 + 3)^2 + (-1 + 2)^2}$$
$$d = \sqrt{(5)^2 + (1)^2}$$
$$d = \sqrt{25 + 1}$$
$$d = \sqrt{26}$$

Since this is a parallelogram, the distance between D and C is the same as the distance from A to B; likewise, the distance from B to C is the same as the distance from A to D. Therefore, the perimeter of the parallelogram is $2\sqrt{53} + 2\sqrt{26}$.

51. The correct answer is C. First convert the given equation to slope-intercept form, as follows:

$$-2x - 3y = -15$$
$$-3y = 2x - 15$$
$$y = \frac{-2}{3}x + 5$$

The slope of the line is $\dfrac{-2}{3}$, and the y-intercept is 5. Now, you can draw the line in the (x, y) coordinate plane. After plotting a few points on the graph, it is clear that the line passes through every quadrant except for the 3rd, as shown in the figure below.

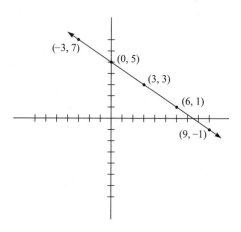

Also, note that the line crosses the y-axis at 5, and has a negative slope. This should help you to eliminate some answer choices quickly.

52. The correct answer is H. Since two points determine a line, it is possible to find an equation for line a because you are given that it passes through the points (2, 5) and (1, 4). To find an equation, first calculate the slope using the slope formula $\dfrac{(y_2 - y_1)}{(x_2 - x_1)}$.

$$\dfrac{(5 - 4)}{(2 - 1)}$$
$$= \dfrac{1}{1} = 1$$

Now that you know the slope is 1, use the point-slope formula for a line $(y - y_1) = m(x - x_1)$ for slope m and point (x_1, y_1). You can use either point in this calculation:

$$y - 4 = 1(x - 1)$$
$$y - 4 = x - 1$$
$$y = x + 3$$

53. **The correct answer is D.** To solve, simplify the expression $3^0 + 3^2 + 3^{-2}$. Apply a couple of exponent rules. First, any nonzero number to the zero power is 1. Also, negative exponents indicate reciprocals, meaning $3^{-2} = \dfrac{1}{3^2} = \dfrac{1}{9}$. Therefore $3^0 + 3^2 + 3^{-2} = 1 + 9 + \dfrac{1}{9} = 10\dfrac{1}{9}$.

54. **The correct answer is K.** The circumference of a circle is given by the formula $C = d\pi$, where d equals the diameter of the circle. The formula for the area of a circle is $A = \pi r^2$, where r is the radius of the circle. Since you are given that the circumference of the circle is 10π, you know that the diameter of the circle is 10, and therefore, the radius is 5 $\left(\dfrac{10}{2}\right)$. You can now find the area of the circle:

$$A = \pi(5^2)$$
$$A = 25\pi$$

55. **The correct answer is A.** You are given the endpoints of the diameter of the circle, so you can use the distance formula to determine the value of the diameter:

$$d = \sqrt{(1 - (-2))^2 + (4 - 8)^2}$$
$$d = \sqrt{(1 + 2)^2 + (-4)^2}$$
$$d = \sqrt{(3)^2 + (-4)^2}$$
$$d = \sqrt{9 + 16}$$
$$d = \sqrt{25}$$
$$d = 5$$

The radius is half of the diameter, so for this circle it is 2.5 $\left(\dfrac{5}{2}\right)$.

56. **The correct answer is G.** You can find the vertical asymptotes of a function by finding the values that would set the denominator equal to zero (the values that are disallowed in the domain). To find these values, set the denominator equal to zero and solve:

$$x^2 + 3x - 10 = 0$$

Find two values that, when multiplied, equal -10, and when added together equal 3 (the only possible values are 5 and -2).

$$(x + 5)(x - 2) = 0$$
$$x + 5 = 0 \text{ or } x - 2 = 0$$

Set both binomials equal to 0.

$$x = -5 \text{ or } x = 2$$

This tells you that you cannot have either -5 or 2 in the domain, and therefore these are the two vertical asymptotes of the function (where the graph can't go).

57. **The correct answer is B.** You are given that the polynomial has roots $-\dfrac{3}{5}$ and $\dfrac{1}{3}$, which means that the values of $-\dfrac{3}{5}$ and $\dfrac{1}{3}$ for x result in the value of the entire polynomial zero. To solve, you could substitute the given values into the polynomials in the answer choices. You could also generate your own polynomial using factors that correspond to each root. For instance, the root $-\dfrac{3}{5}$ corresponds to the factor $(5x + 3)$. Similarly the root $\dfrac{1}{3}$ corresponds to the factor $(3x - 1)$.

58. **The correct answer is F.** To find the value of a in the equation $log_2 2 + log_2 32 = log_4 a$, first simplify the expression $log_2 2 + log_2 32$. According to the rules of logarithms, $log_2 2 + log_2 32 = log_2(2 \cdot 32) = log_2(64)$. By definition of a logarithm, $log_2(64) = x$ means $64 = 2^x$. Therefore $x = 6$. Since $log_4 a = 6$, $a = 4^6 = 4{,}096$.

59. **The correct answer is C.** You are given that $h(x) = f(x) + g(x)$, and also the values for $f(x)$ and $g(x)$. Use these values to solve for $h(x)$:

$$h(x) = (3x^2 - 5x - 11) + (-3x^2 + 23x - 16)$$
$$h(x) = 3x^2 - 3x^2 - 5x + 23x - 11 - 16$$
$$h(x) = 18x - 27$$
$$h(x) = 9(2x - 3)$$

After solving, it is clear that $h(x)$ will always be divisible by 9.

60. **The correct answer is J.** Given that the sum of a and b has a maximum value (8), a will be greatest when b takes its lowest possible value. Since $b \geq 0$, a could be as great as 8 and still satisfy $a + b \leq 8$. Therefore, $2a$ can be as great as $2(8) = 16$.

CHAPTER 7

PRACTICE TEST 2 WITH EXPLANATIONS

ANSWER SHEET

ACT MATHEMATICS TEST 2
Answer Sheet

MATHEMATICS

1 Ⓐ Ⓑ Ⓒ Ⓓ Ⓔ	16 Ⓕ Ⓖ Ⓗ Ⓙ Ⓚ	31 Ⓐ Ⓑ Ⓒ Ⓓ Ⓔ	46 Ⓕ Ⓖ Ⓗ Ⓙ Ⓚ
2 Ⓕ Ⓖ Ⓗ Ⓙ Ⓚ	17 Ⓐ Ⓑ Ⓒ Ⓓ Ⓔ	32 Ⓕ Ⓖ Ⓗ Ⓙ Ⓚ	47 Ⓐ Ⓑ Ⓒ Ⓓ Ⓔ
3 Ⓐ Ⓑ Ⓒ Ⓓ Ⓔ	18 Ⓕ Ⓖ Ⓗ Ⓙ Ⓚ	33 Ⓐ Ⓑ Ⓒ Ⓓ Ⓔ	48 Ⓕ Ⓖ Ⓗ Ⓙ Ⓚ
4 Ⓕ Ⓖ Ⓗ Ⓙ Ⓚ	19 Ⓐ Ⓑ Ⓒ Ⓓ Ⓔ	34 Ⓕ Ⓖ Ⓗ Ⓙ Ⓚ	49 Ⓐ Ⓑ Ⓒ Ⓓ Ⓔ
5 Ⓐ Ⓑ Ⓒ Ⓓ Ⓔ	20 Ⓕ Ⓖ Ⓗ Ⓙ Ⓚ	35 Ⓐ Ⓑ Ⓒ Ⓓ Ⓔ	50 Ⓕ Ⓖ Ⓗ Ⓙ Ⓚ
6 Ⓕ Ⓖ Ⓗ Ⓙ Ⓚ	21 Ⓐ Ⓑ Ⓒ Ⓓ Ⓔ	36 Ⓕ Ⓖ Ⓗ Ⓙ Ⓚ	51 Ⓐ Ⓑ Ⓒ Ⓓ Ⓔ
7 Ⓐ Ⓑ Ⓒ Ⓓ Ⓔ	22 Ⓕ Ⓖ Ⓗ Ⓙ Ⓚ	37 Ⓐ Ⓑ Ⓒ Ⓓ Ⓔ	52 Ⓕ Ⓖ Ⓗ Ⓙ Ⓚ
8 Ⓕ Ⓖ Ⓗ Ⓙ Ⓚ	23 Ⓐ Ⓑ Ⓒ Ⓓ Ⓔ	38 Ⓕ Ⓖ Ⓗ Ⓙ Ⓚ	53 Ⓐ Ⓑ Ⓒ Ⓓ Ⓔ
9 Ⓐ Ⓑ Ⓒ Ⓓ Ⓔ	24 Ⓕ Ⓖ Ⓗ Ⓙ Ⓚ	39 Ⓐ Ⓑ Ⓒ Ⓓ Ⓔ	54 Ⓕ Ⓖ Ⓗ Ⓙ Ⓚ
10 Ⓕ Ⓖ Ⓗ Ⓙ Ⓚ	25 Ⓐ Ⓑ Ⓒ Ⓓ Ⓔ	40 Ⓕ Ⓖ Ⓗ Ⓙ Ⓚ	55 Ⓐ Ⓑ Ⓒ Ⓓ Ⓔ
11 Ⓐ Ⓑ Ⓒ Ⓓ Ⓔ	26 Ⓕ Ⓖ Ⓗ Ⓙ Ⓚ	41 Ⓐ Ⓑ Ⓒ Ⓓ Ⓔ	56 Ⓕ Ⓖ Ⓗ Ⓙ Ⓚ
12 Ⓕ Ⓖ Ⓗ Ⓙ Ⓚ	27 Ⓐ Ⓑ Ⓒ Ⓓ Ⓔ	42 Ⓕ Ⓖ Ⓗ Ⓙ Ⓚ	57 Ⓐ Ⓑ Ⓒ Ⓓ Ⓔ
13 Ⓐ Ⓑ Ⓒ Ⓓ Ⓔ	28 Ⓕ Ⓖ Ⓗ Ⓙ Ⓚ	43 Ⓐ Ⓑ Ⓒ Ⓓ Ⓔ	58 Ⓕ Ⓖ Ⓗ Ⓙ Ⓚ
14 Ⓕ Ⓖ Ⓗ Ⓙ Ⓚ	29 Ⓐ Ⓑ Ⓒ Ⓓ Ⓔ	44 Ⓕ Ⓖ Ⓗ Ⓙ Ⓚ	59 Ⓐ Ⓑ Ⓒ Ⓓ Ⓔ
15 Ⓐ Ⓑ Ⓒ Ⓓ Ⓔ	30 Ⓕ Ⓖ Ⓗ Ⓙ Ⓚ	45 Ⓐ Ⓑ Ⓒ Ⓓ Ⓔ	60 Ⓕ Ⓖ Ⓗ Ⓙ Ⓚ

△ △ △ △ △ △ △ △ △ △

MATHEMATICS TEST

60 Minutes—60 Questions

DIRECTIONS: Solve each of the problems in the time allowed, then fill in the corresponding bubble on your answer sheet (page 139). Do not spend too much time on any one problem; skip the more difficult problems and go back to them later. You may use a calculator on this test. For this test you should assume that figures are NOT necessarily drawn to scale, that all geometric figures lie in a plane, and that the word *line* is used to indicate a straight line.

1. In triangle ABC below, the measure of angle B is 70 degrees, and the measure of angle A is half the measure of angle B. What is the measure of angle C?

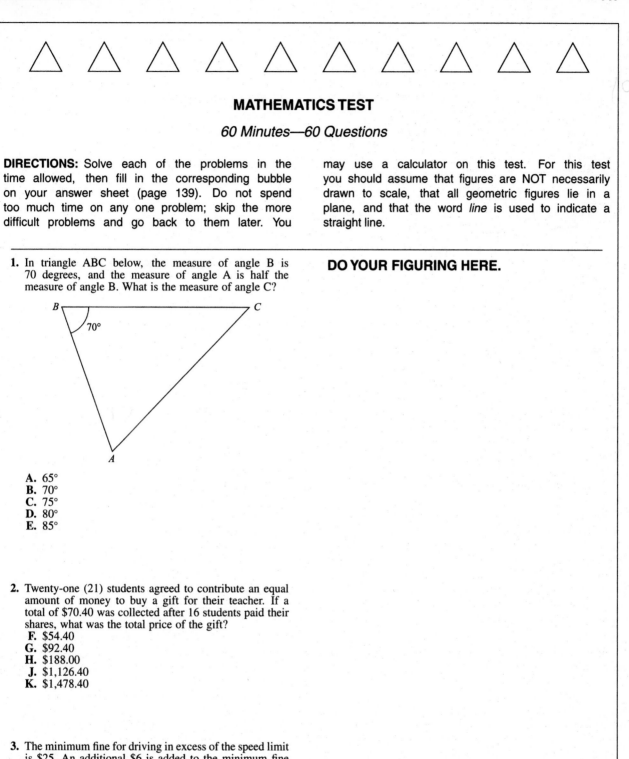

   A. 65°
   B. 70°
   C. 75°
   D. 80°
   E. 85°

2. Twenty-one (21) students agreed to contribute an equal amount of money to buy a gift for their teacher. If a total of $70.40 was collected after 16 students paid their shares, what was the total price of the gift?
   F. $54.40
   G. $92.40
   H. $188.00
   J. $1,126.40
   K. $1,478.40

3. The minimum fine for driving in excess of the speed limit is $25. An additional $6 is added to the minimum fine for each mile per hour (mph) in excess of the speed limit. Omar was issued a $103 fine for speeding in a 55-mph speed limit zone. For driving at what speed, in mph, was Omar fined?
   A. 13
   B. 52
   C. 62
   D. 68
   E. 72

DO YOUR FIGURING HERE.

GO ON TO THE NEXT PAGE.

4. In a circuit, $E = IR$, where E = number of volts, I = number of amperes, and R = number of ohms. How much resistance, in ohms, does a circuit possess if the number of volts is 24 and the current is 8 amperes?

  F. 2
  G. 3
  H. 4
  J. 24
  K. 32

5. In the figure below, line s is parallel to line t, and line p is a transversal crossing both lines s and t. Which of the following lists 3 angles that are equal in measure?

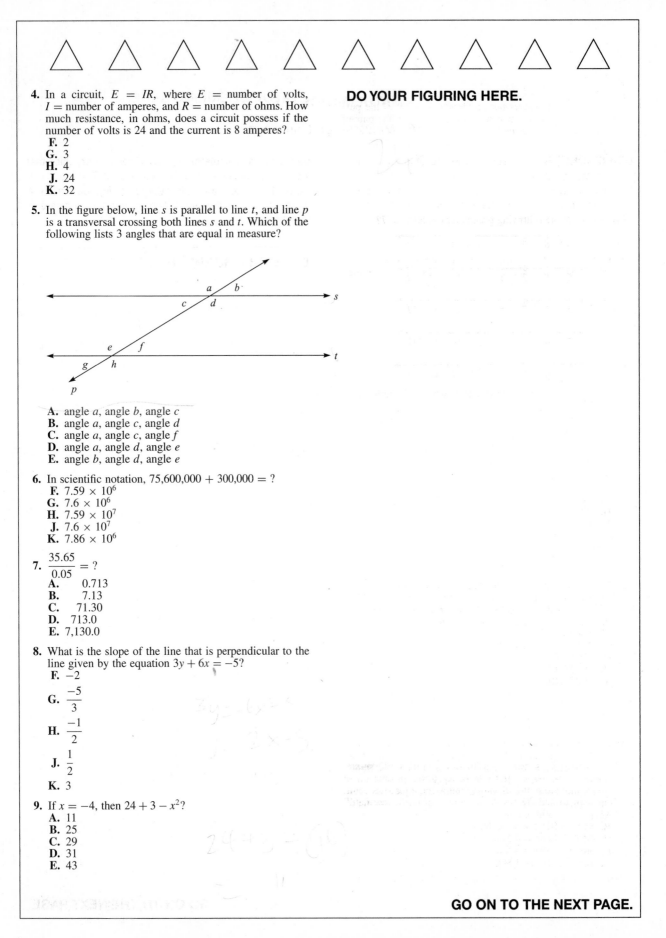

  A. angle a, angle b, angle c
  B. angle a, angle c, angle d
  C. angle a, angle c, angle f
  D. angle a, angle d, angle e
  E. angle b, angle d, angle e

6. In scientific notation, $75{,}600{,}000 + 300{,}000 = ?$

  F. 7.59×10^6
  G. 7.6×10^6
  H. 7.59×10^7
  J. 7.6×10^7
  K. 7.86×10^6

7. $\dfrac{35.65}{0.05} = ?$

  A.   0.713
  B.   7.13
  C.   71.30
  D. 713.0
  E. 7,130.0

8. What is the slope of the line that is perpendicular to the line given by the equation $3y + 6x = -5$?

  F. -2
  G. $\dfrac{-5}{3}$
  H. $\dfrac{-1}{2}$
  J. $\dfrac{1}{2}$
  K. 3

9. If $x = -4$, then $24 + 3 - x^2$?

  A. 11
  B. 25
  C. 29
  D. 31
  E. 43

DO YOUR FIGURING HERE.

GO ON TO THE NEXT PAGE.

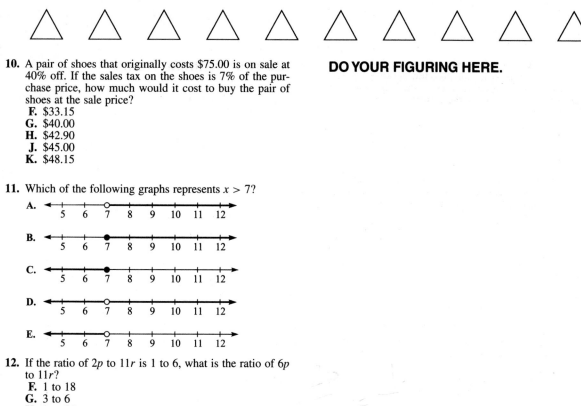

10. A pair of shoes that originally costs $75.00 is on sale at 40% off. If the sales tax on the shoes is 7% of the purchase price, how much would it cost to buy the pair of shoes at the sale price?

F. $33.15
G. $40.00
H. $42.90
J. $45.00
K. $48.15

DO YOUR FIGURING HERE.

11. Which of the following graphs represents $x > 7$?

A. ←——|——|——○————|——|——|——|——|——→
    5   6   7   8   9   10 11 12

B. ←——|——|——●——|——|——|——|——|——→
    5   6   7   8   9   10 11 12

C. ←——|——|——●——|——|——|——|——|——→
    5   6   7   8   9   10 11 12

D. ←——|——|——○——|——|——|——|——|——→
    5   6   7   8   9   10 11 12

E. ←——|——|——○——|——|——|——|——|——→
    5   6   7   8   9   10 11 12

12. If the ratio of $2p$ to $11r$ is 1 to 6, what is the ratio of $6p$ to $11r$?

F. 1 to 18
G. 3 to 6
H. 3 to 33
J. 1 to 6
K. 3 to 22

13. Which of the following equations could be used to determine the value of x?

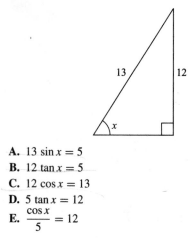

A. $13 \sin x = 5$
B. $12 \tan x = 5$
C. $12 \cos x = 13$
D. $5 \tan x = 12$
E. $\dfrac{\cos x}{5} = 12$

14. A rectangular soccer field has an area of 4,500 square meters. The length of the field is 10 meters more than twice the width. Which of the following equations could be used to find the width, w, in feet, of the soccer field?

F. $w^2 = 4{,}500 - 10w$
G. $2(w + 10) + w = 4{,}500$
H. $w + 10(2w) = 4{,}500$
J. $w(2w + 10) = 4{,}500$
K. $w(w^2 + 10) = 4{,}500$

GO ON TO THE NEXT PAGE.

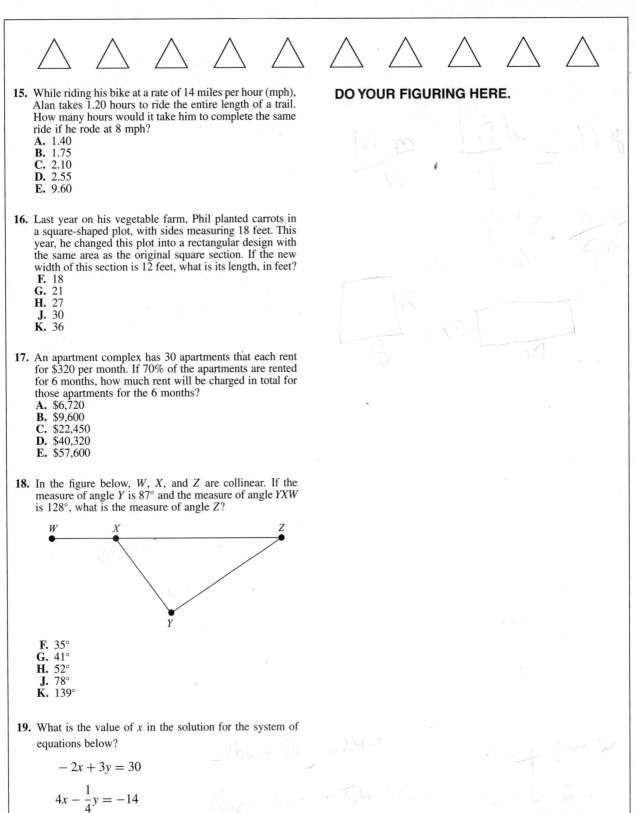

15. While riding his bike at a rate of 14 miles per hour (mph), Alan takes 1.20 hours to ride the entire length of a trail. How many hours would it take him to complete the same ride if he rode at 8 mph?

- **A.** 1.40
- **B.** 1.75
- **C.** 2.10
- **D.** 2.55
- **E.** 9.60

DO YOUR FIGURING HERE.

16. Last year on his vegetable farm, Phil planted carrots in a square-shaped plot, with sides measuring 18 feet. This year, he changed this plot into a rectangular design with the same area as the original square section. If the new width of this section is 12 feet, what is its length, in feet?

- **F.** 18
- **G.** 21
- **H.** 27
- **J.** 30
- **K.** 36

17. An apartment complex has 30 apartments that each rent for \$320 per month. If 70% of the apartments are rented for 6 months, how much rent will be charged in total for those apartments for the 6 months?

- **A.** \$6,720
- **B.** \$9,600
- **C.** \$22,450
- **D.** \$40,320
- **E.** \$57,600

18. In the figure below, W, X, and Z are collinear. If the measure of angle Y is 87° and the measure of angle YXW is 128°, what is the measure of angle Z?

- **F.** 35°
- **G.** 41°
- **H.** 52°
- **J.** 78°
- **K.** 139°

19. What is the value of x in the solution for the system of equations below?

$$-2x + 3y = 30$$

$$4x - \frac{1}{4}y = -14$$

- **A.** −27
- **B.** −16
- **C.** −9
- **D.** −4
- **E.** −3

GO ON TO THE NEXT PAGE.

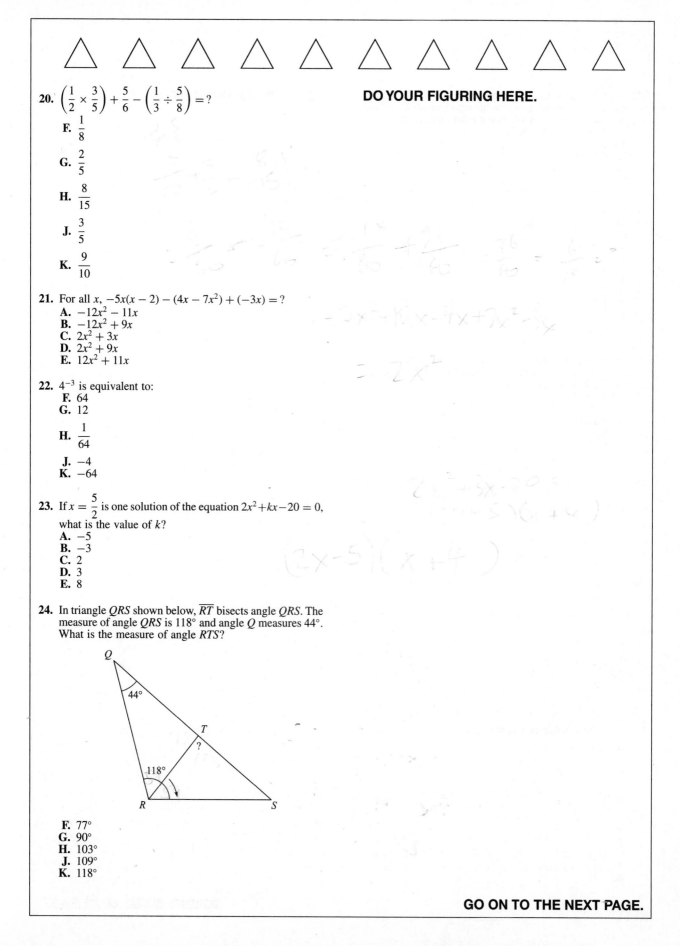

20. $\left(\dfrac{1}{2} \times \dfrac{3}{5}\right) + \dfrac{5}{6} - \left(\dfrac{1}{3} \div \dfrac{5}{8}\right) = ?$

DO YOUR FIGURING HERE.

   F. $\dfrac{1}{8}$

   G. $\dfrac{2}{5}$

   H. $\dfrac{8}{15}$

   J. $\dfrac{3}{5}$

   K. $\dfrac{9}{10}$

21. For all x, $-5x(x - 2) - (4x - 7x^2) + (-3x) = ?$
   A. $-12x^2 - 11x$
   B. $-12x^2 + 9x$
   C. $2x^2 + 3x$
   D. $2x^2 + 9x$
   E. $12x^2 + 11x$

22. 4^{-3} is equivalent to:
   F. 64
   G. 12
   H. $\dfrac{1}{64}$
   J. -4
   K. -64

23. If $x = \dfrac{5}{2}$ is one solution of the equation $2x^2 + kx - 20 = 0$, what is the value of k?
   A. -5
   B. -3
   C. 2
   D. 3
   E. 8

24. In triangle QRS shown below, $\overline{RT}$ bisects angle QRS. The measure of angle QRS is 118° and angle Q measures 44°. What is the measure of angle RTS?

   F. 77°
   G. 90°
   H. 103°
   J. 109°
   K. 118°

GO ON TO THE NEXT PAGE.

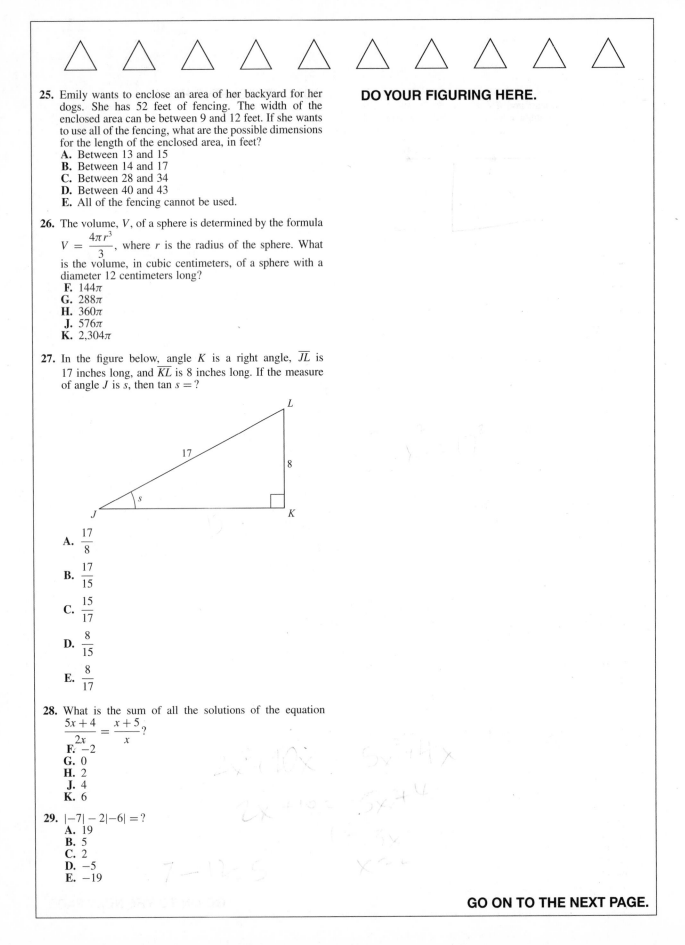

25. Emily wants to enclose an area of her backyard for her dogs. She has 52 feet of fencing. The width of the enclosed area can be between 9 and 12 feet. If she wants to use all of the fencing, what are the possible dimensions for the length of the enclosed area, in feet?

A. Between 13 and 15
B. Between 14 and 17
C. Between 28 and 34
D. Between 40 and 43
E. All of the fencing cannot be used.

26. The volume, V, of a sphere is determined by the formula $V = \dfrac{4\pi r^3}{3}$, where r is the radius of the sphere. What is the volume, in cubic centimeters, of a sphere with a diameter 12 centimeters long?

F. 144π
G. 288π
H. 360π
J. 576π
K. $2,304\pi$

27. In the figure below, angle K is a right angle, $\overline{JL}$ is 17 inches long, and $\overline{KL}$ is 8 inches long. If the measure of angle J is s, then $\tan s = ?$

A. $\dfrac{17}{8}$

B. $\dfrac{17}{15}$

C. $\dfrac{15}{17}$

D. $\dfrac{8}{15}$

E. $\dfrac{8}{17}$

28. What is the sum of all the solutions of the equation $\dfrac{5x+4}{2x} = \dfrac{x+5}{x}?$

F. -2
G. 0
H. 2
J. 4
K. 6

29. $|-7| - 2|-6| = ?$

A. 19
B. 5
C. 2
D. -5
E. -19

GO ON TO THE NEXT PAGE.

DO YOUR FIGURING HERE.

△ △ △ △ △   △ △ △ △ △

30. In the figure below, $\overline{KO}$ is parallel to $\overline{LN}$; points J, K, L, and M are collinear; and $\overline{KN}$ is the same length as $\overline{LN}$. If the measure of angle LNK is 40°, what is the measure of angle JKO?

DO YOUR FIGURING HERE.

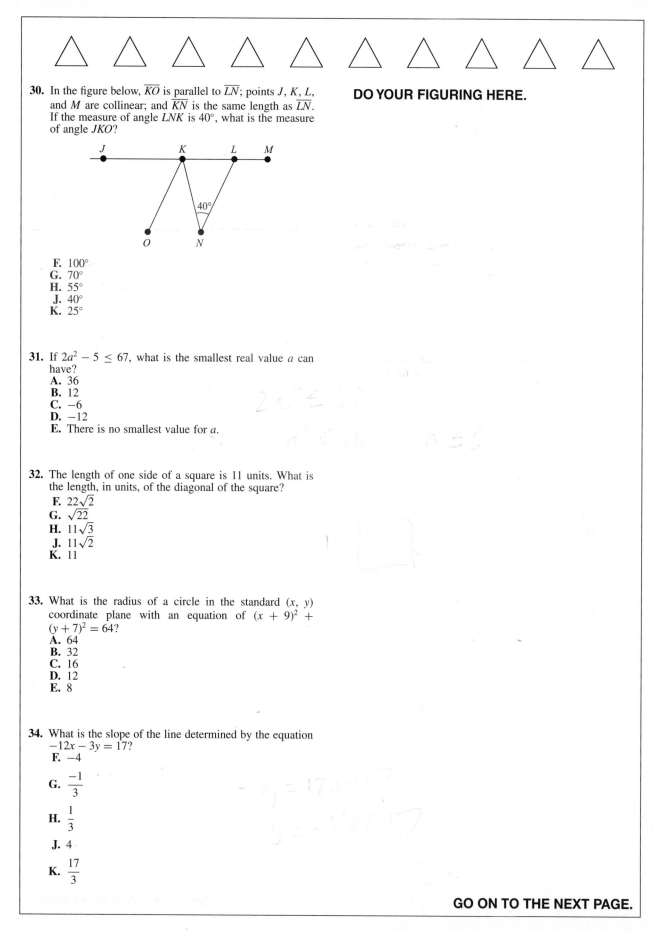

   F. 100°
   G. 70°
   H. 55°
   J. 40°
   K. 25°

31. If $2a^2 - 5 \leq 67$, what is the smallest real value a can have?
   A. 36
   B. 12
   C. −6
   D. −12
   E. There is no smallest value for a.

32. The length of one side of a square is 11 units. What is the length, in units, of the diagonal of the square?
   F. $22\sqrt{2}$
   G. $\sqrt{22}$
   H. $11\sqrt{3}$
   J. $11\sqrt{2}$
   K. 11

33. What is the radius of a circle in the standard (x, y) coordinate plane with an equation of $(x + 9)^2 + (y + 7)^2 = 64$?
   A. 64
   B. 32
   C. 16
   D. 12
   E. 8

34. What is the slope of the line determined by the equation $-12x - 3y = 17$?
   F. −4
   G. $\dfrac{-1}{3}$
   H. $\dfrac{1}{3}$
   J. 4
   K. $\dfrac{17}{3}$

GO ON TO THE NEXT PAGE.

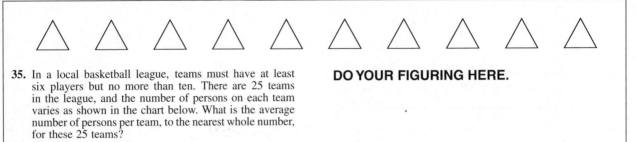

35. In a local basketball league, teams must have at least six players but no more than ten. There are 25 teams in the league, and the number of persons on each team varies as shown in the chart below. What is the average number of persons per team, to the nearest whole number, for these 25 teams?

Number of players on team	6	7	6	9	10
Number of teams	3	6	4	9	3

A. 5
B. 6
C. 7
D. 8
E. 9

DO YOUR FIGURING HERE.

36. In the figure below, the circle centered at K is contained within the square $ABCD$. The length of $\overline{KL}$ is 7 inches. If the circle is cut out of the square, how much of the area, in square inches, of the square, will remain?

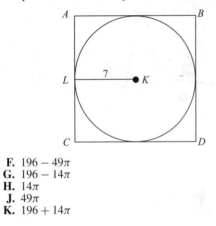

F. $196 - 49\pi$
G. $196 - 14\pi$
H. 14π
J. 49π
K. $196 + 14\pi$

37. What is the equation of the line that has the same slope as the line $2x - 8y = 13$ but with the same y-intercept as the line $y + 5 = -3x$?

A. $y = -3x - \dfrac{13}{8}$

B. $y = -\dfrac{1}{4}x + 5$

C. $y = \dfrac{1}{4}x - 5$

D. $y = 2x + \dfrac{13}{8}$

E. $y = 3x - 5$

GO ON TO THE NEXT PAGE.

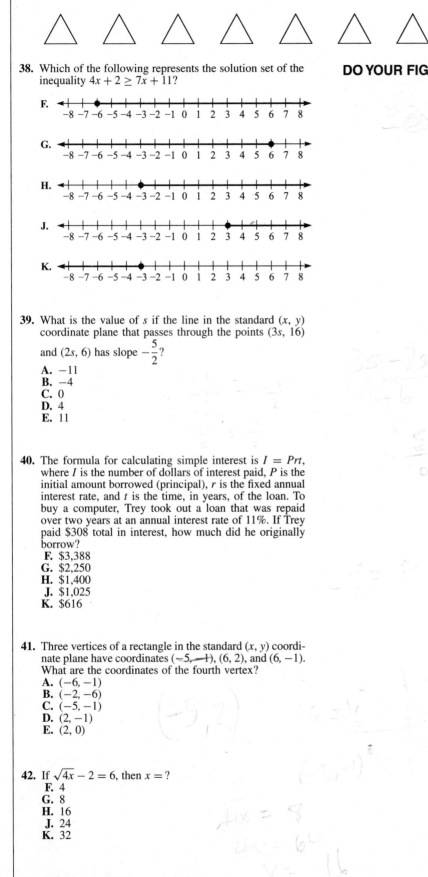

38. Which of the following represents the solution set of the inequality $4x + 2 \geq 7x + 11$?

DO YOUR FIGURING HERE.

39. What is the value of s if the line in the standard (x, y) coordinate plane that passes through the points $(3s, 16)$ and $(2s, 6)$ has slope $-\dfrac{5}{2}$?

A. -11
B. -4
C. 0
D. 4
E. 11

40. The formula for calculating simple interest is $I = Prt$, where I is the number of dollars of interest paid, P is the initial amount borrowed (principal), r is the fixed annual interest rate, and t is the time, in years, of the loan. To buy a computer, Trey took out a loan that was repaid over two years at an annual interest rate of 11%. If Trey paid $308 total in interest, how much did he originally borrow?

F. $3,388
G. $2,250
H. $1,400
J. $1,025
K. $616

41. Three vertices of a rectangle in the standard (x, y) coordinate plane have coordinates $(-5, -1)$, $(6, 2)$, and $(6, -1)$. What are the coordinates of the fourth vertex?

A. $(-6, -1)$
B. $(-2, -6)$
C. $(-5, -1)$
D. $(2, -1)$
E. $(2, 0)$

42. If $\sqrt{4x} - 2 = 6$, then $x = ?$

F. 4
G. 8
H. 16
J. 24
K. 32

GO ON TO THE NEXT PAGE.

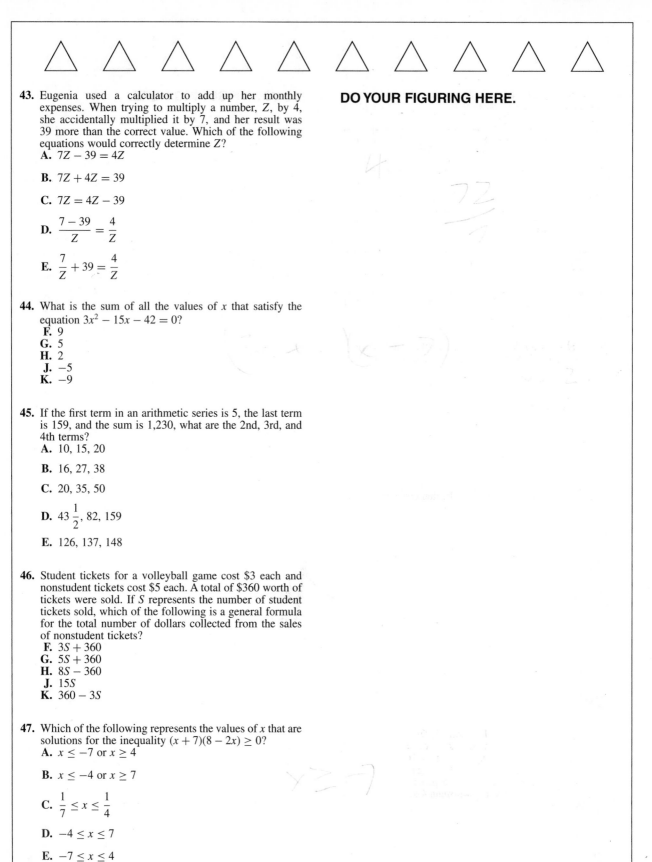

43. Eugenia used a calculator to add up her monthly expenses. When trying to multiply a number, Z, by 4, she accidentally multiplied it by 7, and her result was 39 more than the correct value. Which of the following equations would correctly determine Z?

A. $7Z - 39 = 4Z$

B. $7Z + 4Z = 39$

C. $7Z = 4Z - 39$

D. $\dfrac{7 - 39}{Z} = \dfrac{4}{Z}$

E. $\dfrac{7}{Z} + 39 = \dfrac{4}{Z}$

44. What is the sum of all the values of x that satisfy the equation $3x^2 - 15x - 42 = 0$?

F. 9
G. 5
H. 2
J. -5
K. -9

45. If the first term in an arithmetic series is 5, the last term is 159, and the sum is 1,230, what are the 2nd, 3rd, and 4th terms?

A. 10, 15, 20

B. 16, 27, 38

C. 20, 35, 50

D. $43\dfrac{1}{2}$, 82, 159

E. 126, 137, 148

46. Student tickets for a volleyball game cost $3 each and nonstudent tickets cost $5 each. A total of $360 worth of tickets were sold. If S represents the number of student tickets sold, which of the following is a general formula for the total number of dollars collected from the sales of nonstudent tickets?

F. $3S + 360$
G. $5S + 360$
H. $8S - 360$
J. $15S$
K. $360 - 3S$

47. Which of the following represents the values of x that are solutions for the inequality $(x + 7)(8 - 2x) \geq 0$?

A. $x \leq -7$ or $x \geq 4$

B. $x \leq -4$ or $x \geq 7$

C. $\dfrac{1}{7} \leq x \leq \dfrac{1}{4}$

D. $-4 \leq x \leq 7$

E. $-7 \leq x \leq 4$

DO YOUR FIGURING HERE.

GO ON TO THE NEXT PAGE.

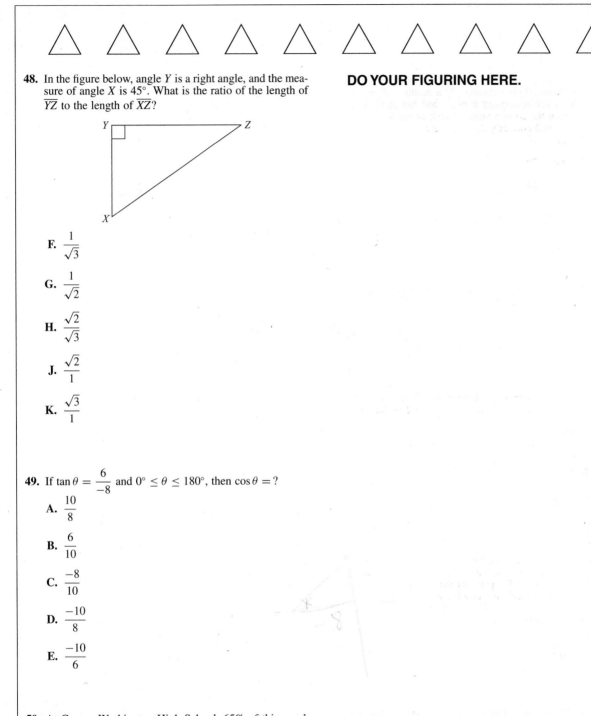

48. In the figure below, angle Y is a right angle, and the measure of angle X is 45°. What is the ratio of the length of $\overline{YZ}$ to the length of $\overline{XZ}$?

DO YOUR FIGURING HERE.

F. $\dfrac{1}{\sqrt{3}}$

G. $\dfrac{1}{\sqrt{2}}$

H. $\dfrac{\sqrt{2}}{\sqrt{3}}$

J. $\dfrac{\sqrt{2}}{1}$

K. $\dfrac{\sqrt{3}}{1}$

49. If $\tan\theta = \dfrac{6}{-8}$ and $0° \le \theta \le 180°$, then $\cos\theta = ?$

A. $\dfrac{10}{8}$

B. $\dfrac{6}{10}$

C. $\dfrac{-8}{10}$

D. $\dfrac{-10}{8}$

E. $\dfrac{-10}{6}$

50. At George Washington High School, 65% of this year's senior class members have taken at least 6 science courses. Of the remaining class members, 40% have taken 4 or 5 science courses. Assuming no seniors took more than 6 science courses, what percent of the senior class members have taken fewer than 4 science courses?

F. 0%

G. 8%

H. 14%

J. 21%

K. 35%

GO ON TO THE NEXT PAGE.

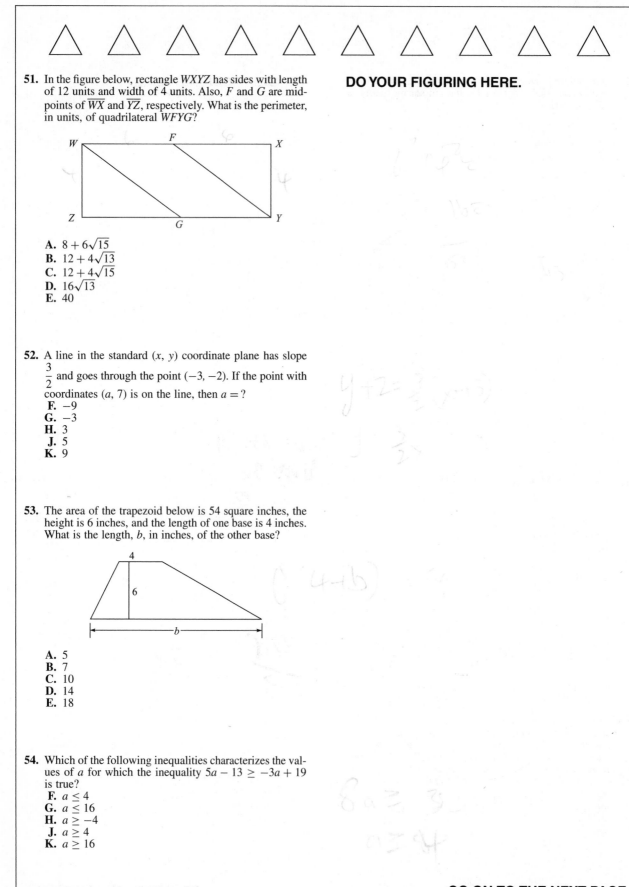

51. In the figure below, rectangle *WXYZ* has sides with length of 12 units and width of 4 units. Also, *F* and *G* are midpoints of $\overline{WX}$ and $\overline{YZ}$, respectively. What is the perimeter, in units, of quadrilateral *WFYG*?

DO YOUR FIGURING HERE.

    A. $8 + 6\sqrt{15}$
    B. $12 + 4\sqrt{13}$
    C. $12 + 4\sqrt{15}$
    D. $16\sqrt{13}$
    E. 40

52. A line in the standard (x, y) coordinate plane has slope $\dfrac{3}{2}$ and goes through the point $(-3, -2)$. If the point with coordinates $(a, 7)$ is on the line, then $a = ?$
    F. -9
    G. -3
    H. 3
    J. 5
    K. 9

53. The area of the trapezoid below is 54 square inches, the height is 6 inches, and the length of one base is 4 inches. What is the length, *b*, in inches, of the other base?

    A. 5
    B. 7
    C. 10
    D. 14
    E. 18

54. Which of the following inequalities characterizes the values of *a* for which the inequality $5a - 13 \geq -3a + 19$ is true?
    F. $a \leq 4$
    G. $a \leq 16$
    H. $a \geq -4$
    J. $a \geq 4$
    K. $a \geq 16$

GO ON TO THE NEXT PAGE.

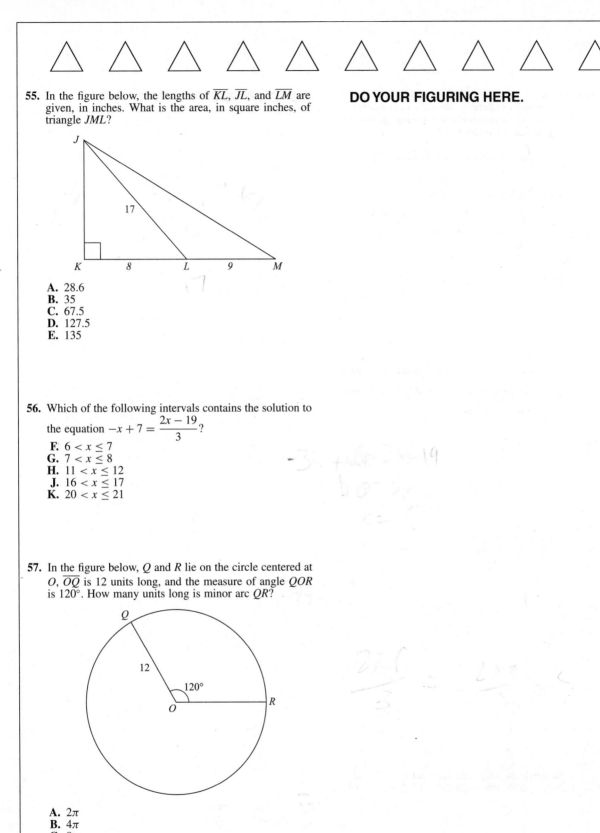

55. In the figure below, the lengths of $\overline{KL}$, $\overline{JL}$, and $\overline{LM}$ are given, in inches. What is the area, in square inches, of triangle *JML*?

DO YOUR FIGURING HERE.

A. 28.6
B. 35
C. 67.5
D. 127.5
E. 135

56. Which of the following intervals contains the solution to the equation $-x + 7 = \dfrac{2x - 19}{3}$?

F. $6 < x \le 7$
G. $7 < x \le 8$
H. $11 < x \le 12$
J. $16 < x \le 17$
K. $20 < x \le 21$

57. In the figure below, Q and R lie on the circle centered at O, $\overline{OQ}$ is 12 units long, and the measure of angle QOR is 120°. How many units long is minor arc QR?

A. 2π
B. 4π
C. 8π
D. 16π
E. 24π

GO ON TO THE NEXT PAGE.

DO YOUR FIGURING HERE.

58. Given the graph in the standard (x, y) coordinate plane below, which of the following statements is true about the slopes m_1 and m_2 of line 1 and line 2, respectively?

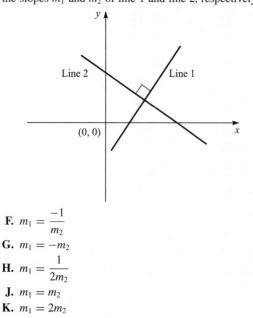

F. $m_1 = \dfrac{-1}{m_2}$

G. $m_1 = -m_2$

H. $m_1 = \dfrac{1}{2m_2}$

J. $m_1 = m_2$

K. $m_1 = 2m_2$

59. In the right triangle below, the length of $\overline{ST}$ is 7 inches and the length of $\overline{SU}$ is 25 inches. What is the cosine of angle U?

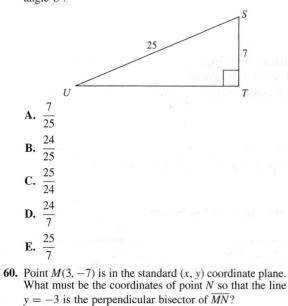

A. $\dfrac{7}{25}$

B. $\dfrac{24}{25}$

C. $\dfrac{25}{24}$

D. $\dfrac{24}{7}$

E. $\dfrac{25}{7}$

60. Point $M(3, -7)$ is in the standard (x, y) coordinate plane. What must be the coordinates of point N so that the line $y = -3$ is the perpendicular bisector of $\overline{MN}$?

    F. $(1, -7)$
    G. $(3, -9)$
    H. $(3, -5)$
    J. $(3, -3)$
    K. $(3, 1)$

END OF THE MATHEMATICS TEST
STOP! IF YOU HAVE TIME LEFT OVER, CHECK YOUR WORK ON THIS SECTION ONLY.

ANSWER KEY

Mathematics Test

1. C	16. H	31. C	46. K
2. G	17. D	32. J	47. E
3. D	18. G	33. E	48. G
4. G	19. E	34. F	49. C
5. D	20. J	35. D	50. J
6. H	21. C	36. F	51. B
7. D	22. H	37. C	52. H
8. J	23. D	38. K	53. D
9. A	24. H	39. B	54. J
10. K	25. B	40. H	55. C
11. A	26. G	41. C	56. G
12. G	27. D	42. H	57. C
13. D	28. H	43. A	58. F
14. J	29. D	44. G	59. B
15. C	30. G	45. B	60. K

SCORING WORKSHEET

On each ACT multiple-choice test (English, Mathematics, Reading, and Science Reasoning) you will receive a SCALED SCORE on a scale of 1 to 36. Use the following guidelines to determine your approximate SCALED SCORE on the ACT Mathematics Diagnostic Test that you just completed.

Step 1 Determine your RAW SCORE.

Your RAW SCORE is the number of questions that you answered correctly. Because there are 60 questions on the ACT Mathematics Test, the highest possible RAW SCORE is 60.

Step 2 Determine your SCALED SCORE using the following Scoring Worksheet.

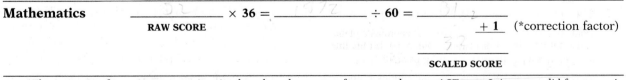

Mathematics _____ × **36** = _____ ÷ **60** = _____
     RAW SCORE   **+ 1** (*correction factor)

                                              _____
                                              SCALED SCORE

*The correction factor is an approximation based on the average from several recent ACT tests. It is most valid for scores in the middle 50% (approximately 16–24 scaled composite score) of the scoring range. The scores are all approximate. Actual ACT scoring scales vary from one administration to the next based upon several factors.

ANSWERS AND EXPLANATIONS

1. **The correct answer is C.** You are given that angle B measures 70° and that the measure of angle A is half that of B. Therefore, angle A must measure $35°$ $\left(\frac{70}{2}\right)$. Since the three angles of a triangle add up to 180°, angle C must equal $180° - 70° - 35°$, or 75°.

2. **The correct answer is G.** The problem states that the students *agreed to contribute an equal amount of money* for the gift. If $70.40 was collected from 16 students, then each of them contributed $4.40 $\left(\frac{\$70.40}{16} = \$4.40\right)$. Since 21 students are involved, the total bill for the gift is $4.40 \times 21 =$ $92.40. You could have safely eliminated answer choices J and K because they are too large; you know that about $\frac{2}{3}$ of the students have paid their share, and the total collection is only $70.40. Also, answer choice F cannot be correct because it is less than $70.40.

3. **The correct answer is D.** Omar paid a total of $103 for his speeding ticket. You are given that the basic fine for speeding is $25, so he was charged an additional $78 ($103 − $25). If the charge for each mile per hour over the speed limit is $6, then Omar was driving 13 mph $\left(\frac{\$78}{\$6} = 13\right)$ over the 55 mph speed limit, or 68 mph.

4. **The correct answer is G.** To solve this problem, substitute the given values into the equation. You are given that the number of volts is 24 and that the current is 8 amperes. Substitute these values into the equation, as follows:

$$E = IR$$
$$24 = 8R$$
$$R = 3$$

Therefore, the circuit possesses a resistance of 3 ohms.

5. **The correct answer is D.** When parallel lines are cut by a transversal, the angles created have special relationships. For instance, opposite angles are congruent (have the same measure), which means that angles a and d are equal, and angles e and h are also equal. Also, same-side interior angles are equal, which means that angles a and e are equal. Only answer choice D includes angles that have the same measure.

6. **The correct answer is H.** To solve this problem, first complete the addition (75,600,000 + 300,000 = 75,900,000). To convert to scientific notation, you must first find the coefficient. The coefficient must be greater than 1 but less than 10 (a good rule of thumb is to put a decimal after the first number and then drop the 0's). In this problem, the coefficient is 7.59, so eliminate answer choices G, J, and K. You also need a base. In scientific notation, the base is always 10, and you must determine the power to which 10 is raised. Count the number of places from the decimal point to the end of the number. Here there are 7 places, so 10 is raised to the 7th power. Therefore, the number is expressed as 7.59×10^7.

7. **The correct answer is D.** To solve this problem, you can use simple division; carefully enter the numbers in your calculator:

$$35.65 \div 0.05 = 713.0.$$

You could also use long division to solve this problem.

8. **The correct answer is J.** To solve this problem, first convert the given equation to slope-intercept form ($y = mx + b$, where m is the slope of the line):

$$3y + 6x = -5$$
$$3y = -6x - 5$$
$$y = -2x - \frac{5}{3}$$

The slope of this line is −2. Since perpendicular slopes are negative reciprocals, the correct answer is $\frac{1}{2}$.

9. **The correct answer is A.** The problem states that $x = -4$, so to solve, substitute −4 wherever there is an instance of x (carefully track the negative signs!):

$$24 + 3 - x^2$$
$$= 24 + 3 - (-4)^2$$
$$= 24 + 3 - (16) = 11$$

10. **The correct answer is K.** As stated in the problem, the shoes are 40% off. Therefore, they are selling for 60% of their original cost ($75.00 × 0.6 = $45.00). The sales tax is 7%, so the total sales tax is $3.15 ($45 × 0.07). In all, the pair of shoes will cost $45.00 + $3.15 = $48.15.

11. **The correct answer is A.** The graph of $x > 7$ is represented by an open point at 7 and a line going to the right of 7. The only choice that correctly shows this is A.

12. **The correct answer is G.** You are given that the ratio of $2p$ to $11r$ is 1 to 6, and you know that $6p$ is equivalent to $3 \times 2p$. Therefore, the ratio of $6p$ to $11r$ is 3 to 6.

13. **The correct answer is D.** To solve this problem, first find the missing value of the leg of the triangle that is adjacent to x. Use the Pythagorean Theorem:

$$a^2 + 12^2 = 13^2$$
$$a^2 + 144 = 169$$
$$a^2 = 25$$
$$a = \sqrt{25}$$
$$a = 5$$

For x, $\sin = \dfrac{12}{13}$, $\cos = \dfrac{5}{13}$, and $\tan = \dfrac{12}{5}$. Test the answer choices to see which one correctly represents its respective trigonometric function:

Answer choice A: $13 \sin x = 5$; $\sin x = \dfrac{5}{13}$. Eliminate answer choice A.

Answer choice B: $12 \tan x = 5$; $\tan x = \dfrac{5}{12}$. Eliminate answer choice B.

Answer choice C: $12 \cos x = 13$; $\cos x = \dfrac{13}{12}$. Eliminate answer choice C.

Answer choice D: $5 \tan x = 12$; $\tan x = \dfrac{12}{5}$. This is the correct answer.

Answer choice D is the only answer that correctly represents one of the trigonometric functions for x.

14. **The correct answer is J.** The area of a rectangle is given by length × width. You are given that the area is 4,500 square meters and that the length is 10 meters more than twice the width. The length can be expressed as $2w + 10$. To solve for w, use the area formula:

$$l \times w = A$$
$$2w + 10 \times w = 4{,}500$$

Find the common factor:

$$w(2w + 10) = 4{,}500$$

15. **The correct answer is C.** To solve this problem, use the distance formula (Distance = Rate × Time) to first determine the length of the trail. If Alan traveled at 14 mph for 1.2 hours, then the trail must be $14 \times 1.2 = 16.8$ miles long. Use the same formula to find out how long it would take Alan to complete the same ride at 8 mph:

$$16.8 = 8t$$
$$t = 2.1$$

It would take Alan 2.1 hours to complete the trail at a speed of 8 mph.

16. **The correct answer is H.** To solve this problem, you first need to calculate the area of the original plot. If it was a square shape with side lengths measuring 18 feet, then the area is $18 \times 18 = 324$ square feet. The section is changed to a rectangular shape but still has the same area. You can solve the problem by using the formula for the area of a rectangle (Area = Length × Width), since you already know the area and the width:

$$324 = l \times 12$$
$$l = 27$$

17. **The correct answer is D.** To solve this problem, first determine how many apartments are being rented. If 70% of the 30 are being rented, then there are 21 (30×0.7) apartments being rented. If rent is \$320 a month and they are each rented out for 6 months, then the total amount of rent charged will be $21 \times 320 \times 6 = \$40{,}320$. Watch out for answer choice A, which is a partial answer, representing the amount of rent collected for the apartments in 1 month.

18. **The correct answer is G.** In this problem, you are given that the measure of angle YXW is 128°. Since this angle forms a line with angle X, the two must add up to 180°. Therefore, angle X must equal $180 - 128 = 52°$. Likewise, the three angles of a triangle must add up to 180°. You know that angle Y is 87° and angle X is 52°, so angle Z must equal $180 - 87 - 52 = 41°$.

19. **The correct answer is E.** To solve this problem, you first need to eliminate one of the variables. In this problem, it makes the most sense to eliminate x. This can be done by multiplying the first equation by 2:

$$2(-2x + 3y) = 2(30)$$
$$= -4x + 6y = 60$$

Now add the two equations:

$$-4x + 6y = 60$$
$$+4x - \frac{1}{4}y = -14$$
$$\overline{\hspace{3cm}}$$
$$5\frac{3}{4}y = 46$$

Finally, solve for y ($5\frac{7}{4}$ is equivalent to 5.75):

$$5.75y = 46$$
$$y = 8$$

Now that you know the value of y, you can solve one of the equations to find x (solve the most simple equation):

$$-2x + 3(8) = 30$$
$$-2x + 24 = 30$$
$$-2x = 6$$
$$x = -3$$

20. **The correct answer is J.** To solve this problem, begin by performing the multiplication and division within the parentheses:

$$\left(\frac{1}{2} \times \frac{3}{5}\right) = \frac{3}{10}$$

$$\left(\frac{1}{3} \div \frac{5}{8}\right) = \frac{8}{15}$$

Now find the common denominator, perform the addition and subtraction (remember to perform the operations from left to right), reduce and solve:

$$\frac{3}{10} + \frac{5}{6} - \frac{8}{15}$$

$$= \frac{9}{30} + \frac{25}{30} - \frac{16}{30} = \frac{18}{30}$$

$$\frac{18}{30} = \frac{3}{5}$$

21. **The correct answer is C.** To solve this problem, first perform the multiplication in the first part of the problem (carefully track the negative signs):

$$-5x(x - 2) = -5x^2 + 10x$$

Now, write out the entire equation and perform the addition and subtraction (again, track the negative signs):

$$-5x^2 + 10x - 4x + 7x^2 - 3x$$

Group like terms together:

$$= (-5x^2 + 7x^2) + (10x - 4x - 3x)$$
$$= 2x^2 + 3x$$

22. **The correct answer is H.** A general rule of exponents says that $x^{-n} = \dfrac{1}{x^n}$. Following this rule, 4^{-3} would be $\dfrac{1}{4^3} = \dfrac{1}{64}$.

23. **The correct answer is D.** You are given that $x = \dfrac{5}{2}$ is one of the solutions to the equation, so backtrack to find the factor:

$$x = \frac{5}{2}$$
$$2x = 5$$
$$2x - 5 = 0$$

This solution must be multiplied by $x + 4$, as that is the only term that would result in the equation $2x^2 + kx - 20 = 0$. To solve for k, simply use the FOIL method for the two binomials:

$$(2x - 5)(x + 4) = 0$$
$$2x^2 + 8x - 5x - 20 = 0$$
$$2x^2 + 3x - 20 = 0$$

Therefore, k is equal to 3.

24. **The correct answer is H.** The three angles of a triangle always add up to 180°. Since you are given the measures of angles Q (44°) and R (118°), the measure of angle S must be $180 - 44 - 118 = 18°$. You are given that $\overline{RT}$ bisects angle QRS, so in each of the two smaller triangles angle R equals 59°. You now have two of the angles in triangle RTS, so the measure of angle RTS must be $180 - 18 - 59 = 103°$.

25. **The correct answer is B.** You are given that Emily has and wants to use all 52 feet of fencing and that the width of the enclosure is going to be between 9 and 12 feet. You can use the formula for perimeter to find the possible dimensions for the length:

$$2W + 2L = \text{Perimeter}$$
$$2(9) + 2L = 52, \text{ or } 2(12) + 2L = 52$$
$$18 + 2L = 52, \text{ or } 24 + 2L = 52$$
$$2L = 34, \text{ or } 2L = 28$$
$$L = 17, \text{ or } L = 14$$

The length of the dog enclosure must be between 14 and 17 feet.

26. **The correct answer is G.** The diameter is twice the radius, so, for this sphere, the radius is 6 centimeters $\left(\dfrac{12}{2}\right)$. Input this value into the equation for the volume of a sphere and solve:

$$V = \frac{4\pi(6^3)}{3}$$
$$V = \frac{4\pi(216)}{3}$$
$$V = \frac{864\pi}{3}$$
$$V = 288\pi$$

27. **The correct answer is D.** To solve this problem, find the missing side length by using the Pythagorean Theorem:

$$a^2 + b^2 = c^2$$
$$8^2 + b^2 = 17^2$$
$$64 + b^2 = 289$$
$$b^2 = 225$$
$$b = \sqrt{225}$$
$$b = 15$$

The tangent of an angle is the ratio of the side opposite the angle to the adjacent side (opposite/adjacent). Therefore, $\tan s = \dfrac{8}{15}$.

28. **The correct answer is H.** To solve this problem, first use cross-multiplication to eliminate the denominators:

$$\frac{5x + 4}{2x} = \frac{x + 5}{x}$$

$$x(5x + 4) = 2x(x + 5)$$

Now, perform the necessary operations to solve for x:

$$5x^2 + 4x = 2x^2 + 10x$$
$$3x^2 - 6x = 0$$
$$3x(x - 2) = 0$$
$$3x = 0 \text{ and } x - 2 = 0$$
$$x = 0 \text{ and } x = 2$$

The sum of the solutions for the equation is $0 + 2$, or 2.

29. **The correct answer is D.** The absolute value of a real number is its numerical value without regard to its sign. To solve this problem, first find the absolute values in the equation.

$$|-7| = 7$$
$$|-6| = 6$$

Next, perform the necessary multiplication and subtraction (perform the multiplication first):

$$7 - 2(6) =$$
$$= 7 - 12 = -5$$

30. **The correct answer is G.** Since $\overline{KO}$ is parallel to $\overline{LN}$, angle JKO is equal to angle KLN. Also, because $\overline{KN}$ is the same length as $\overline{LN}$, triangle KNL is isosceles. The two missing angles must be the same and must add up to $140°$ ($180° - 40°$). Therefore, the angles must each equal $70°$ ($70° + 70° + 40° = 180°$). Because angle KLN measures $70°$, angle JKO must have the same measurement.

31. **The correct answer is C.** To solve this problem, first reduce the inequality:

$$2a^2 - 5 \le 67$$
$$2a^2 \le 72$$
$$a^2 \le 36$$
$$a \le 6$$

Eliminate answer choices A and B because you know that a must be either equal to or less than 6. Now, work through the remaining answer choices, substituting the values for a in the inequality:
Answer choice C: $2(-6)^2 - 5 \le 67$

$$2(36) - 5 \le 67$$
$$72 - 5 \le 67$$
$$67 \le 67$$

Any number less than -6 will yield an answer greater than 67, which would make the inequality untrue.

32. **The correct answer is J.** To solve this problem, it is helpful to draw a picture of the square to give yourself a visual representation of what you are trying to find.

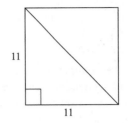

Since all of the angles in a square measure $90°$, the diagonal splits the square into two triangles with angles measuring $45°$, $45°$, and $90°$, as seen in the picture. For a $45°$-$45°$-$90°$ triangle, the sides measure 1, 1, and $\sqrt{2}$, respectively. You already know that the length of each of the sides of the square is 11, so the length of the diagonal must be $11\sqrt{2}$.

33. **The correct answer is E.** The standard equation for a circle with center (h, k) and radius r is $(x - h)^2 + (y - k)^2 = r^2$. In the equation given in this problem, $r^2 = 64$, so the radius must be $\sqrt{64} = 8$.

34. **The correct answer is F.** To find the slope of the line, first put the equation in slope-intercept form ($y = mx + b$), where m represents the slope:

$$-12x - 3y = 17$$
$$-3y = 12x + 17$$
$$y = -4x - \frac{17}{3}$$

The slope of the line is -4.

35. **The correct answer is D.** To solve this problem, you first need to determine how many players are in the league. Multiply each of the "number of players on the team" by their respective "number of teams":

$$6 \times 3 = 18$$
$$7 \times 6 = 42$$
$$6 \times 4 = 24$$
$$9 \times 9 = 81$$
$$10 \times 3 = 30$$

Now, add all of these numbers together:

$$18 + 42 + 24 + 81 + 30 = 195$$

There are 195 players in the league. Since you are given that there are 25 teams in the league, the average number of players per team is $195 \div 25 = 7.8$. The question asks you to round to the nearest whole number, so the correct answer is 8.

36. **The correct answer is F.** The circle is centered at K, so line segment KL is the radius of the circle. The area of a circle is given by the formula $A = \pi r^2$. For this circle, the area would be $\pi(7^2) = 49\pi$. Since the radius of the circle is 7, the diameter is 14, which is also the measure of the sides of the square. The area of the square is $14 \times 14 = 196$. Therefore, if the circle was cut out of the square, the remaining area would be $196 - 49\pi$.

37. **The correct answer is C.** To solve this problem, first find the slope of the first line by changing the equation to slope-intercept form ($y = mx + b$):

$$2x - 8y = 13$$
$$-8y = -2x + 13$$
$$y = \frac{1}{4}x - \frac{13}{8}$$

The slope of this line is $\frac{1}{4}$. Eliminate answer choices A, B, D, and E. The correct answer must be C. If you have time, you can confirm by finding the y-intercept of the second line:

$$y + 5 = -3x$$
$$y = -3x - 5$$

The y-intercept of this equation is -5.
A line with the same slope as the first line and the same y-intercept as the second line would have the equation $y = \frac{1}{4}x - 5$.

38. **The correct answer is K.** To solve this problem, first solve the inequality for x:

$$4x + 2 \geq 7x + 11$$
$$-9 \geq 3x$$
$$-3 \geq x$$

The inequality means "x is less than or equal to -3." This is represented by a closed point at -3 and a line going to the left. The only answer choice that shows this is K.

39. **The correct answer is B.** In this problem, you are given two points on a line and the slope of the line. To solve for s, use the equation $(y_2 - y_1) = m(x_2 - x_1)$, where m is the slope of the line, and (x_1, y_1) and (x_2, y_2) are the given points on the line:

$$6 - 16 = -\frac{5}{2}(2s - 3s)$$
$$-10 = -\frac{5}{2}(-s)$$
$$-10 = \frac{5}{2}s$$
$$-20 = 5s$$
$$-4 = s$$

40. **The correct answer is H.** In this problem, you are given the time over which the loan is to be paid back (t), the interest rate (r), and the total amount of interest paid (I). You are asked to find the amount borrowed (P). To solve, substitute the given values into the formula for calculating interest:

$$I = Prt$$
$$308 = P(0.11)(2)$$
$$308 = 0.22P$$
$$P = 1400$$

Trey took out a \$1,400 loan.

41. **The correct answer is C.** To solve this problem, draw out the (x, y) coordinate plane and plot the three given points, as shown below:

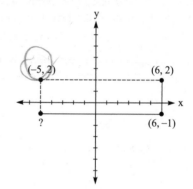

You can see that the missing point must be in the 3rd quadrant (both x and y coordinates are negative) in order to form a rectangle. This eliminates answer choices D and E. Because the figure is a rectangles, opposite sides are parallel, which means the x-coordinate of the missing point must be $-s$, and the y-coordinate must be -1.

42. **The correct answer is H.** To solve this problem, first isolate the variable in the equation:

$$\sqrt{4x} - 2 = 6$$
$$\sqrt{4x} = 8$$

Next, square both sides to get rid of the square root and then solve for x:

$$(\sqrt{4x})^2 = 8^2$$
$$4x = 64$$
$$x = 16$$

43. **The correct answer is A.** By pressing the "7" button instead of the "4," Eugenia's result was 39 more than the correct answer. Since the correct answer would be $4Z$, her mistake yields $4Z + 39$, which is equal to $7Z$. Therefore, the equation to determine Z can be expressed by $7Z - 39 = 4Z$.

44. The correct answer is G. The first step is to determine the binomials to which the given polynomial can be reduced. Find two numbers that, when multiplied together, equal 42. The only options are: 1 and 42, 2 and 21, and 6 and 7. The most logical pair (and easiest to work with) to test would be 6 and 7, as shown next:

$$(3x + 6)(x - 7) = 0$$
$$3x + 6 = 0 \text{ and } x - 7 = 0$$
$$3x = -6 \text{ and } x = 7$$
$$x = -2 \text{ and } x = 7$$

The sum of the solutions is $-2 + 7 = 5$.

45. The correct answer is B. In this problem, you are given the sum of the series (1,230) and the values of the first (5) and last (159) terms. The equation for finding the sum of the first n terms of a series is $S_n = \dfrac{n}{2(a_1 + a_n)}$. Here, a_1 is the first term in the series. Use this formula to determine the number of values that are in the series (159 is the nth number in the series):

$$1{,}230 = \dfrac{n}{2(5 + 159)}$$
$$2{,}460 = n(164)$$
$$15 = n$$

Now you know that 159 is the 15th term in the series. Since it is also the last term, there must be 15 terms total in the series. To find the 2nd, 3rd, and 4th terms of the series, you must first find the common difference (d). This can be found by using the formula for finding the nth term of an arithmetic series, which is $a_n = a_1 + (n - 1)d$. Use the values that you have for the first and last term of the series to solve for d:

$$159 = 5 + (15 - 1)d$$
$$159 = 5 + 14d$$
$$154 = 14d$$
$$d = 11$$

The common difference is 11. This is the number that is added to each term to get the next term in the series. Since the first number in the series is 5, the 2nd must be 16 ($5 + 11$), the 3rd is 27 ($16 + 11$), and the 4th is 38 ($27 + 11$).

46. The correct answer is K. You are given that $360 total worth of tickets were sold and that student tickets cost $3. To determine the number of dollars collected from nonstudent tickets, subtract $3S$ from the total number of dollars collected. This is expressed mathematically as $360 - 3S$.

47. The correct answer is E. To solve this problem, set up two different inequalities:

$$x + 7 \geq 0 \text{ and } 8 - 2x \geq 0$$
$$= x \geq -7 \text{ and } 8 \geq 2x$$
$$= x \geq -7 \text{ and } x \leq 4$$
$$= -7 \leq x \leq 4$$

48. The correct answer is G. You are given that angle Y is 90° and that angle X is 45°, so Z must be 45° as well ($90 + 45 + 45 = 180$). For a 45°-45°-90° triangle, the sides measure 1-1-$\sqrt{2}$, respectively. Therefore, the ratio of $\overline{YZ}$ to $\overline{XZ}$ would be $\dfrac{1}{\sqrt{2}}$.

49. The correct answer is C. To solve this problem, begin by drawing a diagram using the (x, y) coordinate plane, as shown below:

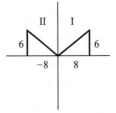

Since $0° \leq \theta° \leq 180°$, θ must be in either Quadrant I or II. You are given that $\tan \theta = \dfrac{6}{-8}$, so you know that θ is in Quadrant II, because the adjacent side is negative. Using the Pythagorean Theorem, you can find the missing side of the triangle:

$$6^2 + (-8)^2 = c^2$$
$$36 + 64 = c^2$$
$$100 = c^2$$
$$c = 10$$

The cosine of an angle is given by adjacent/hypotenuse, so for θ it is $\dfrac{-8}{10}$.

50. The correct answer is J. If 65% of the senior class members have taken at least 6 science courses, then 35% have taken fewer than 6 science courses. Of these remaining students, 40% have taken 4 or 5 science courses. To find the percentage of the entire class that this represents, multiply 0.35 by 0.40, which equals 0.14. This tells you that 14% of the senior class members took 4 or 5 science courses. Therefore, the percentage of the senior class that took fewer than 4 science courses would be 21% ($35 - 14$).

51. The correct answer is B. Since F and G are midpoints, they split $\overline{WX}$ and $\overline{ZY}$ each into two sections of 6 units. They also form two equal triangles (*WZG* and *FXY*). Looking at triangle *WZG*, you already know that $\overline{WZ}$ is 4 units (the width of the rectangle), and that $\overline{ZG}$ is 6 units. Use the Pythagorean Theorem to find the value of $\overline{WG}$:

$$4^2 + 6^2 = c^2$$
$$16 + 36 = c^2$$
$$52 = c^2$$
$$c = \sqrt{52}$$
$$c = \sqrt{4} \times \sqrt{13}$$
$$c = 2\sqrt{13}$$

Now you can find the perimeter of quadrilateral *WFYG*. $\overline{WF}$ and $\overline{GY}$ both equal 6, and $\overline{WG}$ and $\overline{FY}$ both equal $2\sqrt{13}$, so the perimeter is:

$$2L + 2W$$
$$2(6) + 2(2\sqrt{13})$$
$$12 + 4\sqrt{13}$$

52. **The correct answer is H.** To solve this problem, set up an equation in the form $(y_2 - y_1) = m(x_2 - x_1)$:

$$(7 - (-2)) = \frac{3}{2}(a - (-3))$$
$$(7 + 2) = \frac{3}{2}(a + 3)$$
$$9 = \frac{3}{2}a + 4\frac{1}{2}$$
$$4\frac{1}{2} = \frac{3}{2}a$$
$$a = 3$$

53. **The correct answer is D.** To find the area of a trapezoid, take the sum of the bases, multiply by the height of the trapezoid, and divide by 2. Use the values that you are given to solve for the missing base length:

$$54 = \frac{6(4 + b)}{2}$$
$$108 = 24 + 6b$$
$$84 = 6b$$
$$b = 14$$

The other base measures 14 inches.

54. **The correct answer is J.** Don't let the wording of this problem trip you up. It is simply asking you to solve the inequality for *a*:

$$5a - 13 \geq -3a + 19$$
$$8a \geq 32$$
$$a \geq 4$$

55. **The correct answer is C.** The area for a triangle is given by the formula $A = \frac{1}{2}bh$ (base × height). You are given the length of the base ($\overline{LM} = 9$), and you need to find the height. Notice that two right triangles are formed (*JKL* and *JKM*). For triangle *JKL*, you already have the values of two sides, so you can use the Pythagorean Theorem to find the third:

$$a^2 + b^2 = c^2$$
$$a^2 + 8^2 = 17^2$$
$$a^2 + 64 = 289$$
$$a^2 = 225$$
$$a = 15$$

Therefore, the length of $\overline{JK}$ is 15 inches. You can use this value to solve for the area of triangle *JML*, as it represents the height of the triangle:

$$A = \frac{1}{2}(9)(15)$$
$$A = \frac{1}{2}(135)$$
$$A = 67.5$$

56. **The correct answer is G.** This question asks you to solve the given equation. To do so, use cross-multiplication:

$$-x + 7 = \frac{2x - 19}{3}$$
$$3(-x + 7) = 2x - 19$$
$$-3x + 21 = 2x - 19$$
$$40 = 5x$$
$$8 = x$$

The only interval that includes $x = 8$ is the one given in answer choice G.

57. **The correct answer is C.** The formula for the length of an arc of a circle is given by $s = r\theta$, where s = arc length, r = radius of the circle, and θ = measure of the central angle, in radians. Also, the minor arc of a circle is the shorter of two arcs between two points on a circle. For this problem you know that the radius is 12 units long, and the central angle is 120° $\left(\dfrac{2\pi}{3}\ \text{in radians}\right)$. You can now set up an equation to solve:

$$s = r\theta$$
$$s = 12\left(\frac{2\pi}{3}\right)$$
$$s = \frac{24\pi}{3}$$
$$s = 8\pi$$

The measure of the minor arc is 8π.

58. **The correct answer is F.** The two lines depicted in the picture are perpendicular. By definition, perpendicular lines have negative reciprocal slopes. Therefore, when the slope of one line is x, the slope of a line perpendicular to that line will be $-\left(\dfrac{1}{x}\right)$. This relationship is represented in answer choice F.

59. **The correct answer is B.** The cosine of an angle is given by adjacent/hypotenuse. For angle U, the length of the adjacent side is missing. Use the Pythagorean Theorem to determine what it is:

$$a^2 + b^2 = c^2$$
$$7^2 + b^2 = 25^2$$
$$49 + b^2 = 625$$
$$b^2 = 576$$
$$b = 24$$

The cosine of angle U would be $\dfrac{24}{25}$.

60. **The correct answer is K.** To solve this problem, draw a picture of the (x, y) coordinate plane to give you a visual representation.

First, draw the line $y = -3$, and then plot all of the points that are given as possible answers, as shown below:

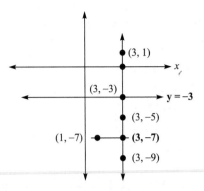

The correct answer must form a line with the point $(3, -7)$ that is perpendicular to $y = -3$. You can eliminate answer choice F, as this forms a line parallel to $y = -3$. Also, the correct answer must be as far away from $y = -3$ as $(3, -7)$ is (same point on x-axis, 4 away on y-axis.) The only choice that correctly matches both criteria is the point $(3, 1)$, answer choice K.

CHAPTER 8

PRACTICE TEST 3 WITH EXPLANATIONS

ACT MATHEMATICS TEST 3
Answer Sheet

MATHEMATICS

#				#				#				#			
1	Ⓐ Ⓑ Ⓒ Ⓓ Ⓔ			16	Ⓕ Ⓖ Ⓗ Ⓙ Ⓚ			31	Ⓐ Ⓑ Ⓒ Ⓓ Ⓔ			46	Ⓕ Ⓖ Ⓗ Ⓙ Ⓚ		
2	Ⓕ Ⓖ Ⓗ Ⓙ Ⓚ			17	Ⓐ Ⓑ Ⓒ Ⓓ Ⓔ			32	Ⓕ Ⓖ Ⓗ Ⓙ Ⓚ			47	Ⓐ Ⓑ Ⓒ Ⓓ Ⓔ		
3	Ⓐ Ⓑ Ⓒ Ⓓ Ⓔ			18	Ⓕ Ⓖ Ⓗ Ⓙ Ⓚ			33	Ⓐ Ⓑ Ⓒ Ⓓ Ⓔ			48	Ⓕ Ⓖ Ⓗ Ⓙ Ⓚ		
4	Ⓕ Ⓖ Ⓗ Ⓙ Ⓚ			19	Ⓐ Ⓑ Ⓒ Ⓓ Ⓔ			34	Ⓕ Ⓖ Ⓗ Ⓙ Ⓚ			49	Ⓐ Ⓑ Ⓒ Ⓓ Ⓔ		
5	Ⓐ Ⓑ Ⓒ Ⓓ Ⓔ			20	Ⓕ Ⓖ Ⓗ Ⓙ Ⓚ			35	Ⓐ Ⓑ Ⓒ Ⓓ Ⓔ			50	Ⓕ Ⓖ Ⓗ Ⓙ Ⓚ		
6	Ⓕ Ⓖ Ⓗ Ⓙ Ⓚ			21	Ⓐ Ⓑ Ⓒ Ⓓ Ⓔ			36	Ⓕ Ⓖ Ⓗ Ⓙ Ⓚ			51	Ⓐ Ⓑ Ⓒ Ⓓ Ⓔ		
7	Ⓐ Ⓑ Ⓒ Ⓓ Ⓔ			22	Ⓕ Ⓖ Ⓗ Ⓙ Ⓚ			37	Ⓐ Ⓑ Ⓒ Ⓓ Ⓔ			52	Ⓕ Ⓖ Ⓗ Ⓙ Ⓚ		
8	Ⓕ Ⓖ Ⓗ Ⓙ Ⓚ			23	Ⓐ Ⓑ Ⓒ Ⓓ Ⓔ			38	Ⓕ Ⓖ Ⓗ Ⓙ Ⓚ			53	Ⓐ Ⓑ Ⓒ Ⓓ Ⓔ		
9	Ⓐ Ⓑ Ⓒ Ⓓ Ⓔ			24	Ⓕ Ⓖ Ⓗ Ⓙ Ⓚ			39	Ⓐ Ⓑ Ⓒ Ⓓ Ⓔ			54	Ⓕ Ⓖ Ⓗ Ⓙ Ⓚ		
10	Ⓕ Ⓖ Ⓗ Ⓙ Ⓚ			25	Ⓐ Ⓑ Ⓒ Ⓓ Ⓔ			40	Ⓕ Ⓖ Ⓗ Ⓙ Ⓚ			55	Ⓐ Ⓑ Ⓒ Ⓓ Ⓔ		
11	Ⓐ Ⓑ Ⓒ Ⓓ Ⓔ			26	Ⓕ Ⓖ Ⓗ Ⓙ Ⓚ			41	Ⓐ Ⓑ Ⓒ Ⓓ Ⓔ			56	Ⓕ Ⓖ Ⓗ Ⓙ Ⓚ		
12	Ⓕ Ⓖ Ⓗ Ⓙ Ⓚ			27	Ⓐ Ⓑ Ⓒ Ⓓ Ⓔ			42	Ⓕ Ⓖ Ⓗ Ⓙ Ⓚ			57	Ⓐ Ⓑ Ⓒ Ⓓ Ⓔ		
13	Ⓐ Ⓑ Ⓒ Ⓓ Ⓔ			28	Ⓕ Ⓖ Ⓗ Ⓙ Ⓚ			43	Ⓐ Ⓑ Ⓒ Ⓓ Ⓔ			58	Ⓕ Ⓖ Ⓗ Ⓙ Ⓚ		
14	Ⓕ Ⓖ Ⓗ Ⓙ Ⓚ			29	Ⓐ Ⓑ Ⓒ Ⓓ Ⓔ			44	Ⓕ Ⓖ Ⓗ Ⓙ Ⓚ			59	Ⓐ Ⓑ Ⓒ Ⓓ Ⓔ		
15	Ⓐ Ⓑ Ⓒ Ⓓ Ⓔ			30	Ⓕ Ⓖ Ⓗ Ⓙ Ⓚ			45	Ⓐ Ⓑ Ⓒ Ⓓ Ⓔ			60	Ⓕ Ⓖ Ⓗ Ⓙ Ⓚ		

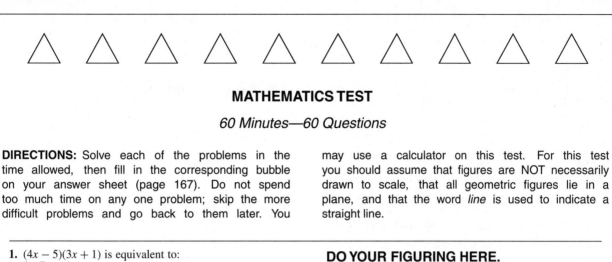

MATHEMATICS TEST

60 Minutes—60 Questions

DIRECTIONS: Solve each of the problems in the time allowed, then fill in the corresponding bubble on your answer sheet (page 167). Do not spend too much time on any one problem; skip the more difficult problems and go back to them later. You may use a calculator on this test. For this test you should assume that figures are NOT necessarily drawn to scale, that all geometric figures lie in a plane, and that the word *line* is used to indicate a straight line.

DO YOUR FIGURING HERE.

1. $(4x - 5)(3x + 1)$ is equivalent to:
   A. $7x - 4$
   B. $12x^2 - 5$
   C. $7x^2 + 11x - 4$
   D. $12x^2 - 11x - 5$
   E. $16x + 20$

2. What is the perimeter, in inches, of a rectangle if it has a length of 11 inches and a width of 6 inches?
   F. 17
   G. 34
   H. 36
   J. 66
   K. 132

3. Adam attempted 33 field goals throughout the football season and made 26 of them. Approximately what percentage of his field goals did he make during the season?
   A. 27%
   B. 33%
   C. 66%
   D. 72%
   E. 79%

4. What (x, y) pair is the solution to the system of equations below?

   $$-2x + 4y = -18$$
   $$4x - 5y = 30$$

   F. $(5, -2)$
   G. $(3, 3)$
   H. $(0, 0)$
   J. $(-3, -3)$
   K. $(-5, 2)$

5. If the measure of each interior angle in a regular polygon is 90, how many sides does the polygon have?
   A. 8
   B. 6
   C. 5
   D. 4
   E. 3

GO ON TO THE NEXT PAGE.

△ △ △ △ △ △ △ △ △ △

6. For all positive integers x, what is the greatest common factor of the numbers $256x$ and $144x$?
  F. 12
  G. 16
  H. x
  J. $16x$
  K. $24x$

7. Kathleen and Natalie are putting new carpet in their apartment. Kathleen used $22\frac{3}{4}$ square yards of carpet in the living room, and Natalie used $12\frac{1}{2}$ square yards of carpet in the dining room. If 50 square yards of carpet was purchased, how many square yards were left after laying new carpet down in both rooms?
  A. $12\frac{3}{4}$

  B. $14\frac{1}{4}$

  C. $14\frac{1}{2}$

  D. $14\frac{3}{4}$

  E. $16\frac{1}{4}$

8. In the figure below, parallel lines q and r are intersected by line s. What is the value of x ?

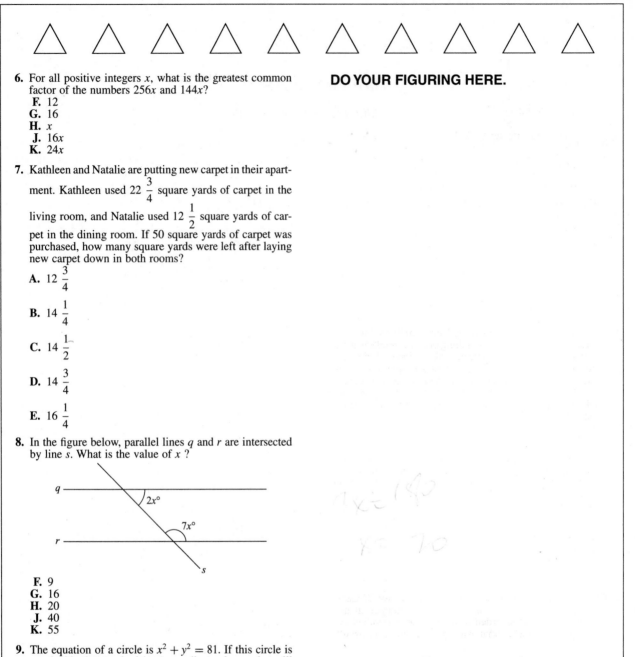

  F. 9
  G. 16
  H. 20
  J. 40
  K. 55

9. The equation of a circle is $x^2 + y^2 = 81$. If this circle is graphed in the standard (x, y) coordinate plane, what will be the y-intercepts?
  A. $(0, 3)$ and $(0, -3)$
  B. $(0, 9)$ and $(0, -9)$
  C. $(0, 12)$ and $(0, -12)$
  D. $(0, 18)$ and $(0, -18)$
  E. $(0, 27)$ and $(0, -27)$

10. A new rectangular soccer field is being constructed at John Adams High School. The length of the field must be $(4x - 3)$ yards and the width must be $5x$ yards. Which of the following expressions in terms of x gives the number of square yards of grass needed to cover the field?
  F. $x - 3$
  G. $9x - 3$
  H. $20x - 15x^2$
  J. $15x^2 + 9x$
  K. $20x^2 - 15x$

DO YOUR FIGURING HERE.

GO ON TO THE NEXT PAGE.

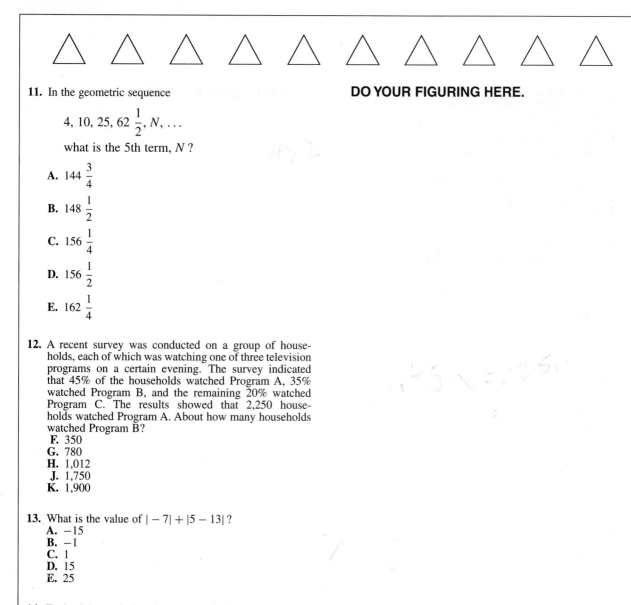

11. In the geometric sequence

$$4, 10, 25, 62\frac{1}{2}, N, \ldots$$

what is the 5th term, N?

A. $144\frac{3}{4}$

B. $148\frac{1}{2}$

C. $156\frac{1}{4}$

D. $156\frac{1}{2}$

E. $162\frac{1}{4}$

12. A recent survey was conducted on a group of house-holds, each of which was watching one of three television programs on a certain evening. The survey indicated that 45% of the households watched Program A, 35% watched Program B, and the remaining 20% watched Program C. The results showed that 2,250 house-holds watched Program A. About how many households watched Program B?
 F. 350
 G. 780
 H. 1,012
 J. 1,750
 K. 1,900

13. What is the value of $|-7| + |5 - 13|$?
 A. -15
 B. -1
 C. 1
 D. 15
 E. 25

14. Each night at closing time over a full workweek, Cory counted the number of customers who shopped at his store that day and recorded it in the table shown below. For that workweek, what was the average number of customers per day at Cory's store?

Day	Number of customers
Monday	20
Tuesday	26
Wednesday	21
Thursday	17
Friday	31

 F. 26
 G. 23
 H. 21
 J. 20
 K. 18

GO ON TO THE NEXT PAGE.

△   △   △   △   △   △   △   △   △   △

15. Sasha is going to Italy over his spring break. When he arrives, he has to exchange his U.S. dollars for euros. If the exchange rate between the number of U.S. dollars (u) and euros (e) is expressed in the equation $0.77u = e$, approximately how many euros will Sasha receive in exchange for his 675 U.S. dollars?
A. 877
B. 730
C. 520
D. 493
E. 465

16. At approximately what speed, in miles per hour, would you be traveling on your bike if you traveled 3.5 miles in 12 minutes?
F. 3.4
G. 8.3
H. 14.0
J. 15.2
K. 17.5

17. There is a bowl with 48 different marbles in it. In the bowl, there are 14 red marbles, 12 blue, 9 green, 8 yellow, and 5 white. If Corbin reaches into the bowl without looking, what is the probability that he will draw a marble that is either blue or white?

A. $\dfrac{21}{48}$

B. $\dfrac{17}{48}$

C. $\dfrac{12}{48}$

D. $\dfrac{9}{48}$

E. $\dfrac{5}{48}$

18. If $n = 2$, what is the value of $n(-6)^n - 9n$?
F. 126
G. 81
H. 54
J. 18
K. −90

19. Which of the following is a factor of $(2z^2 - z - 15)$?
A. $2z - 5$
B. $2z - 15$
C. $z^2 - 3$
D. $z + 15$
E. $z - 3$

20. If the point with coordinates $(-2, y_1)$ lies on the graph of $y = -4x + 5$, what is the value of y_1?
F. 13
G. 8
H. 3
J. 1
K. −3

DO YOUR FIGURING HERE.

GO ON TO THE NEXT PAGE.

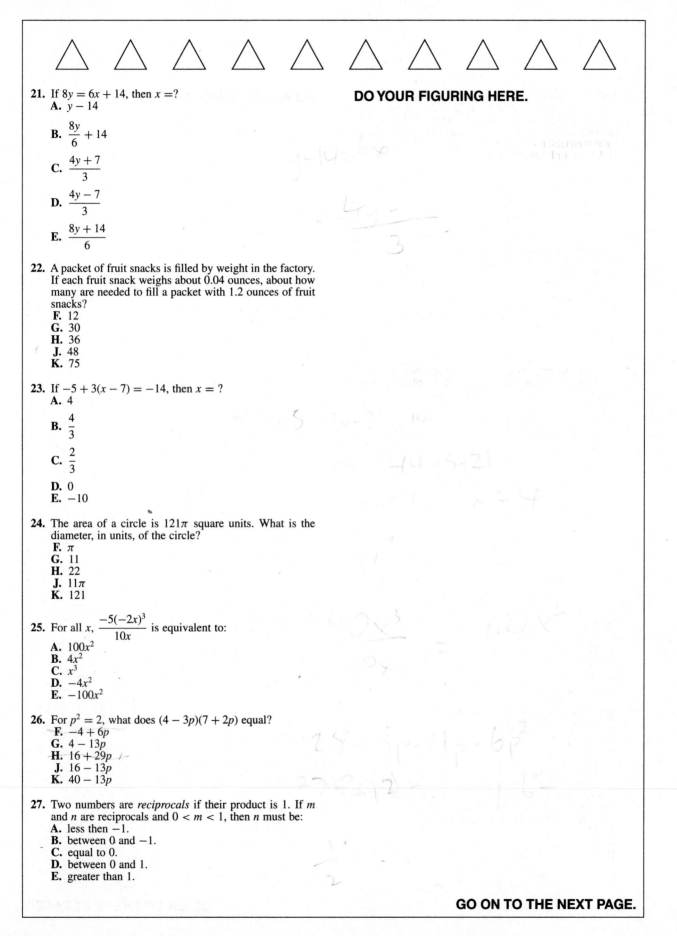

21. If $8y = 6x + 14$, then $x =$?
  A. $y - 14$

  B. $\dfrac{8y}{6} + 14$

  C. $\dfrac{4y + 7}{3}$

  D. $\dfrac{4y - 7}{3}$

  E. $\dfrac{8y + 14}{6}$

22. A packet of fruit snacks is filled by weight in the factory. If each fruit snack weighs about 0.04 ounces, about how many are needed to fill a packet with 1.2 ounces of fruit snacks?
  F. 12
  G. 30
  H. 36
  J. 48
  K. 75

23. If $-5 + 3(x - 7) = -14$, then $x = $?
  A. 4

  B. $\dfrac{4}{3}$

  C. $\dfrac{2}{3}$

  D. 0
  E. -10

24. The area of a circle is 121π square units. What is the diameter, in units, of the circle?
  F. π
  G. 11
  H. 22
  J. 11π
  K. 121

25. For all x, $\dfrac{-5(-2x)^3}{10x}$ is equivalent to:
  A. $100x^2$
  B. $4x^2$
  C. x^3
  D. $-4x^2$
  E. $-100x^2$

26. For $p^2 = 2$, what does $(4 - 3p)(7 + 2p)$ equal?
  F. $-4 + 6p$
  G. $4 - 13p$
  H. $16 + 29p$
  J. $16 - 13p$
  K. $40 - 13p$

27. Two numbers are *reciprocals* if their product is 1. If m and n are reciprocals and $0 < m < 1$, then n must be:
  A. less then -1.
  B. between 0 and -1.
  C. equal to 0.
  D. between 0 and 1.
  E. greater than 1.

DO YOUR FIGURING HERE.

GO ON TO THE NEXT PAGE.

△ △ △ △ △ △ △ △ △ △

28. Which of the following is equivalent to

$$(5x - 2x^2) - (3x - 11) + (x^2 - 6)?$$

F. $x^4 - 2x^2 - 17$
G. $-x^4 + 2x^2 + 5$
H. $-x^4 + 2x^2 - 17$
J. $-x^2 + 2x + 5$
K. $-x^2 + 2x - 17$

DO YOUR FIGURING HERE.

29. The edges of a cube are 4 inches long. What is the surface area, in square inches, of this cube?
A. 144
B. 96
C. 64
D. 24
E. 16

30. A ladder is set up at a 50° angle to the second-store window of a house, which is 28 feet tall. Which of the following equations gives the height x, in feet, of the ladder?

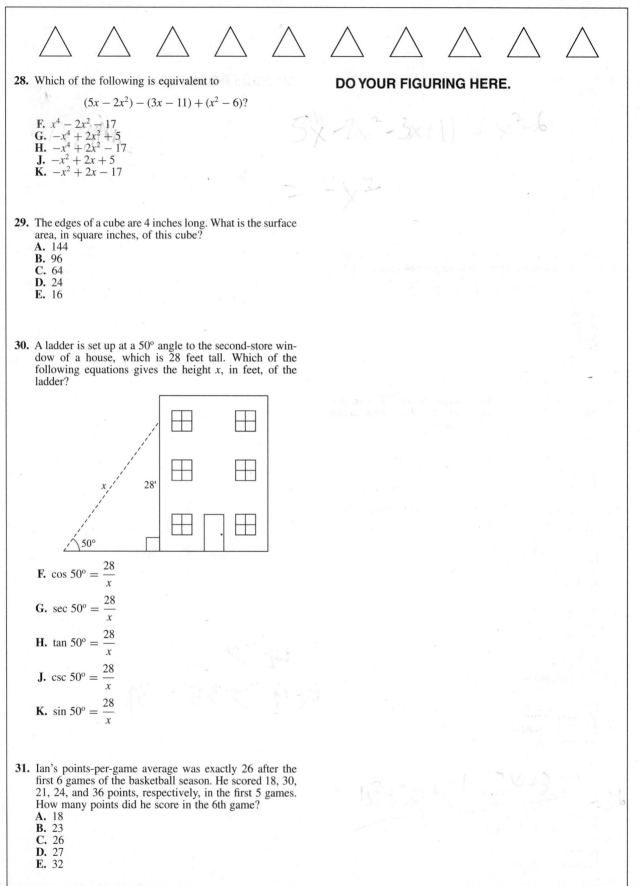

F. $\cos 50° = \dfrac{28}{x}$

G. $\sec 50° = \dfrac{28}{x}$

H. $\tan 50° = \dfrac{28}{x}$

J. $\csc 50° = \dfrac{28}{x}$

K. $\sin 50° = \dfrac{28}{x}$

31. Ian's points-per-game average was exactly 26 after the first 6 games of the basketball season. He scored 18, 30, 21, 24, and 36 points, respectively, in the first 5 games. How many points did he score in the 6th game?
A. 18
B. 23
C. 26
D. 27
E. 32

GO ON TO THE NEXT PAGE.

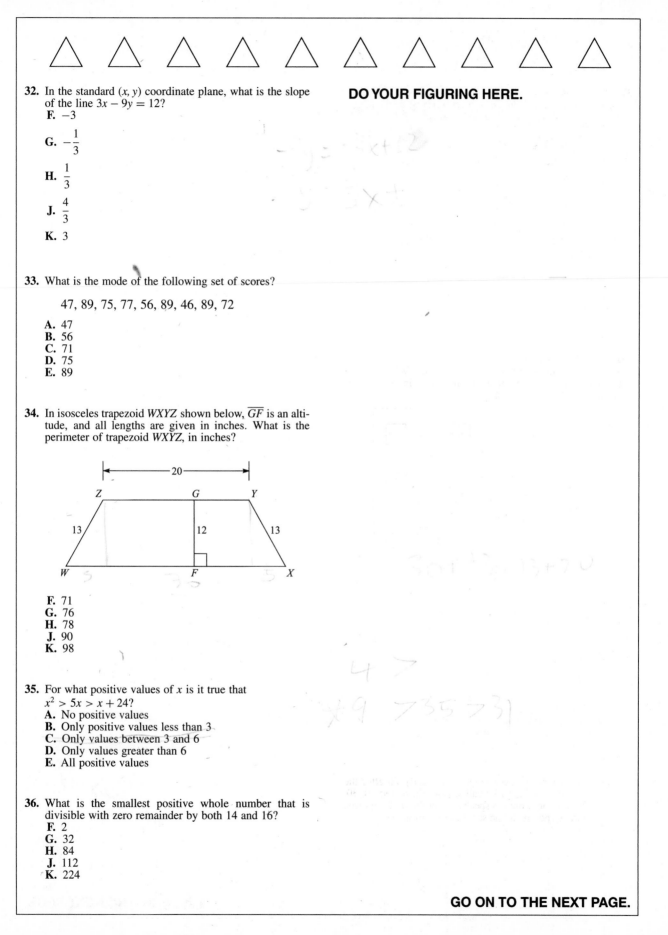

32. In the standard (x, y) coordinate plane, what is the slope of the line $3x - 9y = 12$?

   F. -3

   G. $-\dfrac{1}{3}$

   H. $\dfrac{1}{3}$

   J. $\dfrac{4}{3}$

   K. 3

DO YOUR FIGURING HERE.

33. What is the mode of the following set of scores?

     47, 89, 75, 77, 56, 89, 46, 89, 72

   A. 47
   B. 56
   C. 71
   D. 75
   E. 89

34. In isosceles trapezoid $WXYZ$ shown below, $\overline{GF}$ is an altitude, and all lengths are given in inches. What is the perimeter of trapezoid $WXYZ$, in inches?

   F. 71
   G. 76
   H. 78
   J. 90
   K. 98

35. For what positive values of x is it true that $x^2 > 5x > x + 24$?
   A. No positive values
   B. Only positive values less than 3
   C. Only values between 3 and 6
   D. Only values greater than 6
   E. All positive values

36. What is the smallest positive whole number that is divisible with zero remainder by both 14 and 16?
   F. 2
   G. 32
   H. 84
   J. 112
   K. 224

GO ON TO THE NEXT PAGE.

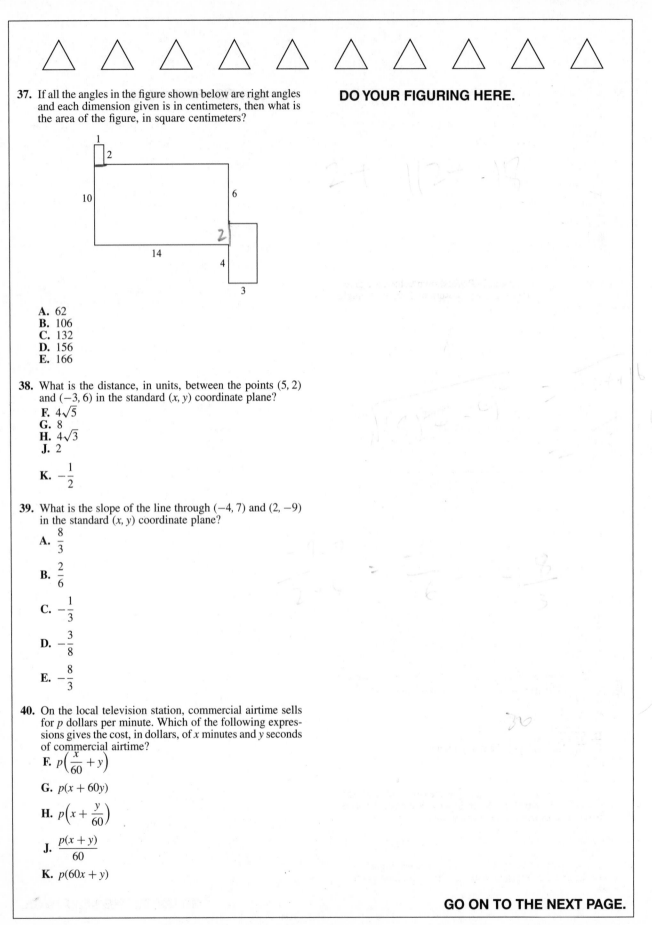

37. If all the angles in the figure shown below are right angles and each dimension given is in centimeters, then what is the area of the figure, in square centimeters?

DO YOUR FIGURING HERE.

A. 62
B. 106
C. 132
D. 156
E. 166

38. What is the distance, in units, between the points $(5, 2)$ and $(-3, 6)$ in the standard (x, y) coordinate plane?
   F. $4\sqrt{5}$
   G. 8
   H. $4\sqrt{3}$
   J. 2
   K. $-\dfrac{1}{2}$

39. What is the slope of the line through $(-4, 7)$ and $(2, -9)$ in the standard (x, y) coordinate plane?
   A. $\dfrac{8}{3}$
   B. $\dfrac{2}{6}$
   C. $-\dfrac{1}{3}$
   D. $-\dfrac{3}{8}$
   E. $-\dfrac{8}{3}$

40. On the local television station, commercial airtime sells for p dollars per minute. Which of the following expressions gives the cost, in dollars, of x minutes and y seconds of commercial airtime?
   F. $p\left(\dfrac{x}{60} + y\right)$
   G. $p(x + 60y)$
   H. $p\left(x + \dfrac{y}{60}\right)$
   J. $\dfrac{p(x + y)}{60}$
   K. $p(60x + y)$

GO ON TO THE NEXT PAGE.

△ △ △ △ △ △ △ △ △ △

41. For all positive values of j, k, and s, which of the following is equivalent to $\dfrac{j^5(j^2)(k^3)^4}{s^{-7}}$?

    A. $j^{10}k^7s^7$

    B. $j^7k^7s^7$

    C. $j^7k^{12}s^7$

    D. $\dfrac{j^{10}k^7}{s^7}$

    E. $\dfrac{j^7k^{12}}{s^7}$

42. The dimensions of triangle PQR, shown below, are given in inches. What is the area, in square feet, of triangle PQR?

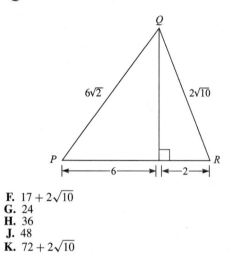

    F. $17 + 2\sqrt{10}$
    G. 24
    H. 36
    J. 48
    K. $72 + 2\sqrt{10}$

43. On February 1, Mr. Weiss' electric meter read 5,468 kilowatt-hours (kwh). On March 1, the meter read 7,678 kwh, but the utility company did not send an agent to take the reading. Instead, they estimated that Mr. Weiss had used 2,150 kwh of electricity that month and billed him for that estimated amount. If each kwh costs $0.12, what, if any, amount of money will Mr. Weiss owe the utility company beyond what he was actually billed?
    A. $3.87
    B. $4.08
    C. $5.25
    D. $7.20
    E. He does not owe them any money

44. If 2 interior angles of a triangle measure 40° and 85°, respectively, which of the following describes the location of the shortest side of the triangle?
    F. Always opposite the 40° angle
    G. Always between the 40° and the 85° angle
    H. Always opposite the 85° angle
    J. Opposite either the 85° or the unknown angle
    K. Cannot be determined from the information given

DO YOUR FIGURING HERE.

GO ON TO THE NEXT PAGE.

45. On the number line below, what is the coordinate of the point between Y and Z that is three times as far from point Z as from point Y?

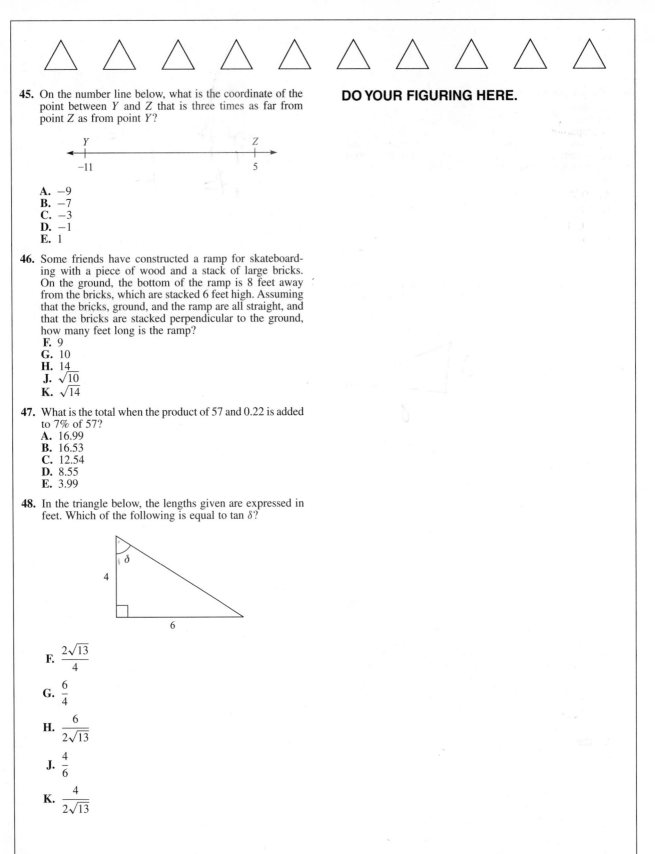

A. -9
B. -7
C. -3
D. -1
E. 1

46. Some friends have constructed a ramp for skateboarding with a piece of wood and a stack of large bricks. On the ground, the bottom of the ramp is 8 feet away from the bricks, which are stacked 6 feet high. Assuming that the bricks, ground, and the ramp are all straight, and that the bricks are stacked perpendicular to the ground, how many feet long is the ramp?
F. 9
G. 10
H. 14
J. $\sqrt{10}$
K. $\sqrt{14}$

47. What is the total when the product of 57 and 0.22 is added to 7% of 57?
A. 16.99
B. 16.53
C. 12.54
D. 8.55
E. 3.99

48. In the triangle below, the lengths given are expressed in feet. Which of the following is equal to $\tan \delta$?

F. $\dfrac{2\sqrt{13}}{4}$

G. $\dfrac{6}{4}$

H. $\dfrac{6}{2\sqrt{13}}$

J. $\dfrac{4}{6}$

K. $\dfrac{4}{2\sqrt{13}}$

DO YOUR FIGURING HERE.

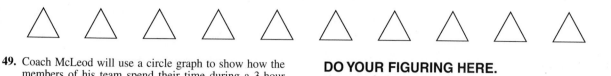

49. Coach McLeod will use a circle graph to show how the members of his team spend their time during a 3-hour practice. The size of the sector representing each drill is proportional to the time spent in that drill. During practice, the team members spend 36 minutes on the punt return drill. How many degrees should the central angle measure in the sector representing the punt return drill?

A. 30.5°

B. 36°

C. 49.75°

D. 72°

E. 144°

DO YOUR FIGURING HERE.

50. If $r \neq 0$, s is a real number, $r^3 = 2s$, and $r^5 = 18s$, then what is one possible value of r?

F. 3

G. 5

H. 9

J. s^2

K. Cannot be determined from the information given

51. The volume of a sphere is given by the formula $V = \frac{4}{3}\pi r^3$ and its surface area by the formula $S = 4\pi r^2$, where r is the radius of the sphere. What is the surface area of a sphere, in square inches, if its volume is $\frac{2,048\pi}{3}$?

A. 32π

B. 144π

C. 256π

D. 324π

E. 512π

GO ON TO THE NEXT PAGE.

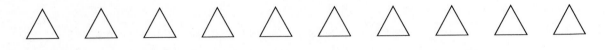

52. Jim and Steve both work as lifeguards at the local beach. Their lookout towers are located about 22 yards apart, at the same elevation. A victim is spotted waving for help in the water at angles of 39° and 54° from the line of sight between the lookout towers, as indicated in the diagram below. Which of the following expressions, if any, gives the approximate distance, in yards, between the victim and Steve's tower?

(Note: The *law of sines* states that the ratio of the sine of an angle to the length of the side opposite an angle is the same for all interior angles in the same triangle.)

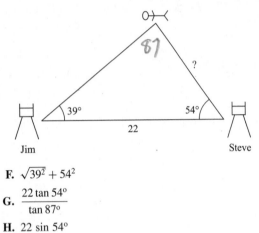

Jim   Steve

F. $\sqrt{39^2 + 54^2}$

G. $\dfrac{22 \tan 54°}{\tan 87°}$

H. $22 \sin 54°$

J. $\dfrac{22 \sin 39°}{\sin 87°}$

K. The distance cannot be approximated without more information.

53. For a population that grows at a constant rate of $r\%$ per year, the formula $P(t) = p_o \left(1 + \dfrac{r}{100}\right)^t$ models the population t years after an initial population of p_o is counted. The population of the city of Midtown was 557,000 in 2005. Assume the population grows at a constant rate of 2% per year. According to this formula, which of the following is an expression for the population of Midtown in the year 2010?

A. $(557{,}000 \times 1.02)^5$
B. $(557{,}000 \times 1.2)^5$
C. $557{,}000(1.02)^5$
D. $557{,}000(1.2)^5$
E. $557{,}000(3)^5$

54. In the standard (x, y) coordinate plane, line k_1 has an equation of $2x + 6y = 11$. If line k_2 is perpendicular to line k_1, what is the slope of line k_2?

F. 3
G. $\dfrac{11}{6}$
H. 1
J. $-\dfrac{1}{3}$
K. -3

DO YOUR FIGURING HERE.

GO ON TO THE NEXT PAGE.

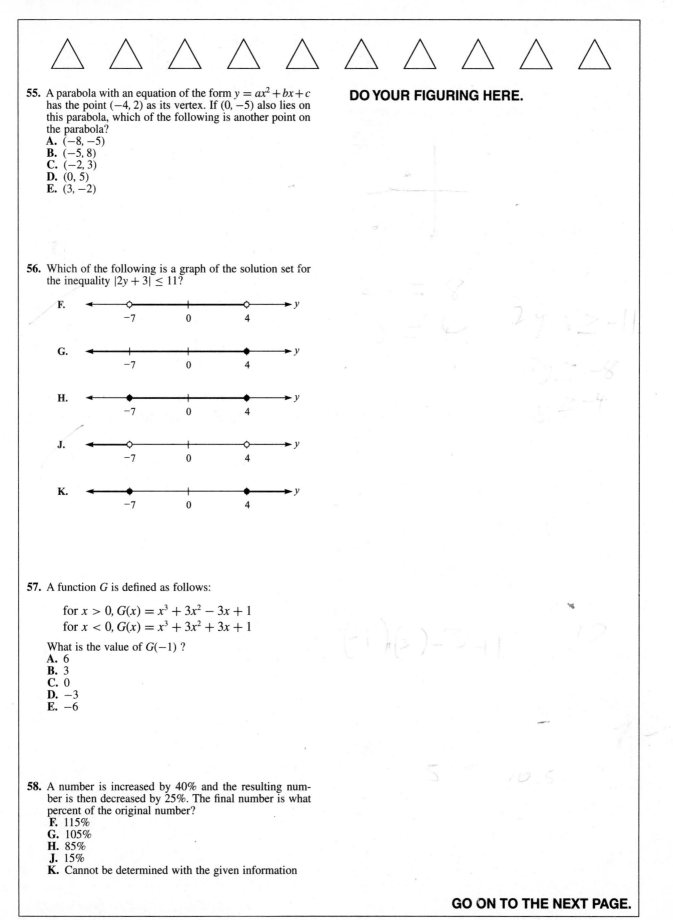

55. A parabola with an equation of the form $y = ax^2 + bx + c$ has the point $(-4, 2)$ as its vertex. If $(0, -5)$ also lies on this parabola, which of the following is another point on the parabola?
   A. $(-8, -5)$
   B. $(-5, 8)$
   C. $(-2, 3)$
   D. $(0, 5)$
   E. $(3, -2)$

DO YOUR FIGURING HERE.

56. Which of the following is a graph of the solution set for the inequality $|2y + 3| \leq 11$?

   F.

   G.

   H.

   J.

   K.

57. A function G is defined as follows:

   for $x > 0$, $G(x) = x^3 + 3x^2 - 3x + 1$
   for $x < 0$, $G(x) = x^3 + 3x^2 + 3x + 1$

   What is the value of $G(-1)$?
   A. 6
   B. 3
   C. 0
   D. −3
   E. −6

58. A number is increased by 40% and the resulting number is then decreased by 25%. The final number is what percent of the original number?
   F. 115%
   G. 105%
   H. 85%
   J. 15%
   K. Cannot be determined with the given information

GO ON TO THE NEXT PAGE.

8 △ △ △ △ △ △ △ △ 8

59. If $a > 0$ and $b < 0$, which of the following *must* be true for the value of $b - a$?
   A. $b - a > a$
   B. $b - a > 0$
   C. $b - a > b$
   D. $b - a > ab$
   E. $b - a < b$

DO YOUR FIGURING HERE.

60. The length of one side of a square is decreased by 40%. By approximately what percent would the length of an adjacent side have to be *increased* so that the area of the new figure (a rectangle) is the same as the area of the original square?
   F. 33%
   G. 40%
   H. 55%
   J. 67%
   K. 75%

END OF THE MATHEMATICS TEST
STOP! IF YOU HAVE TIME LEFT OVER, CHECK YOUR WORK ON THIS SECTION ONLY.

ANSWER KEY

Mathematics Test

1. D	16. K	31. D	46. G
2. G	17. B	32. H	47. B
3. E	18. H	33. E	48. G
4. F	19. E	34. G	49. D
5. A	20. F	35. D	50. F
6. J	21. D	36. J	51. C
7. D	22. G	37. C	52. J
8. H	23. A	38. F	53. C
9. B	24. H	39. E	54. F
10. K	25. B	40. H	55. A
11. C	26. J	41. C	56. H
12. J	27. E	42. G	57. C
13. D	28. J	43. D	58. G
14. G	29. B	44. F	59. E
15. C	30. K	45. B	60. J

SCORING WORKSHEET

On each ACT multiple-choice test (English, Mathematics, Reading, and Science Reasoning) you will receive a SCALED SCORE on a scale of 1 to 36. Use the following guidelines to determine your approximate SCALED SCORE on the ACT Mathematics Diagnostic Test that you just completed.

Step 1   Determine your RAW SCORE.

Your RAW SCORE is the number of questions that you answered correctly. Because there are 60 questions on the ACT Mathematics Test, the highest possible RAW SCORE is 60.

Step 2   Determine your SCALED SCORE using the following Scoring Worksheet.

Mathematics   _____ × **36** = _____ ÷ **60** = _____
                      RAW SCORE   **+ 1**   (*correction factor)

                                                                      _____
                                                                      SCALED SCORE

*The correction factor is an approximation based on the average from several recent ACT tests. It is most valid for scores in the middle 50% (approximately 16–24 scaled composite score) of the scoring range. The scores are all approximate. Actual ACT scoring scales vary from one administration to the next based upon several factors.

ANSWERS AND EXPLANATIONS

1. **The correct answer is D.** To solve this problem, use the Distributive Property to expand $(4x-5)(3x+1)$. You might know this as the FOIL method because you multiply the *f*irst terms together, then the *o*utside terms, then *i*nside terms, and finally the *l*ast terms. In this case $(4x - 5)(3x + 1) = (4x)(3x) + (4x)(1) - (5)(3x) - (5)(1) = 12x^2 + 4x - 15x - 5$. Combine like terms to get $12x^2 - 11x - 5$.

2. **The correct answer is G.** To solve this problem, recall that perimeter is the distance around a shape. To find the perimeter of a rectangle add the lengths of each side. Conveniently, opposite sides of rectangles have equal lengths. Since the rectangle's length is 11 inches and its width is 6 inches, the perimeter is $2(11) + 2(6) = 22 + 12 = 34$ inches.

3. **The correct answer is E.** To solve this problem, divide the number made by the number attempted, then multiply by 100 to get the percent. Since Adam attempted 33 field goals and made 26, the percentage made is $\frac{26}{33} \times 100 = 78.\overline{78}\%$, which rounds up to 79%.

4. **The correct answer is F.** One way to solve this problem is to solve one of the equations for x or y and use substitution. It does not matter which equation you solve first:

$$-2x + 4y = -18$$
$$-2x = -4y - 18$$
$$x = \frac{-4}{-2}y - \frac{18}{-2} = 2y + 9$$

Now substitute $2y + 9$ for x into the equation $4x - 5y = 30$:

$$4(2y + 9) - 5y = 30$$
$$8y + 36 - 5y = 30$$
$$3y + 36 = 30$$
$$3y = -6$$
$$y = -2$$

At this point it is not necessary to find the x-coordinate because only one answer choice has a y-coordinate of -2. The correct answer could also have been found by substituting in each answer choice into both of the equations. The correct answer choice works in both equations.

5. **The correct answer is D.** A polygon whose interior angles each measure 90 is a rectangle (or a square, which is a special rectangle). You could also have applied the formula $S = 180(n - 2)$, where S is the sum of the measures of the interior angles of a regular polygon. A regular polygon with n congruent angles, so $S = 90n$:

$$90n = 180(n - 2)$$
$$90n = 180n - 360$$
$$90n = 360$$
$$n = 4$$

6. **The correct answer is J.** It is clear that x is a factor of both $256x$ and $144x$. Eliminate answer choices F and G. Now find the greatest common factor of 256 and 144.

Factors of 256:   1, 2, 4, 8, **16**, 32, 64, 128, 256

Factors of 144:   1, 2, 3, 4, 6, 8, 9, 12, **16**, 18, 24, 36, 48, 72, 144

The greatest common factor is $16x$.

7. **The correct answer is D.** To solve this problem, find the total quantity of carpet used and subtract that sum from 50. To add $22\frac{3}{4}$ and $12\frac{1}{2}$, first find common denominators: the least common multiple of 2 and 4, which is 4. Now convert $12\frac{1}{2}$ to $12\frac{2}{4}$. Add the numbers to get $22 + 12 + \frac{3}{4} + \frac{2}{4} = 22 + 12 + \frac{5}{4} = 22 + 12 + 1 + \frac{1}{4} = 35\frac{1}{4}$. Subtracting $35\frac{1}{4}$ from 50 yields $14\frac{3}{4}$.

8. **The correct answer is H.** By definition, the angles with measure $2x°$ and $7x°$ are interior angles. Interior angles that are formed by cutting two parallel lines by a transversal are supplementary, meaning their sum is $180°$. Therefore $2x + 7x = 180$. Solve for x:

$$2x + 7x = 180$$
$$9x = 180$$
$$x = 20$$

9. **The correct answer is B.** Circles have an equation of the form $(x-h)^2 + (y-k)^2 = r^2$, where the circle has center (h, k) and radius r. A circle with equation $x^2 + y^2 = 81$ has its center at $(0, 0)$ because $(x - 0)^2 = x^2$ and $(y - k)^2 = y^2$, and a radius of $\sqrt{81} = 9$. Therefore, the circle will intersect the y-axis 9 units above and 9 units below the origin at points $(0, 9)$ and $(0, -9)$.

10. **The correct answer is K.** The area of a rectangle is found by multiplying length by width. Since width of the field is $(4x - 3)$ yards and the

length is $5x$ yards, the area is given by $5x(4x - 3)$. To simplify, use the Distributive Property to get $(5x)(4x) - (5x)(3) = 20x^2 - 15x$.

11. **The correct answer is C.** To solve this problem, recall that a geometric sequence is formed by multiplying each successive term by a constant number to get the next term. Call this constant number k, so that $4k = 10$, $10k = 25$, $25k = 62\frac{1}{2}$, and so on... In all of these cases, $k = 2.5$. Therefore, the 5th term can be found by multiplying the 4th term, $62\frac{1}{2}$, by the quantity 2.5. The result is 156.25, or $156\frac{1}{4}$.

12. **The correct answer is J.** Let H represent the total number of households. If 45% of H watched Program A, and that proportion equaled 2,250 households, then $0.45H = 2,250$.

$$0.45H = 2,250$$
$$H = 5,000.$$

Since $H = 5,000$, the number of households that watched Program B is 35% of H, or $0.35(5,000) = 1,750$ households.

13. **The correct answer is D.** Recall that $|-7|$ means "the absolute value of -7." Absolute values represent the distance a number is from 0. Since all distances are positive, absolute values are always positive. Thus, $|-7| = 7$. Likewise, $|5 - 13| = |-8| = 8$. The expression $|-7| + |5 - 13|$ becomes $7 + 8$, or 15.

14. **The correct answer is G.** In this case, average refers to the "mean." To find the mean, add the values then divide that sum by the total number of values. Since there are 5 values, (Monday through Friday) divide the sum by 5: $\frac{(20 + 26 + 21 + 17 + 31)}{5} = \frac{115}{5} = 23.$

15. **The correct answer is C.** In this problem, $u = 675$. Since $0.77u = e$, $0.77(675) = e = 519.75$, or about 520 euros. Because the exchange rate is less than 1, you could have eliminated answer choices A and B.

16. **The correct answer is K.** If you traveled 3.5 miles in 12 minutes, then you traveled $\frac{3.5}{12}$ or about 0.291 miles per minute. Since there are 60 minutes in each hour, simply multiply the quantity 0.291 by 60 to get 17.46, or about 17.5 miles per hour.

17. **The correct answer is B.** Since there are 12 blue and 5 white marbles, there are 17 marbles that Corbin could draw out of a total of 48 marbles.

Therefore, the probability that Corbin draws a marble that is either blue or white is $\frac{17}{48}$.

18. **The correct answer is H.** To solve $n(-6)^n - 9n$ for $n = 2$, substitute 2 for n in the expression as follows:

$$2(-6)^2 - 9(2)$$
$$= 2(36) - 18$$
$$= 72 - 18 = 54$$

19. **The correct answer is E.** To solve this problem, factor the quadratic equation $2z^2 - z - 15$ as follows:

$$(2z + 5)(z - 3)$$

You are asked to find one factor and only $(z - 3)$ is among the choices, so answer choice E must be correct.

20. **The correct answer is F.** To find the y-coordinate of a particular x-value on the line $y = -4x + 5$, simply "plug in" the x-value: $y_1 = -4(-2) + 5 = 8 + 5 = 13$.

21. **The correct answer is D.** To answer this question, solve $8y = 6x + 14$ for x:

$$8y = 6x + 14$$
$$8y - 14 = 6x$$
$$\frac{8y - 14}{6} = x; \text{ simplify by dividing by 2.}$$
$$\frac{4y - 7}{3} = x$$

22. **The correct answer is G.** To solve this problem, divide the total weight of a packet (1.2 ounces) by the weight of an individual snack (0.04 ounces). The result is $\frac{1.2}{0.04} = 30$. There are 30 fruit snacks in a packet.

23. **The correct answer is A.** Solve this problem step by step as shown below (carefully track the negative signs):

$$-5 + 3(x - 7) = -14$$
$$3(x - 7) = -9$$
$$x - 7 = -3$$
$$x = 4$$

24. **The correct answer is H.** The area of a circle is given by πr^2, where r is the radius. Since the area is given as 121π, $r = \sqrt{121} = 11$. The diameter of a circle is equal to twice the length of the radius, or $2(11) = 22$.

25. **The correct answer is B.** To simplify, follow the proper order of operations:

$$\frac{-5(-2x)^3}{10x}$$

Compute exponents first:

$$= \frac{-5\left(-8x^3\right)}{10x}$$

Perform the multiplication in the numerator next:

$$= \frac{40x^3}{10x}$$

Simplify and cancel terms:

$$= 4x^2$$

26. The correct answer is J. To solve this problem, first distribute $(4 - 3p)(7 + 2p)$ using the FOIL method, as shown next:

$$(4 - 3p)(7 + 2p)$$
$$= (4)(7) + (4)(2p) - (3p)(7) - (3p)(2p)$$
$$= 28 + 8p - 21p - 6p^2$$

You are given that $p^2 = 2$, so simplify and make the substitution:

$$28 - 13p - 6(2)$$
$$= 16 - 13p$$

27. The correct answer is E. This is a good time to use a "stand in" to calculate the correct answer. Since $0 < m < 1$, pick a number for m that satisfies the requirements, such as $\frac{1}{2}$. The reciprocal of $\frac{1}{2}$ is 2 because $2\left(\frac{1}{2}\right) = 1$. Therefore if $m = \frac{1}{2}$, then $n = 2$. The only choice that works is that n must be greater than 1. You can try other values for m and n with the same results.

28. The correct answer is J. To solve this problem, distribute subtraction to each term within the parentheses, then combine like terms, as shown below:

$$(5x - 2x^2) - (3x - 11) + (x^2 - 6)$$
$$= 5x - 2x^2 - 3x + 11 + x^2 - 6$$
$$= -2x^2 + x^2 + 5x - 3x + 11 - 6$$
$$= -x^2 + 2x + 5$$

29. The correct answer is B. To solve this problem, recall that a cube has 6 square-shaped faces. Therefore the surface area is equal to 6 times the area of one of the square faces. Since an edge of the cube has length 4, one face has area $4^2 = 16$. The total surface area is $6(16) = 96$ square inches.

30. The correct answer is K. To solve this problem, recall that the sine of an angle in a right triangle is the ratio of the opposite side to the hypotenuse. In this case the side opposite the $50°$ angle has length 28 and the hypotenuse has length x; $\sin 50° = \frac{28}{x}$.

31. The correct answer is D. In this question, average refers to mean. The mean score of the first 6 games is 26. If the number of points Ian scored in the 6th game is given by x, then $\frac{(18 + 30 + 21 + 24 + 36 + x)}{6} = 26$. Solve for x:

$$\frac{(18 + 30 + 21 + 24 + 36 + x)}{6} = 26$$
$$(129 + x) = 6(26) = 156$$
$$x = 156 - 129 = 27$$

32. The correct answer is H. To find the slope of the line $3x - 9y = 12$, convert the equation to slope-intercept form ($y = mx + b$, where m is the slope and b is the y-intercept):

$$3x - 9y = 12$$
$$-9y = -3x + 12$$
$$y = \frac{-3}{-9}x + \frac{12}{-9}$$
$$m(slope) = \frac{-3}{-9} = \frac{1}{3}$$

33. The correct answer is E. To solve this problem, recall that mode is the value that appears most often in the list. First, rearrange the list in order of value to get 46, 47, 56, 72, 75, 77, 89, 89, 89. You can see 89 appears 3 times in the list.

34. The correct answer is G. To solve this problem, think of the bottom side as having the length of the top side plus two additional lengths (the small legs of right triangles formed below):

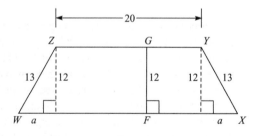

Since the height and hypotenuse are given, use the Pythagorean Theorem to find the length of the missing leg:

$$12^2 + a^2 = 13^2$$
$$144 + a^2 = 169$$
$$a^2 = 25$$
$$a = 5$$

The length of each leg is 5, making the total length of the bottom side $20 + 2(5) = 30$. The perimeter is then $20 + 13 + 13 + 30 = 76$.

35. The correct answer is D. To solve this problem, use sample values to evaluate the validity of the statement $x^2 > 5x > x + 24$. Since the answer choices use the values 3 and 6, it is logical to start with those values, then try others.

$x = 3$	$3^2 > 5(3) > 3 + 24$	False
$x = 6$	$6^2 > 5(6) > 6 + 24$	False
$x = 7$	$7^2 > 5(7) > 7 + 24$	True

Therefore, the statement must be valid only for values of x greater than 6.

36. **The correct answer is J.** To solve this problem, find the least common multiple of 14 and 16. Multiples of 14 include 14, 28, 42, 56, 70, 84, 98, 112 … Multiples of 16 include 16, 32, 48, 64, 80, 96, 112 … It is easy to see that 112 is the smallest positive whole number that is divisible with zero remainder by both 14 and 16. You could find a common multiple by finding the product of 14 and 16, but in this case it is not the *least* common multiple. Watch out for answer choice F, which is the smallest common factor (other than 1) of both 14 and 16.

37. **The correct answer is C.** To solve this problem, break the figure into three rectangles as shown below:

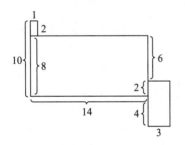

The dimensions of the large rectangle can be determined by subtracting the length of the small rectangle at the top (2) from 10 to get 8. The large rectangle has length 14 and width 8, making its area $(14)(8) = 112$. The area of the whole figure must be greater than 112, so eliminate answer choices A and B. The smallest rectangle has length 1 and width 2, making its area $(1)(2) = 2$. Finally the dimensions of the third rectangle can be found by determining the length of the "gap" on its upper left side. The gap is $8 - 6 = 2$, making the total length of that side $2 + 4 = 6$. Its area is $(6)(3) = 18$. The total area is $112 + 18 + 2 = 132$.

38. **The correct answer is F.** To find the distance between the points $(5, 2)$ and $(-3, 6)$, use the distance formula (the distance between the points (x_1, y_1) and (x_2, y_2) is $d = \sqrt{(x_2 - x_1)^2 + (y_2 - y_1)^2}$:

$$\sqrt{(-3 - 5)^2 + (6 - 2)^2}$$
$$= \sqrt{(-8)^2 + (4)^2}$$
$$= \sqrt{64 + 16} = \sqrt{80}$$
$$= \sqrt{16} \times \sqrt{5} = 4\sqrt{5}$$

39. **The correct answer is E.** The slope of a line can be found by using the slope formula (the slope of a line between two points (x_1, y_1) and (x_2, y_2) $\frac{y_2 - y_1}{x_2 - x_1}$ as follows:

$$\frac{y_2 - y_1}{x_2 - x_1}$$

Substitute $(-4, 7)$ and $(2, -9)$

$$\frac{-9 - 7}{2 - (-4)} = \frac{-16}{6} = -\frac{8}{3}$$

40. **The correct answer is H.** Since x represents minutes of airtime and y represents seconds of airtime, find the total number of minutes of commercial airtime. To do so, convert the number of seconds into minutes by dividing by 60 (60 seconds in a minute): $\frac{y}{60}$. The total minutes is therefore $x + \frac{y}{60}$. Since commercial airtime sells for p dollars per minute, the total cost is $p\left(x + \frac{y}{60}\right)$.

41. **The correct answer is C.** This problem requires the use of three different exponent rules. First, to simplify $j^5(j^2)$ simply add the exponents to get j^7. Eliminate answer choices A and D. Second, $(k^3)^4$ can be simplified by multiplying the exponents to get k^{12}. Eliminate answer choice B. Finally, $\frac{1}{s^{-7}} = s^7$. Therefore the correct answer is $j^7 k^{12} s^7$.

42. **The correct answer is G.** Recall that the area of a triangle is $\frac{1}{2}bh$, where b is the length of the base and h is the height. The base of triangle PQR is $6 + 2 = 8$ inches. The height is not given, but can be found using the Pythagorean theorem. A right triangle is formed with legs 2 and h (the height of triangle PQR) and with hypotenuse $2\sqrt{10}$. Use the Pythagorean Theorem:

$$2^2 + h^2 = (2\sqrt{10})^2$$
$$4 + h^2 = 40$$
$$h^2 = 36$$
$$h = 6$$

Therefore, the area is $\frac{1}{2}(8)(6) = \frac{1}{2}(48) = 24$.

43. **The correct answer is D.** The first step is to calculate the amount of electricity Mr. Weiss actually used by finding the difference between the two meter readings: $7,678 - 5,468 = 2,210$ kwh. Although he was estimated to have used 2,150 kwh, he actually used $2,210 - 2,150 = 60$ kwh more. Therefore, Mr. Weiss owes the utility company for 60 kwh beyond what he was actually billed. The amount owed is $60(0.12) = \$7.20$.

44. **The correct answer is F.** The length of a side of a triangle is proportional to the measure of the angle opposite it. The angles of this triangle are 40°, 85°, and since the sum of the angles in a triangle is always 180°, the third angle measure is $180 - (40 + 85) = 55°$. Therefore, the shortest side of this triangle is opposite the smallest angle of 40°.

45. **The correct answer is B.** Since point Y is located at -11 and point Z is located at 5, the distance between them is 16. Think of the 16 units between the two points in four equal sections of 4 units each. A point that is three times as far from point Z as from point Y will be located at the end of the first section of 4 units to the right of Y. Since point Y is located at -11, this point is located at $-11 + 4$, or -7.

46. **The correct answer is G.** The problem describes a right triangle with legs 6 and 8. To find the length of the ramp, use the Pythagorean Theorem, as the ramp represents the hypotenuse of this right triangle:

$$6^2 + 8^2 = c^2$$
$$36 + 64 = c^2$$
$$100 = c^2, c = 10$$

The length of the ramp is 10 feet.

47. **The correct answer is B.** To solve this problem, first compute the two values, then take the sum. The product of 57 and 0.22 is $0.22(57) = 12.54$. Seven percent of 57 is $0.07(57) = 3.99$. The sum of 12.54 and 3.99 is $12.54 + 3.99 = 16.53$.

48. **The correct answer is G.** The tangent of an angle in a right triangle is the ratio of the side opposite to the side adjacent to that angle. The side opposite δ has length 6 and the side adjacent has length 4. Therefore $\tan \delta = \dfrac{6}{4}$.

49. **The correct answer is D.** A three-hour practice consists of 180 minutes ($3 \times 60 = 180$). Each minute of practice represents 2° on a circle graph, as there are 360 degrees in a circle. A 36-minute drill will occupy $2(36) = 72°$ on a circle (pie) graph.

50. **The correct answer is F.** To solve this problem, use substitution. You are given that $r^3 = 2s$ and $r^5 = 18s$. Since $r^5 = 18s$, then $r^5 = 9(2s)$. You are given that $r^3 = 2s$, so $r^5 = 9(r^3)$. Solve for r as follows:

$$r^5 = 9r^3$$
$$r^2 = 9$$
$$r = 3$$

51. **The correct answer is C.** To solve this problem, first find the radius of the sphere. Since the volume is $\dfrac{2,048\pi}{3}$ and the formula is $V = \dfrac{4}{3}\pi r^3$, set these quantities equal and solve for r:

$$\frac{2,048\pi}{3} = \frac{4}{3}\pi r^3$$
$$512 = r^3$$
$$r = 8$$

Now that you know the radius is 8, find the surface area as follows:

$$S = 4\pi r^2$$
$$S = 4\pi(8)^2$$
$$S = 4\pi(64)$$
$$S = 256\pi$$

52. **The correct answer is J.** The first step in solving this problem is to find the unknown angle. Since the sum of the angles in a triangle must be 180°, the unknown angle is $180 - (39 + 54) = 87°$. The *law of sines* states that the ratio of the sine of an angle to the length of the side opposite an angle is the same for all interior angles in the same triangle. Set the unknown side equal to x, and solve:

$$\frac{22}{\sin 87°} = \frac{x}{\sin 39°}$$
$$\frac{22 \sin 39°}{\sin 87°} = x$$

53. **The correct answer is C.** Given that $P(t) = p_o\left(1 + \dfrac{r}{100}\right)^t$, substitute the values $p_o = 557,000$, $r = 2$, and $t = 5$ to get $P(t) = 557,000\left(1 + \dfrac{2}{100}\right)^5$. Next simplify the expression to get $P(t) = 557,000(1 + .02)^5 = 557,000(1.02)^5$.

54. **The correct answer is F.** To solve, first find the slope of line k_1 which has an equation of $2x + 6y = 11$. To do so, convert it to slope-intercept form ($y = mx + b$, where m is the slope and b is the y-intercept).

$$2x + 6y = 11$$
$$6y = -2x + 11$$
$$y = -\frac{2}{6}x + \frac{11}{6}$$

The slope is $-\dfrac{2}{6}$, which reduces to $-\dfrac{1}{3}$.

Since k_2 is perpendicular to k_1, the slopes are negative reciprocals, and the slope of line k_2 is 3.

55. **The correct answer is A.** Parabolas have a line of symmetry that runs through the vertex. Since the point $(0, -5)$ has an x-coordinate that is 4 units to the right of the vertex, there will be a corresponding point with the same y-coordinate four units to the left of the vertex. Since the vertex is $(-4, 2)$, a point 4 units to the left will have an x-coordinate of $-4 - 4 = -8$. Therefore the point is $(-8, -5)$.

56. **The correct answer is H.** To solve this problem, break up $|2y+3| \leq 11$ into two inequalities (because of the absolute value) and solve for y, as shown below:

First inequality	Second inequality
$2y + 3 \leq 11$	$2y + 3 \geq -11$
$2y \leq 8$	$2y \geq -14$
$y \leq 4$	$y \geq -7$

Now look for the graph that shows the intersection of these two inequalities ($4 \geq y \geq -7$). Because the inequalities are inclusive ("less than or equal to" and "greater than or equal to"), the correct graph will have closed circles. Only answer choice H satisfies these conditions.

57. **The correct answer is C.** To solve this problem, substitute -1 for x in the appropriate equation. Since $-1 < 0$, use $G(x) = x^3 + 3x^2 + 3x + 1$ as follows:

$$G(-1) = (-1)^3 + 3(-1)^2 + 3(-1) + 1$$
$$G(-1) = -1 + 3 - 3 + 1 = 0$$

58. **The correct answer is G.** To solve this problem, select a number as a "stand in." A good number to select is 100 since you are using percents. Increasing 100 by 40% yields 140. To decrease 140 by 25%, multiply 140 by 0.75 (which is 100% minus 25%), which gives you 105. Therefore, the resulting number is 105% of the original number.

59. **The correct answer is E.** Given that a is positive and b is negative, the difference $(b - a)$ is negative. Try some numbers: $a = 1$ and $b = -1$; $-1 - 1 = -2$. Since a is positive and nonzero, $b - a$ must be less than b; therefore $b - a < b$ is the correct answer.

60. **The correct answer is J.** This problem might be simplified by using a number as a "stand-in." Use 10 as the original length of the side of the square because it is an easy number to work with. The original area of the square is $10^2 = 100$. If the length of one side is reduced by 40%, leaving 60% of the length intact, the new length is 6, creating a rectangle with a length of 6, a width of 10, and an area of 60. The area of the original square was 100, which means that you must increase the area of the newly created rectangle by $100 - 60$, or 40. Set up a proportion as follows, where x is the percent of increase:

40 is to 60 as x is to 100

$$\frac{40}{60} = \frac{x}{100}$$

Cross-multiply and solve for x:

$$60x = 4,000$$
$$x = 66.6$$

The adjacent side will need to be increased by about 67%.

CHAPTER 9

PRACTICE TEST 4 WITH EXPLANATIONS

ANSWER SHEET

ACT MATHEMATICS TEST 4
Answer Sheet

MATHEMATICS

1 Ⓐ Ⓑ Ⓒ Ⓓ Ⓔ	16 Ⓕ Ⓖ Ⓗ Ⓙ Ⓚ	31 Ⓐ Ⓑ Ⓒ Ⓓ Ⓔ	46 Ⓕ Ⓖ Ⓗ Ⓙ Ⓚ
2 Ⓕ Ⓖ Ⓗ Ⓙ Ⓚ	17 Ⓐ Ⓑ Ⓒ Ⓓ Ⓔ	32 Ⓕ Ⓖ Ⓗ Ⓙ Ⓚ	47 Ⓐ Ⓑ Ⓒ Ⓓ Ⓔ
3 Ⓐ Ⓑ Ⓒ Ⓓ Ⓔ	18 Ⓕ Ⓖ Ⓗ Ⓙ Ⓚ	33 Ⓐ Ⓑ Ⓒ Ⓓ Ⓔ	48 Ⓕ Ⓖ Ⓗ Ⓙ Ⓚ
4 Ⓕ Ⓖ Ⓗ Ⓙ Ⓚ	19 Ⓐ Ⓑ Ⓒ Ⓓ Ⓔ	34 Ⓕ Ⓖ Ⓗ Ⓙ Ⓚ	49 Ⓐ Ⓑ Ⓒ Ⓓ Ⓔ
5 Ⓐ Ⓑ Ⓒ Ⓓ Ⓔ	20 Ⓕ Ⓖ Ⓗ Ⓙ Ⓚ	35 Ⓐ Ⓑ Ⓒ Ⓓ Ⓔ	50 Ⓕ Ⓖ Ⓗ Ⓙ Ⓚ
6 Ⓕ Ⓖ Ⓗ Ⓙ Ⓚ	21 Ⓐ Ⓑ Ⓒ Ⓓ Ⓔ	36 Ⓕ Ⓖ Ⓗ Ⓙ Ⓚ	51 Ⓐ Ⓑ Ⓒ Ⓓ Ⓔ
7 Ⓐ Ⓑ Ⓒ Ⓓ Ⓔ	22 Ⓕ Ⓖ Ⓗ Ⓙ Ⓚ	37 Ⓐ Ⓑ Ⓒ Ⓓ Ⓔ	52 Ⓕ Ⓖ Ⓗ Ⓙ Ⓚ
8 Ⓕ Ⓖ Ⓗ Ⓙ Ⓚ	23 Ⓐ Ⓑ Ⓒ Ⓓ Ⓔ	38 Ⓕ Ⓖ Ⓗ Ⓙ Ⓚ	53 Ⓐ Ⓑ Ⓒ Ⓓ Ⓔ
9 Ⓐ Ⓑ Ⓒ Ⓓ Ⓔ	24 Ⓕ Ⓖ Ⓗ Ⓙ Ⓚ	39 Ⓐ Ⓑ Ⓒ Ⓓ Ⓔ	54 Ⓕ Ⓖ Ⓗ Ⓙ Ⓚ
10 Ⓕ Ⓖ Ⓗ Ⓙ Ⓚ	25 Ⓐ Ⓑ Ⓒ Ⓓ Ⓔ	40 Ⓕ Ⓖ Ⓗ Ⓙ Ⓚ	55 Ⓐ Ⓑ Ⓒ Ⓓ Ⓔ
11 Ⓐ Ⓑ Ⓒ Ⓓ Ⓔ	26 Ⓕ Ⓖ Ⓗ Ⓙ Ⓚ	41 Ⓐ Ⓑ Ⓒ Ⓓ Ⓔ	56 Ⓕ Ⓖ Ⓗ Ⓙ Ⓚ
12 Ⓕ Ⓖ Ⓗ Ⓙ Ⓚ	27 Ⓐ Ⓑ Ⓒ Ⓓ Ⓔ	42 Ⓕ Ⓖ Ⓗ Ⓙ Ⓚ	57 Ⓐ Ⓑ Ⓒ Ⓓ Ⓔ
13 Ⓐ Ⓑ Ⓒ Ⓓ Ⓔ	28 Ⓕ Ⓖ Ⓗ Ⓙ Ⓚ	43 Ⓐ Ⓑ Ⓒ Ⓓ Ⓔ	58 Ⓕ Ⓖ Ⓗ Ⓙ Ⓚ
14 Ⓕ Ⓖ Ⓗ Ⓙ Ⓚ	29 Ⓐ Ⓑ Ⓒ Ⓓ Ⓔ	44 Ⓕ Ⓖ Ⓗ Ⓙ Ⓚ	59 Ⓐ Ⓑ Ⓒ Ⓓ Ⓔ
15 Ⓐ Ⓑ Ⓒ Ⓓ Ⓔ	30 Ⓕ Ⓖ Ⓗ Ⓙ Ⓚ	45 Ⓐ Ⓑ Ⓒ Ⓓ Ⓔ	60 Ⓕ Ⓖ Ⓗ Ⓙ Ⓚ

△ △ △ △ △ △ △ △ △ △

MATHEMATICS TEST

60 Minutes—60 Questions

DIRECTIONS: Solve each of the problems in the time allowed, then fill in the corresponding bubble on your answer sheet (page 193). Do not spend too much time on any one problem; skip the more difficult problems and go back to them later. You may use a calculator on this test. For this test you should assume that figures are NOT necessarily drawn to scale, that all geometric figures lie in a plane, and that the word *line* is used to indicate a straight line.

DO YOUR FIGURING HERE.

1. Katie plans to purchase a motorcycle that costs $4,600. In addition, she has to pay $450 for insurance and $320 for taxes. If Katie has $3,200 saved, what amount must she borrow to be able to buy the motorcycle and pay the expenses?
   A. $630
   B. $1,400
   C. $1,850
   D. $2,170
   E. $7,800

2. What is the greatest common factor of the monomials $18x^2$, $27x^4$, and $30x^3$?
   F. $3x^2$
   G. $3x^4$
   H. $9x^2$
   J. $18x^2$
   K. $30x^3$

3. $6a^7 \times 9a^3$ is equivalent to:
   A. $54a^{21}$
   B. $54a^{10}$
   C. $54a^4$
   D. $15a^{21}$
   E. $15a^{10}$

4. In parallelogram *WXYZ* shown below, $\overline{WY}$ is perpendicular to $\overline{YZ}$ and the measure of angle *WZY* is 72°. What is the measure of angle *XYW* ?

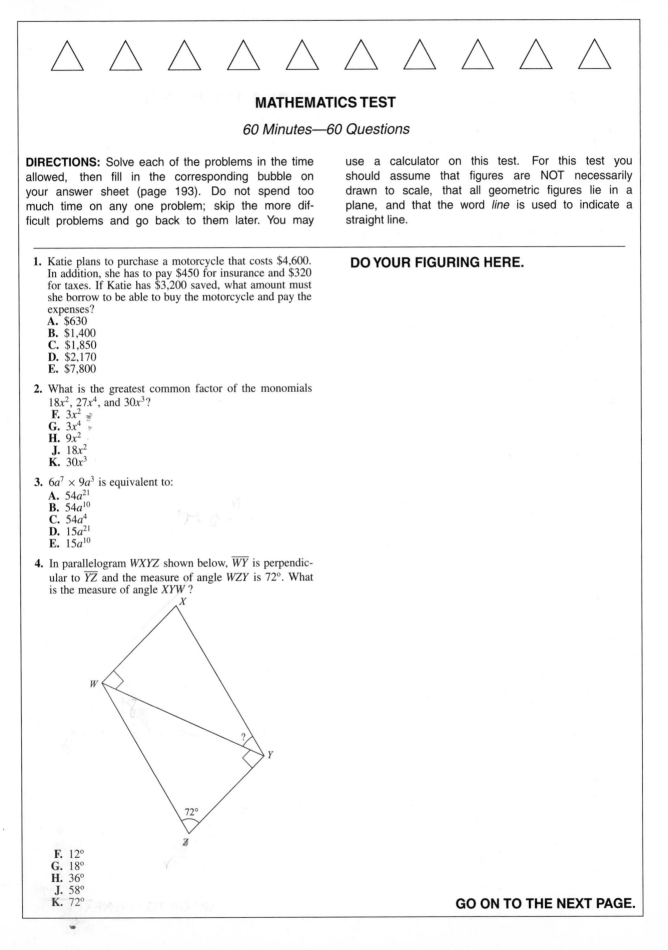

   F. 12°
   G. 18°
   H. 36°
   J. 58°
   K. 72°

GO ON TO THE NEXT PAGE.

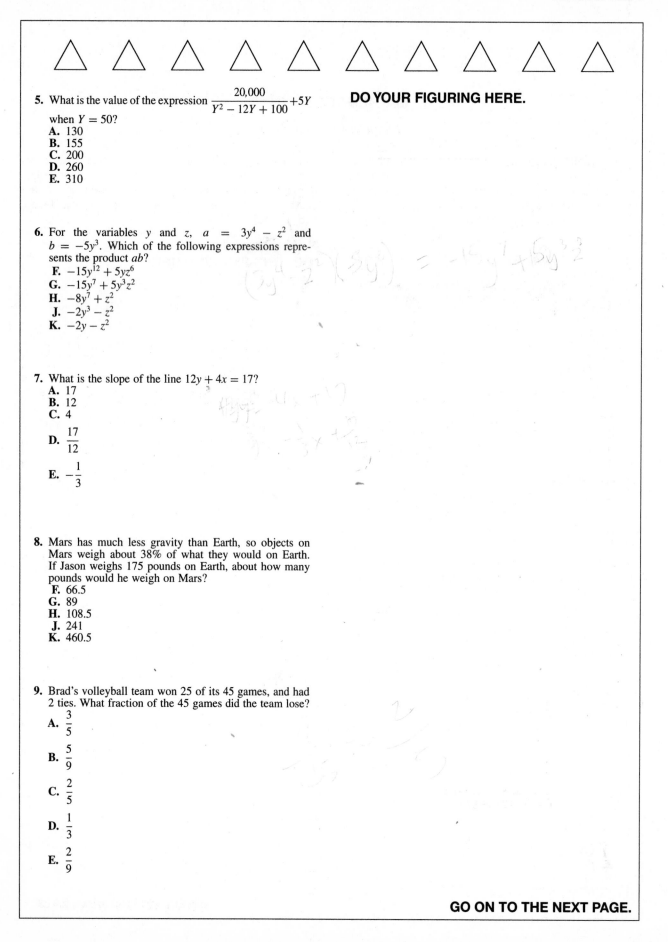

5. What is the value of the expression $\dfrac{20{,}000}{Y^2 - 12Y + 100} + 5Y$ when $Y = 50$?

DO YOUR FIGURING HERE.

 A. 130
 B. 155
 C. 200
 D. 260
 E. 310

6. For the variables y and z, $a = 3y^4 - z^2$ and $b = -5y^3$. Which of the following expressions represents the product ab?

 F. $-15y^{12} + 5yz^6$
 G. $-15y^7 + 5y^3z^2$
 H. $-8y^7 + z^2$
 J. $-2y^3 - z^2$
 K. $-2y - z^2$

7. What is the slope of the line $12y + 4x = 17$?

 A. 17
 B. 12
 C. 4
 D. $\dfrac{17}{12}$
 E. $-\dfrac{1}{3}$

8. Mars has much less gravity than Earth, so objects on Mars weigh about 38% of what they would on Earth. If Jason weighs 175 pounds on Earth, about how many pounds would he weigh on Mars?

 F. 66.5
 G. 89
 H. 108.5
 J. 241
 K. 460.5

9. Brad's volleyball team won 25 of its 45 games, and had 2 ties. What fraction of the 45 games did the team lose?

 A. $\dfrac{3}{5}$
 B. $\dfrac{5}{9}$
 C. $\dfrac{2}{5}$
 D. $\dfrac{1}{3}$
 E. $\dfrac{2}{9}$

GO ON TO THE NEXT PAGE.

10. In the figure below, $\overline{ML}$ is perpendicular to $\overline{LK}$, and points L, K, and J are collinear. If the measure of angle LMK is 62°, what is the measure of angle MKJ?

DO YOUR FIGURING HERE.

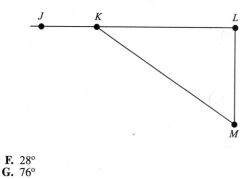

    F. 28°
    G. 76°
    H. 118°
    J. 134°
    K. 152°

11. In trapezoid $WXYZ$ below, angle XWZ and angle WZY are both right angles. If $\overline{WX}$ is 13 inches long, $\overline{XY}$ 10 inches long, and $\overline{WZ}$ 8 inches long, how many inches long is $\overline{ZY}$?

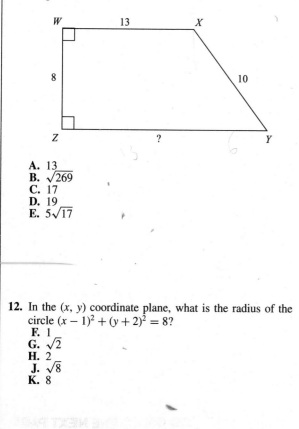

    A. 13
    B. $\sqrt{269}$
    C. 17
    D. 19
    E. $5\sqrt{17}$

12. In the (x, y) coordinate plane, what is the radius of the circle $(x - 1)^2 + (y + 2)^2 = 8$?
    F. 1
    G. $\sqrt{2}$
    H. 2
    J. $\sqrt{8}$
    K. 8

GO ON TO THE NEXT PAGE.

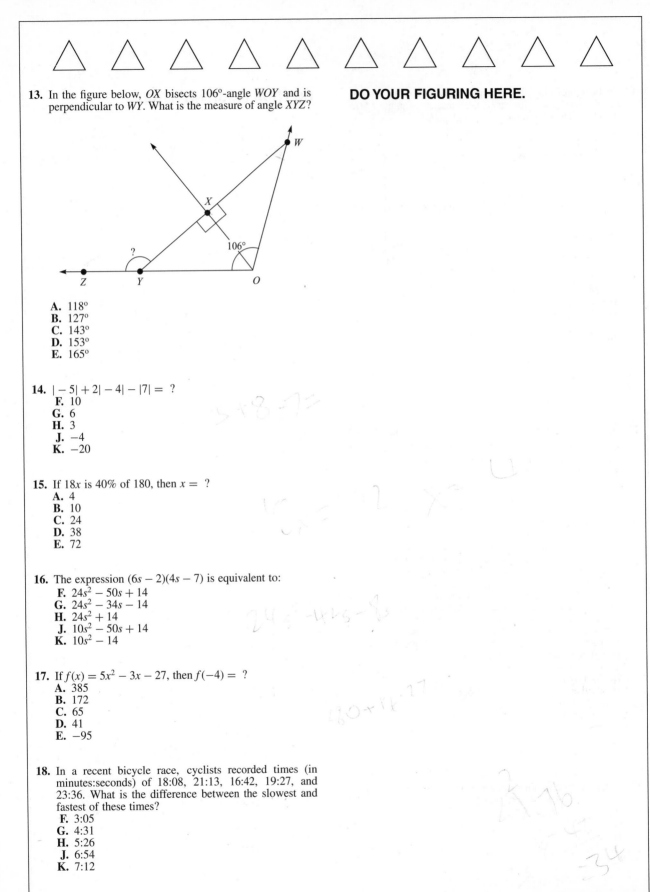

13. In the figure below, *OX* bisects 106°-angle *WOY* and is perpendicular to *WY*. What is the measure of angle *XYZ*?

DO YOUR FIGURING HERE.

- **A.** 118°
- **B.** 127°
- **C.** 143°
- **D.** 153°
- **E.** 165°

14. $|-5| + 2| - 4| - |7| = ?$
- **F.** 10
- **G.** 6
- **H.** 3
- **J.** −4
- **K.** −20

15. If $18x$ is 40% of 180, then $x = ?$
- **A.** 4
- **B.** 10
- **C.** 24
- **D.** 38
- **E.** 72

16. The expression $(6s - 2)(4s - 7)$ is equivalent to:
- **F.** $24s^2 - 50s + 14$
- **G.** $24s^2 - 34s - 14$
- **H.** $24s^2 + 14$
- **J.** $10s^2 - 50s + 14$
- **K.** $10s^2 - 14$

17. If $f(x) = 5x^2 - 3x - 27$, then $f(-4) = ?$
- **A.** 385
- **B.** 172
- **C.** 65
- **D.** 41
- **E.** −95

18. In a recent bicycle race, cyclists recorded times (in minutes:seconds) of 18:08, 21:13, 16:42, 19:27, and 23:36. What is the difference between the slowest and fastest of these times?
- **F.** 3:05
- **G.** 4:31
- **H.** 5:26
- **J.** 6:54
- **K.** 7:12

GO ON TO THE NEXT PAGE.

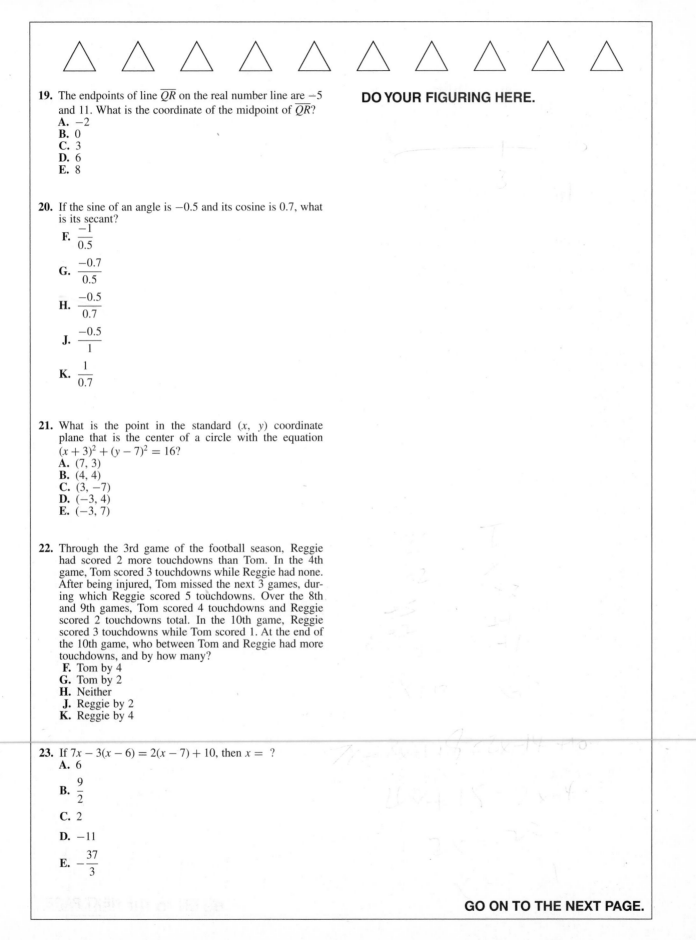

19. The endpoints of line $\overline{QR}$ on the real number line are -5 and 11. What is the coordinate of the midpoint of $\overline{QR}$?
   A. -2
   B. 0
   C. 3
   D. 6
   E. 8

DO YOUR FIGURING HERE.

20. If the sine of an angle is -0.5 and its cosine is 0.7, what is its secant?
   F. $\dfrac{-1}{0.5}$

   G. $\dfrac{-0.7}{0.5}$

   H. $\dfrac{-0.5}{0.7}$

   J. $\dfrac{-0.5}{1}$

   K. $\dfrac{1}{0.7}$

21. What is the point in the standard (x, y) coordinate plane that is the center of a circle with the equation $(x + 3)^2 + (y - 7)^2 = 16$?
   A. $(7, 3)$
   B. $(4, 4)$
   C. $(3, -7)$
   D. $(-3, 4)$
   E. $(-3, 7)$

22. Through the 3rd game of the football season, Reggie had scored 2 more touchdowns than Tom. In the 4th game, Tom scored 3 touchdowns while Reggie had none. After being injured, Tom missed the next 3 games, during which Reggie scored 5 touchdowns. Over the 8th and 9th games, Tom scored 4 touchdowns and Reggie scored 2 touchdowns total. In the 10th game, Reggie scored 3 touchdowns while Tom scored 1. At the end of the 10th game, who between Tom and Reggie had more touchdowns, and by how many?
   F. Tom by 4
   G. Tom by 2
   H. Neither
   J. Reggie by 2
   K. Reggie by 4

23. If $7x - 3(x - 6) = 2(x - 7) + 10$, then $x = $?
   A. 6

   B. $\dfrac{9}{2}$

   C. 2

   D. -11

   E. $-\dfrac{37}{3}$

GO ON TO THE NEXT PAGE.

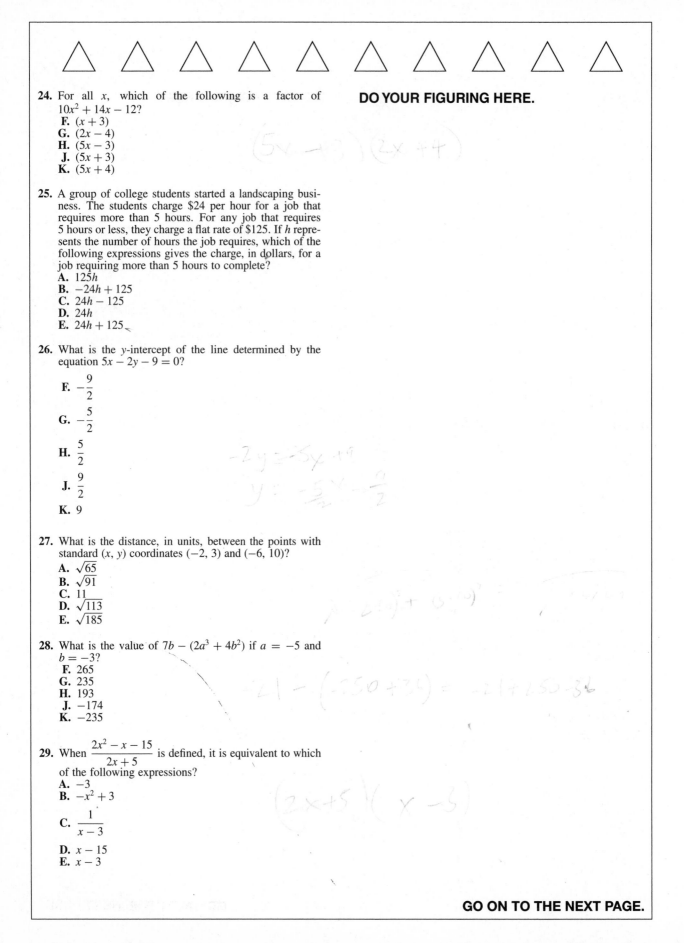

24. For all x, which of the following is a factor of $10x^2 + 14x - 12$?
  F. $(x + 3)$
  G. $(2x - 4)$
  H. $(5x - 3)$
  J. $(5x + 3)$
  K. $(5x + 4)$

DO YOUR FIGURING HERE.

25. A group of college students started a landscaping business. The students charge $24 per hour for a job that requires more than 5 hours. For any job that requires 5 hours or less, they charge a flat rate of $125. If h represents the number of hours the job requires, which of the following expressions gives the charge, in dollars, for a job requiring more than 5 hours to complete?
  A. $125h$
  B. $-24h + 125$
  C. $24h - 125$
  D. $24h$
  E. $24h + 125$

26. What is the y-intercept of the line determined by the equation $5x - 2y - 9 = 0$?

  F. $-\dfrac{9}{2}$

  G. $-\dfrac{5}{2}$

  H. $\dfrac{5}{2}$

  J. $\dfrac{9}{2}$

  K. 9

27. What is the distance, in units, between the points with standard (x, y) coordinates $(-2, 3)$ and $(-6, 10)$?
  A. $\sqrt{65}$
  B. $\sqrt{91}$
  C. 11
  D. $\sqrt{113}$
  E. $\sqrt{185}$

28. What is the value of $7b - (2a^3 + 4b^2)$ if $a = -5$ and $b = -3$?
  F. 265
  G. 235
  H. 193
  J. -174
  K. -235

29. When $\dfrac{2x^2 - x - 15}{2x + 5}$ is defined, it is equivalent to which of the following expressions?
  A. -3
  B. $-x^2 + 3$

  C. $\dfrac{1}{x - 3}$

  D. $x - 15$
  E. $x - 3$

GO ON TO THE NEXT PAGE.

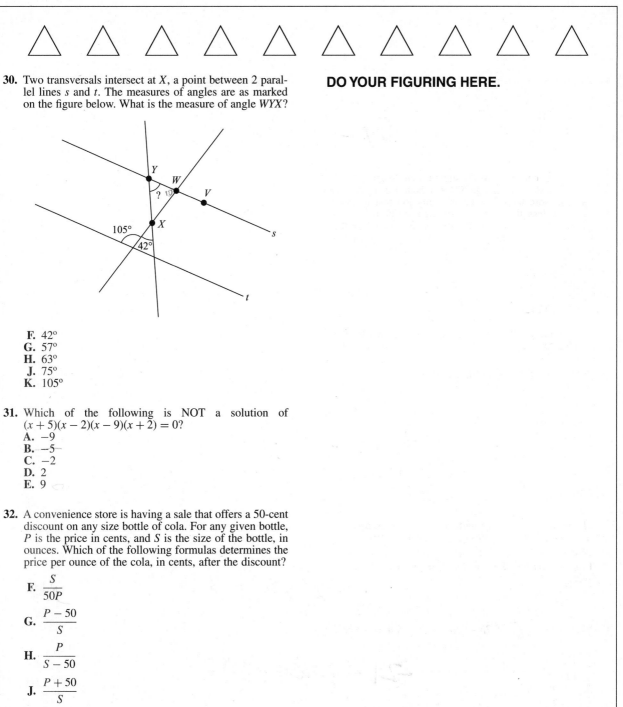

30. Two transversals intersect at X, a point between 2 parallel lines s and t. The measures of angles are as marked on the figure below. What is the measure of angle WYX?

DO YOUR FIGURING HERE.

F. 42°
G. 57°
H. 63°
J. 75°
K. 105°

31. Which of the following is NOT a solution of $(x + 5)(x - 2)(x - 9)(x + 2) = 0$?
A. −9
B. −5
C. −2
D. 2
E. 9

32. A convenience store is having a sale that offers a 50-cent discount on any size bottle of cola. For any given bottle, P is the price in cents, and S is the size of the bottle, in ounces. Which of the following formulas determines the price per ounce of the cola, in cents, after the discount?

F. $\dfrac{S}{50P}$

G. $\dfrac{P - 50}{S}$

H. $\dfrac{P}{S - 50}$

J. $\dfrac{P + 50}{S}$

K. $\dfrac{50P}{S}$

33. Aaron drove to visit a friend. He drove 410 miles in 6 hours and 15 minutes. What was his average speed, to the nearest tenth of a mile per hour?
A. 62.4
B. 63.2
C. 65.6
D. 66.7
E. 68.3

GO ON TO THE NEXT PAGE.

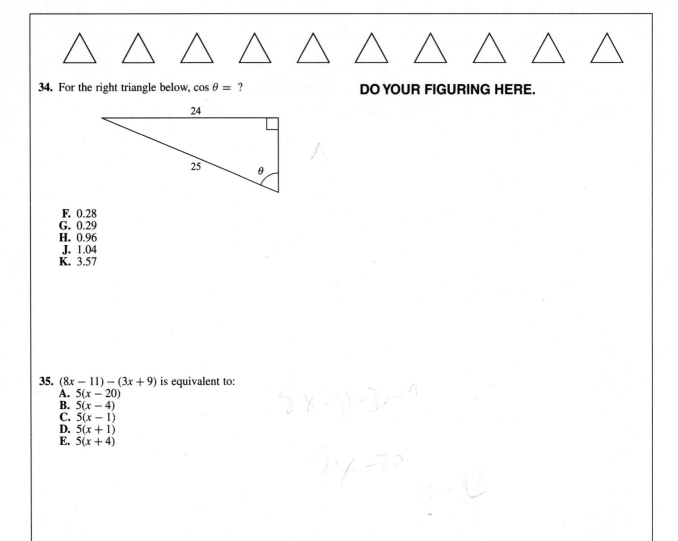

34. For the right triangle below, $\cos \theta = $?

DO YOUR FIGURING HERE.

    F. 0.28
    G. 0.29
    H. 0.96
    J. 1.04
    K. 3.57

35. $(8x - 11) - (3x + 9)$ is equivalent to:
    A. $5(x - 20)$
    B. $5(x - 4)$
    C. $5(x - 1)$
    D. $5(x + 1)$
    E. $5(x + 4)$

36. Molly is planning her birthday party at a local skating rink. For renting the rink, she was given the following prices:

Number of guests	Price
10	$130
15	$180
20	$230
25	$280
30	$330

Which of the following equations, where G represents the number of guests and P represents the price in dollars, best fits the information in the price list?
    F. $P = 50G + 100$
    G. $P = 50G$
    H. $P = 10G + 30$
    J. $P = 5G + 80$
    K. $P = G + 120$

GO ON TO THE NEXT PAGE.

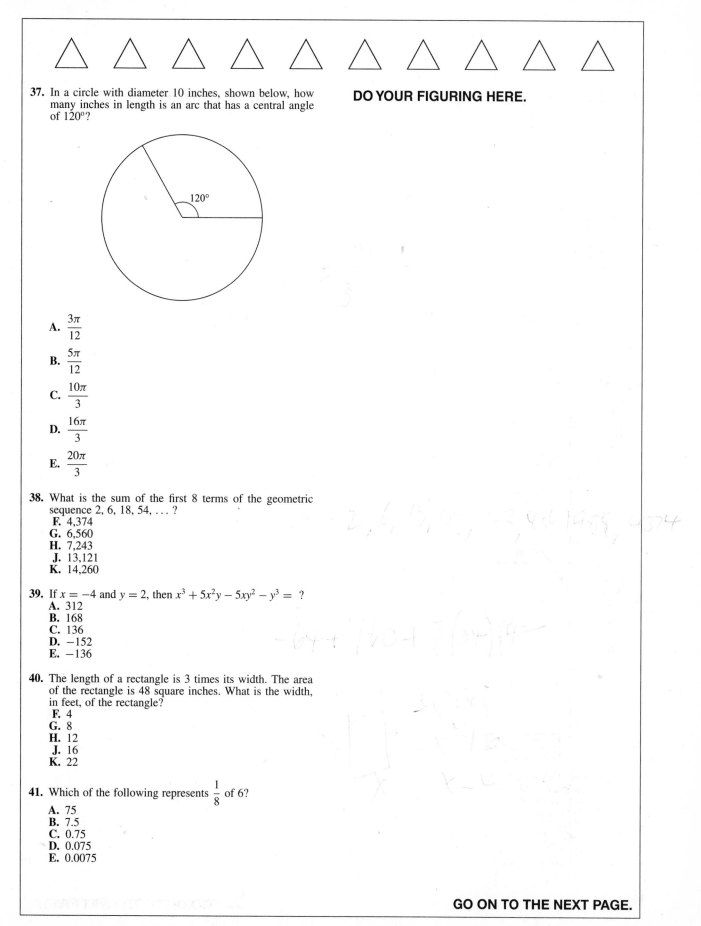

37. In a circle with diameter 10 inches, shown below, how many inches in length is an arc that has a central angle of 120°?

120°

DO YOUR FIGURING HERE.

A. $\dfrac{3\pi}{12}$

B. $\dfrac{5\pi}{12}$

C. $\dfrac{10\pi}{3}$

D. $\dfrac{16\pi}{3}$

E. $\dfrac{20\pi}{3}$

38. What is the sum of the first 8 terms of the geometric sequence 2, 6, 18, 54, … ?
 F. 4,374
 G. 6,560
 H. 7,243
 J. 13,121
 K. 14,260

39. If $x = -4$ and $y = 2$, then $x^3 + 5x^2y - 5xy^2 - y^3 = $?
 A. 312
 B. 168
 C. 136
 D. −152
 E. −136

40. The length of a rectangle is 3 times its width. The area of the rectangle is 48 square inches. What is the width, in feet, of the rectangle?
 F. 4
 G. 8
 H. 12
 J. 16
 K. 22

41. Which of the following represents $\dfrac{1}{8}$ of 6?

 A. 75
 B. 7.5
 C. 0.75
 D. 0.075
 E. 0.0075

GO ON TO THE NEXT PAGE.

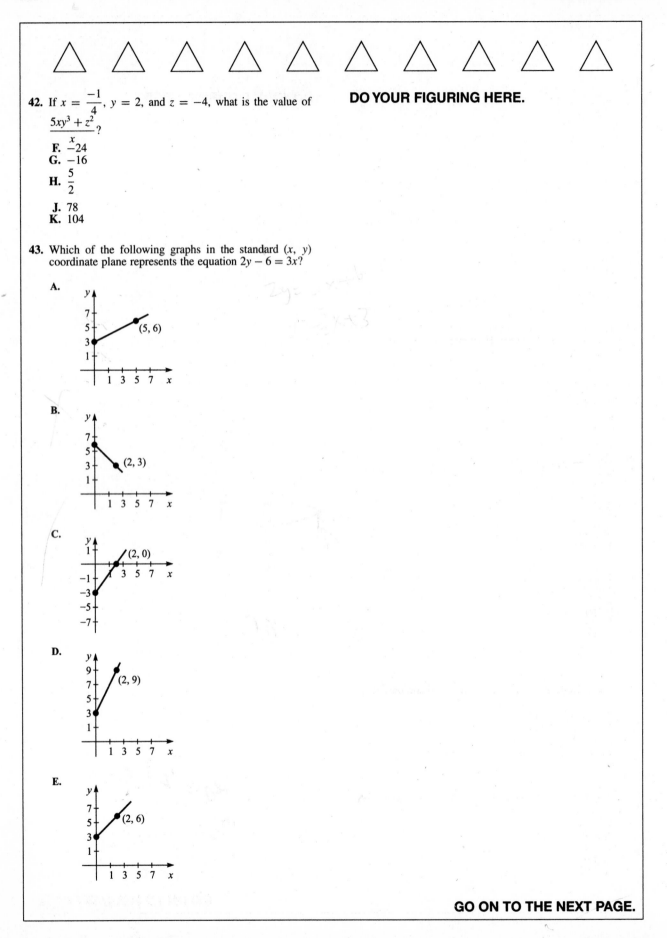

42. If $x = \dfrac{-1}{4}$, $y = 2$, and $z = -4$, what is the value of $\dfrac{5xy^3 + z^2}{x}$?

DO YOUR FIGURING HERE.

   F. -24
   G. -16
   H. $\dfrac{5}{2}$
   J. 78
   K. 104

43. Which of the following graphs in the standard (x, y) coordinate plane represents the equation $2y - 6 = 3x$?

   A.

   B.

   C.

   D.

   E.

GO ON TO THE NEXT PAGE.

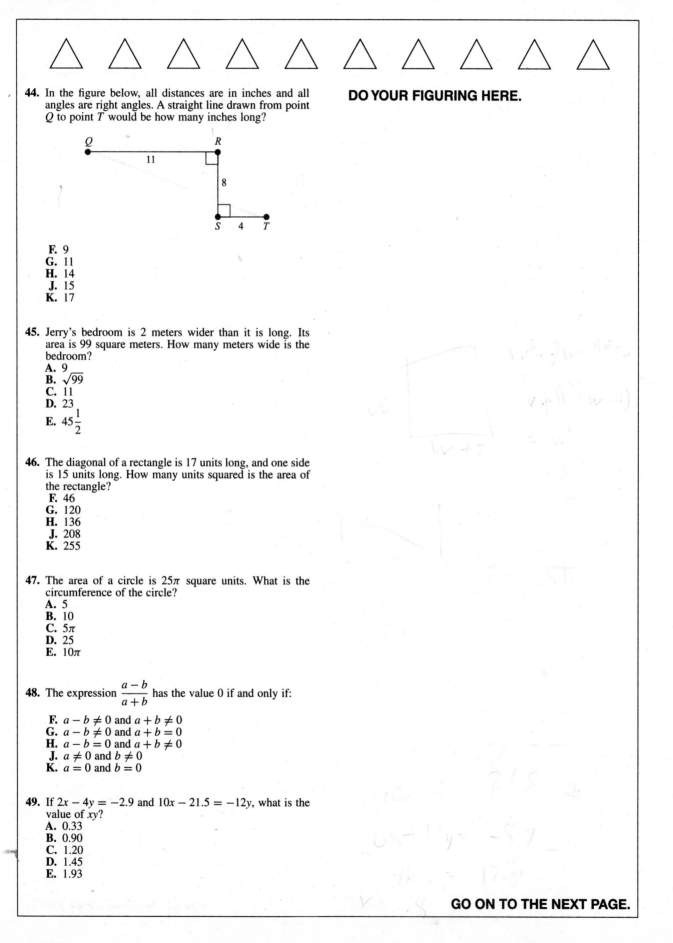

44. In the figure below, all distances are in inches and all angles are right angles. A straight line drawn from point Q to point T would be how many inches long?

DO YOUR FIGURING HERE.

F. 9
G. 11
H. 14
J. 15
K. 17

45. Jerry's bedroom is 2 meters wider than it is long. Its area is 99 square meters. How many meters wide is the bedroom?
A. 9
B. $\sqrt{99}$
C. 11
D. 23
E. $45\frac{1}{2}$

46. The diagonal of a rectangle is 17 units long, and one side is 15 units long. How many units squared is the area of the rectangle?
F. 46
G. 120
H. 136
J. 208
K. 255

47. The area of a circle is 25π square units. What is the circumference of the circle?
A. 5
B. 10
C. 5π
D. 25
E. 10π

48. The expression $\dfrac{a-b}{a+b}$ has the value 0 if and only if:

F. $a - b \neq 0$ and $a + b \neq 0$
G. $a - b \neq 0$ and $a + b = 0$
H. $a - b = 0$ and $a + b \neq 0$
J. $a \neq 0$ and $b \neq 0$
K. $a = 0$ and $b = 0$

49. If $2x - 4y = -2.9$ and $10x - 21.5 = -12y$, what is the value of xy?
A. 0.33
B. 0.90
C. 1.20
D. 1.45
E. 1.93

GO ON TO THE NEXT PAGE.

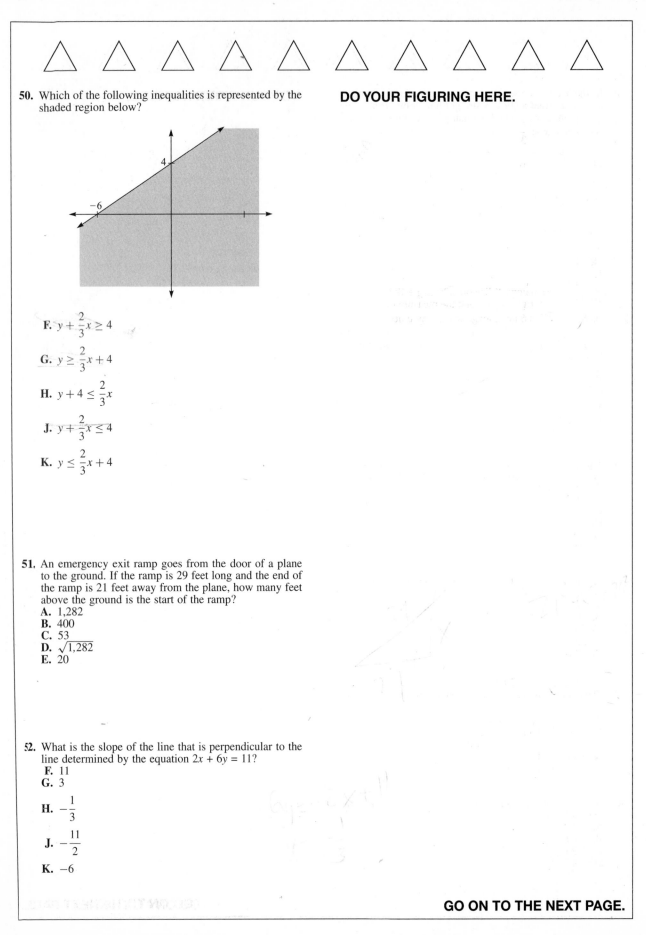

50. Which of the following inequalities is represented by the shaded region below?

DO YOUR FIGURING HERE.

F. $y + \dfrac{2}{3}x \geq 4$

G. $y \geq \dfrac{2}{3}x + 4$

H. $y + 4 \leq \dfrac{2}{3}x$

J. $y + \dfrac{2}{3}x \leq 4$

K. $y \leq \dfrac{2}{3}x + 4$

51. An emergency exit ramp goes from the door of a plane to the ground. If the ramp is 29 feet long and the end of the ramp is 21 feet away from the plane, how many feet above the ground is the start of the ramp?
A. 1,282
B. 400
C. 53
D. $\sqrt{1,282}$
E. 20

52. What is the slope of the line that is perpendicular to the line determined by the equation $2x + 6y = 11$?
F. 11
G. 3
H. $-\dfrac{1}{3}$
J. $-\dfrac{11}{2}$
K. -6

53. Which of the following expresses all and only the values of x that satisfy $|3x - 5| > 13$?

A. $-6 < x < \dfrac{8}{3}$

B. $-\dfrac{8}{3} < x < 6$

C. $x < -6$ or $x > \dfrac{8}{3}$

D. $x < -\dfrac{8}{3}$ or $x > 6$

E. $x < \dfrac{8}{3}$ or $x > -6$

54. In the figure below, X lies on $\overline{WY}$, angle WZY and angle ZXY are both right angles, and the measure of angle ZWX is 60°. If $\overline{ZY}$ is 6 units long, how many units long is $\overline{XY}$?

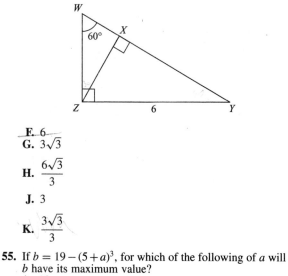

F. 6

G. $3\sqrt{3}$

H. $\dfrac{6\sqrt{3}}{3}$

J. 3

K. $\dfrac{3\sqrt{3}}{3}$

55. If $b = 19 - (5 + a)^3$, for which of the following of a will b have its maximum value?
A. 19
B. 5
C. 1
D. -5
E. -19

56. Chuck drinks 9 bottles of water in 2 days. At this rate, how many bottles of water will Chuck drink in $2 + d$ days?

F. $9 + \dfrac{9d}{2}$

G. $2 + \dfrac{d}{2}$

H. $\dfrac{9}{2} + \dfrac{9}{2d}$

J. $\dfrac{9}{2} + \dfrac{d}{2}$

K. $\dfrac{9}{2} + d$

DO YOUR FIGURING HERE.

GO ON TO THE NEXT PAGE.

9 △ △ △ △ △ △ △ △ 9

57. In the (x, y) coordinate plane, a line passes through the point $(-4, 6)$ and has a slope of $-\dfrac{1}{3}$. What is the x-coordinate of a point on the line having a y-coordinate of 3?
  A. -13
  B. -8
  C. 3
  D. 5
  E. 9

58. A rectangle has a perimeter of 36 units, and its length is twice its width. A right triangle has sides with lengths of 5, 12, and 13 units. What is the difference in the areas of these figures, in square units?
  F. 7
  G. 26
  H. 42
  J. 50
  K. 84

59. How many zeros are there in the integer representation of the product of 3 thousand and 7 billion?
  A. 11
  B. 12
  C. 13
  D. 14
  E. 15

60. If $\cos x = -\dfrac{\sqrt{2}}{2}$ and $\dfrac{\pi}{2} < x < \pi$, what is the value of $\tan x$?
  F. $-\sqrt{2}$
  G. -1
  H. $1\sqrt{2}$
  J. 1
  K. $\sqrt{3}$

DO YOUR FIGURING HERE.

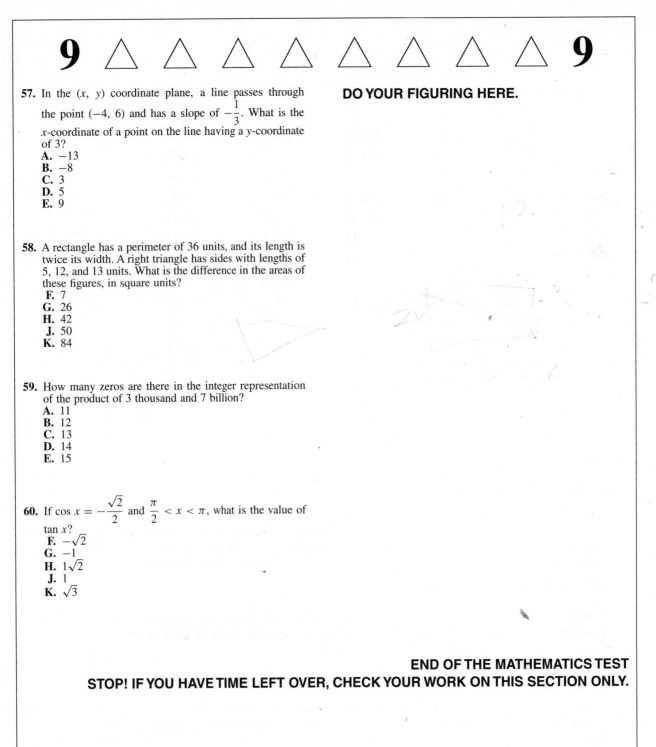

END OF THE MATHEMATICS TEST
STOP! IF YOU HAVE TIME LEFT OVER, CHECK YOUR WORK ON THIS SECTION ONLY.

ANSWER KEY

Mathematics Test

1. D	16. F	31. A	46. G
2. F	17. C	32. G	47. E
3. B	18. J	33. C	48. H
4. G	19. C	34. F	49. B
5. D	20. K	35. B	50. K
6. G	21. E	36. H	51. E
7. E	22. K	37. C	52. G
8. F	23. D	38. G	53. D
9. C	24. H	39. B	54. G
10. K	25. D	40. F	55. E
11. D	26. F	41. C	56. F
12. J	27. A	42. F	57. D
13. C	28. H	43. E	58. H
14. G	29. E	44. K	59. B
15. A	30. H	45. C	60. G

SCORING WORKSHEET

On each ACT multiple-choice test (English, Mathematics, Reading, and Science Reasoning) you will receive a SCALED SCORE on a scale of 1 to 36. Use the following guidelines to determine your approximate SCALED SCORE on the ACT Mathematics Diagnostic Test that you just completed.

Step 1   Determine your RAW SCORE.

Your RAW SCORE is the number of questions that you answered correctly. Because there are 60 questions on the ACT Mathematics Test, the highest possible RAW SCORE is 60.

Step 2   Determine your SCALED SCORE using the following Scoring Worksheet.

Mathematics   _____ × **36** = _____ ÷ **60** = _____

              RAW SCORE   **+ 1**   (*correction factor)

                                                                        _____

                                                                        SCALED SCORE

*The correction factor is an approximation based on the average from several recent ACT tests. It is most valid for scores in the middle 50% (approximately 16–24 scaled composite score) of the scoring range. The scores are all approximate. Actual ACT scoring scales vary from one administration to the next based upon several factors.

ANSWERS AND EXPLANATIONS

1. **The correct answer is D.** To solve this problem, first calculate the total amount that Katie will have to pay for the motorcycle:

   $4,600 (cost)
   +$450 (insurance)
   +$320 (taxes)
   = $5,370 (total)

   Eliminate answer choice E, because she won't have to borrow more than the total cost.

   If she has $3,200 saved, then the amount that she must borrow in order to buy the motorcycle and pay the expenses is $5,370 − $3,200, or $2,170.

2. **The correct answer is F.** The greatest common factor, or GCF, is the greatest factor that divides two or more numbers. Looking at the numbers alone (18, 27, and 30), the greatest number that divides all three of them is 3. Eliminate answer choices H, J, and K. In terms of the variables (x^2, x^4, and x^3), the greatest number that divides all three is x^2. Therefore, the greatest common factor of these monomials is $3x^2$.

3. **The correct answer is B.** To solve this problem, you need to multiply like terms. Remember, when multiplying any two powers of the same base, simply add the powers together:

   $6a^7 \times 9a^3$
   $= (6 \times 9)(a^7 \times a^3)$
   $= 54a^{10}$

   If you started by simply multiplying 6×9, you could have quickly eliminated answer choices D and E.

4. **The correct answer is G.** Within parallelogram $WXYZ$, there are two equal triangles (WYZ and YWX). The measure of angle YZW is 72°; this is also the measure of angle WXY. The three angles of a triangle must add up to 180°, so the measure of angle XYW must equal 180° − 90° − 72°, or 18°.

5. **The correct answer is D.** To solve this problem, substitute 50 for all instances of Y in the equation and solve:

   $$\frac{20,000}{Y^2 - 12Y + 100} + 5Y$$

   $$= \frac{20,000}{(50)^2 - 12(50) + 100} + 5(50)$$

   $$= \frac{20,000}{2,500 - 600 + 100} + 250$$

   $$= \frac{20,000}{2,000} + 250$$

   $$= 10 + 250 = 260$$

6. **The correct answer is G.** This problem asks you to multiply a and b. Remember, when multiplying two powers of the same base, add the powers together. For two powers with different bases, simply keep the powers the same:

   $(3y^4 - z^2)(-5y^3)$
   $= -15y^7 + 5y^3z^2$

   If you started by simply multiplying 3×-5, you could have quickly eliminated answer choices H, J, and K.

7. **The correct answer is E.** To find the slope of this line, you first must convert the equation to slope-intercept form ($y = mx + b$):

   $12y + 4x = 17$
   $12y = -4x + 17$
   $y = \dfrac{-4}{12x} + \dfrac{17}{12}$
   $y = \dfrac{-1}{3x} + \dfrac{17}{12}$

   The slope of the line is $-\dfrac{1}{3}$.

8. **The correct answer is F.** You are given that objects on Mars weigh about 38% of what they would on Earth. Therefore, if Jason weighs 175 pounds on Earth, he would weigh about 175×0.38, or 66.5 pounds on Mars.

9. **The correct answer is C.** Brad's team won 25 of its 45 games and had 2 ties, so they must have lost 18 games (45 − 25 − 2). Set up a fraction to show the relationship between games lost and games played:

   $$\frac{18}{45} = \frac{9 \times 2}{9 \times 5} = \frac{2}{5}$$

10. **The correct answer is K.** You are given that $\overline{ML}$ is perpendicular to $\overline{LK}$, so angle MLK measures 90°. Also given is the value of angle LMK (62°). The three angles of a triangle must add up to 180°, so angle MKL must equal 28°(180° − 90° − 62°). Angle MKL and angle MKJ form a line, so they must also add up to 180°. Therefore, angle MKJ measures 152°(180° − 28°).

11. **The correct answer is D.** To solve this problem, first draw a straight line with length 8 from X to a made-up point (p) to form a right triangle with a height of 8, the same as $\overline{WZ}$. The line from Z to p will be the same length as $\overline{WX}$(13), as shown below:

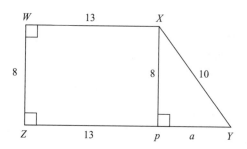

Finally, use the Pythagorean Theorem to determine the missing value in the triangle:

$$a^2 + b^2 = c^2$$
$$a^2 + 8^2 = 10^2$$
$$a^2 + 64 = 100$$
$$a^2 = 36$$
$$a = \sqrt{36}$$
$$a = 6$$

The measure of $\overline{ZY}$ is $13 + 6$, or 19 inches.

12. **The correct answer is J.** The standard form for the equation of a circle is $(x-h)^2 + (y-k)^2 = r^2$, where (h, k) is the circle's center and r is its radius. In this case, $r^2 = 8$, so $r = \sqrt{8}$.

13. **The correct answer is C.** You are given that OX bisects 106°-angle WOY. This means that two 53° angles (angle XOY and angle XOW) have been created. This also forms two separate triangles. Looking at triangle XOY, you have the measures of two of the angles (53° and 90°), so the missing angle (XYO) must measure 37°($180° - 53° - 90°$). This angle forms a line with angle XYZ, and thus the two must add up to 180°, so angle XYZ measures 143° ($180 - 37$).

14. **The correct answer is G.** This problem deals with absolute values. The absolute value of a number is its numerical value without regard to its sign. Simplify the equation by finding the necessary absolute values ($|-5| = 5, |-4| = 4, |7| = 7$):

$$5 + 2(4) - 7$$
$$= 5 + 8 - 7$$
$$= 6$$

15. **The correct answer is A.** To solve this problem, first find 40% of 180:

$$(0.40 \times 180 = 72)$$

You can now set up an equation to solve for x:

$$18x = 72$$
$$x = 4$$

16. **The correct answer is F.** When multiplying binomials, use the FOIL (first, outside, inside, last) method:

$$(6s - 2)(4s - 7) =$$

First: $6s \times 4s = 24s^2$

Outside: $6s \times -7 = -42s$

Inside: $-2 \times 4s = -8s$

Last: $-2 \times -7 = 14$

Now, combine like terms:

$$24s^2 - 42s - 8s + 14$$
$$= 24s^2 - 50s + 14$$

Once you determined that the first value was $24s^2$, you could safely eliminate answer choices J and K.

17. **The correct answer is C.** To solve this problem, substitute –4 for any instance of x in the function:

$$5x^2 - 3x - 27$$
$$= 5(-4^2) - 3(-4) - 27$$
$$= 5(16) + 12 - 27$$
$$= 80 + 12 - 27 = 65$$

18. **The correct answer is J.** To solve this problem, first find the slowest time (23:36) and the fastest time (16:42). You can see that the difference between the two is going to be just under 7 minutes (if you added 7 minutes to 16 minutes 42 seconds you would have 23 minutes 42 seconds). Eliminate answer choices F, G, H, and K. Therefore, the correct answer must be 6 minutes 54 seconds.

19. **The correct answer is C.** To solve this problem, first determine how far it is from each point to 0 (–5 is 5 spaces away from 0, 11 is 11 spaces away from 0). Therefore, the two points are 16 spaces away from each other ($5 + 11 = 16$). The midpoint of the line would be 8 spaces away from each of the endpoints ($-5 + 8 = 3, 11 - 8 = 3$). Therefore, the midpoint of the line is 3.

20. **The correct answer is K.** The definition of secant is $\dfrac{1}{\text{cosine}}$, so for this angle, the secant would be $\dfrac{1}{0.7}$.

21. **The correct answer is E.** The equation of a circle is given by $(x - h)^2 + (y - k)^2 = r^2$, where (h, k) is the center of the circle and r is the radius. In the given circle, h is –3, and k is 7, so the center of the circle is $(-3, 7)$.

22. **The correct answer is K.** One way to solve this problem is to create a chart to track the touchdowns made by each player (for simplicity, assume that Tom did not score any touchdowns in Games 1–3):

Game number	Tom's touchdowns	Reggie's touchdowns
1–3	0	2
4	3	0
5–7	0	5
8 & 9	4	2
10	1	3
Total number of touchdowns	8	12

At the end of 10 games, Reggie is ahead of Tom by 4 touchdowns.

23. **The correct answer is D.** To solve this problem, simplify each side of the equation by performing the necessary multiplication:

$$7x - 3(x - 6) = 2(x - 7) + 10$$
$$7x - 3x + 18 = 2x - 14 + 10$$
$$4x + 18 = 2x - 4$$
$$2x = -22$$
$$x = -11$$

24. **The correct answer is H.** To solve this problem, first simplify the polynomial:

$$10x^2 + 14x - 12$$
$$= 5x^2 + 7x - 6$$

Now factor $5x^2 + 7x - 6$, as follows:

$$5x^2 + 7x - 6$$
$$= (5x - 3)(x + 2)$$

The only answer choice that includes one of the factors of $10x^2 + 14x - 12$ is answer choice H.

25. **The correct answer is D.** You are given that the students charge $24 per hour for a job that requires more than 5 hours. The question asks you for the expression that shows how much they charge for a job requiring more than 5 hours, which is $24 times the number of hours it takes. This can be expressed mathematically as $24h$.

26. **The correct answer is F.** To solve this problem, first write the equation in slope-intercept form ($y = mx + b$):

$$5x - 2y - 9 = 0$$
$$-2y = -5x + 9$$
$$y = \frac{5}{2}x - \frac{9}{2}$$

For an equation in slope-intercept form, the y-intercept is given by b, which in this case is $-\frac{9}{2}$.

27. **The correct answer is A.** The formula for the distance between two points in the (x, y) coordinate plane is $\sqrt{(x_2 - x_1)^2 + (y_2 - y_1)^2}$, where (x_1, y_1) and (x_2, y_2) are the coordinates of the two points. Use the formula with the two points that are given:

$$= \sqrt{(-6 - (-2))^2 + (10 - 3)^2}$$
$$= \sqrt{(-4)^2 + (7)^2}$$
$$= \sqrt{16 + 49}$$
$$= \sqrt{65}$$

This cannot be simplified further, so the distance between the points is $\sqrt{65}$.

28. **The correct answer is H.** To solve this problem, substitute the given values for a and b into the equation as follows:

$$7b - (2a^3 + 4b^2)$$
$$= 7(-3) - (2(-5^3) + 4(-3^2))$$
$$= -21 - (2(-125) + 4(9))$$
$$= -21 - (-250 + 36)$$
$$= -21 - (-214)$$
$$= -21 + 214 = 193$$

29. **The correct answer is E.** To solve this problem, first simplify by factoring the numerator:

$$2x^2 - x - 15 = (2x + 5)(x - 3)$$

You now have $\dfrac{(2x + 5)(x - 3)}{2x + 5,}$ so you can cancel out $2x + 5$ leaving you with $x - 3$.

30. **The correct answer is H.** Before you find the measure of angle WYX, you must find a few missing angles. Notice that the points W, Y, and X form a small triangle. Therefore, the three angles within the triangle must add up to 180°. Angle YXW has the same measurement as the 42° angle that is given in the picture, as they are vertical angles. Angle VWX is an alternate interior angle of the given 105° angle, so they have the same measurement. Because this angle forms a line with angle YWX, the two

must add up to 180°, so angle *YWX* equals 75° (180 − 105). You now have two of the three angles in the triangle (42° and 75°). The missing measurement is that of angle *WYX*, and it must equal 63° (180 − 42 − 75 = 63).

31. The correct answer is A. To find the solutions to the equation, set each of the four binomials equal to 0:

- $(x + 5) = 0$ $x = -5$
- $(x - 2) = 0$ $x = 2$
- $(x - 9) = 0$ $x = 9$
- $(x + 2) = 0$ $x = -2$

The solutions to the equation are −5, −2, 2, and 9. The only answer choice that is not a possible solution is −9.

32. The correct answer is G. If the price of any bottle of cola is P, then the price after the 50-cent discount will be $P - 50$. To determine the price per ounce of the cola, you need to divide the discounted price by the number of ounces in the bottle (S). Therefore, the formula is expressed as $\dfrac{P - 50}{S}$.

33. The correct answer is C. If Aaron drove for 6 hours and 15 minutes, he drove for 6.25 hours $\left(\dfrac{15 \text{ min}}{60 \text{ min}} = 0.25 \text{ hours}\right)$. His average speed can be calculated by dividing the distance he traveled (410 miles) by the time he spent driving (6.25 hours), which equals 65.6 miles per hour.

34. The correct answer is F. To solve this problem, first find the missing length of the leg of the triangle using the Pythagorean Theorem:

$$a^2 + b^2 = c^2$$
$$a^2 + 24^2 = 25^2$$
$$a^2 + 576 = 625$$
$$a^2 = 49$$
$$a = \sqrt{49}$$
$$a = 7$$

The cosine of an angle is given by $\dfrac{\text{adjacent}}{\text{hypotenuse}}$. For angle θ, the cosine is $\dfrac{7}{25}$, which equals 0.28.

35. The correct answer is B. To solve this problem, write out the expression without the parentheses and combine like terms, as shown below:

$$(8x - 11) - (3x + 9) = 8x - 11 - 3x - 9$$
$$= 8x - 3x - 11 - 9$$
$$= 5x - 20$$

Factor out the 5:

$$= 5(x - 4)$$

36. The correct answer is H. According to the information given, the price (P) is always 30 more than 10 times the number of guests (G). For example, $10 \times 10 = 100$ and $130 = 100 + 30$. This can be expressed by the equation $P = 10G + 30$.

37. The correct answer is C. The formula for the arc of a circle is given by $s = r\theta$, where s is the arc length, r is the radius of the circle, and θ is the measure of the central angle, in radians. You are given that the diameter of the circle is 10 inches, so the radius is $\dfrac{10}{2}$, or 5. To convert a degree measure of an angle to radians, multiply by $\dfrac{\pi}{180}$. For 120°:

$$120 \times \dfrac{\pi}{180}$$
$$= \dfrac{120\pi}{180}$$
$$= \dfrac{2\pi}{3}$$

Now, use the values you found for the radius and the degree measure in radians to solve for the arc length:

$$s = 5\left(\dfrac{2\pi}{3}\right)$$
$$s = \dfrac{10\pi}{3}$$

38. The correct answer is G. To find the sum of terms in a geometric sequence, use the formula $S_n = \dfrac{a_1(1 - r^n)}{(1 - r)}$, where S_n is the sum of the first n terms in a sequence, a_1 is the first term in the sequence, r is the common ratio in the sequence, and n is the number of terms you are adding up. For this sequence, the common ratio is 3 ($2 \times 3 = 6$, $6 \times 3 = 18$, etc.). To solve, substitute the values that you have into the formula:

$$S_8 = \dfrac{2(1 - 3^8)}{(1 - 3)}$$
$$S_8 = \dfrac{2(1 - 6{,}561)}{-2}$$
$$S_8 = \dfrac{2(-6{,}560)}{-2}$$
$$S_8 = \dfrac{-13{,}120}{-2}$$
$$S_8 = 6{,}560$$

39. The correct answer is B. To solve this problem, substitute −4 for any instance of x, and 2 for any instance of y (carefully track the negative signs):

$$x^3 + 5x^2y - 5xy^2 - y^3$$
$$= (-4)^3 + 5(-4)^2(2) - 5(-4)(2)^2 - (2)^3$$
$$= -64 + 5(16)(2) - 5(-4)(4) - 8$$
$$= -64 + 160 - (-80) - 8$$
$$= -64 + 160 + 80 - 8 = 168$$

40. **The correct answer is F.** The area of a rectangle is defined as $A = L \times W$. For this rectangle, you are given that the length is 3 times the width and that the area is 48 square inches. Knowing this, you can set up an equation (since the length is 3 times the width, the length can be expressed as $3W$):

$$48 = 3W \times W$$
$$48 = 3W^2$$
$$16 = W^2$$
$$W = \sqrt{16}$$
$$W = 4$$

41. **The correct answer is C.** To solve this problem, multiply $\frac{1}{8}$ by 6, which equals $\frac{3}{4}$, or 0.75 in decimal form. You could also divide 6 by 8 to get the answer. You could also make an educated guess because you know that $\frac{1}{2}$ of 6 is 3, so $\frac{1}{8}$ of 6 must be less than 3.

42. **The correct answer is F.** You are given the values for x, y, and z, so take these and substitute them into $\dfrac{5xy^3 + z^2}{x}$ to solve (carefully track the negative signs):

$$= \frac{5\left(-\dfrac{1}{4}\right)(2^3) + (-4)^2}{-\left(\dfrac{1}{4}\right)}$$

$$= \frac{5\left(-\dfrac{1}{4}\right)(8) + 16}{-\left(\dfrac{1}{4}\right)}$$

$$= \frac{-10 + 16}{-\left(\dfrac{1}{4}\right)}$$

$$= \frac{6}{-\left(\dfrac{1}{4}\right)}$$

$$= 6 \times \frac{-4}{1} = -24$$

43. **The correct answer is E.** To solve this problem, first change the equation so that it is in slope-intercept form ($y = mx + b$):

$$2y - 6 = 3x$$
$$2y = 3x + 6$$
$$y = \frac{3x + 6}{2}$$

The line represented by this equation has a slope of $\dfrac{3}{2}$ and a y-intercept of 3. Eliminate answer choices B and C. Next, determine the slope of the remaining choices:

Answer choice A: $\dfrac{(6 - 3)}{(5 - 0)} = \dfrac{3}{5}$

Answer choice D: $\dfrac{(9 - 3)}{(2 - 0)} = \dfrac{6}{2} = 3$

Answer choice E: $\dfrac{(6 - 3)}{(2 - 0)} = \dfrac{3}{2}$

44. **The correct answer is K.** This problem looks a bit more complicated than it actually is. To solve, first draw a line from Q to T. You can see that by adding a few more lines you can form a right triangle. Creating a new point, X, you can see that $\overline{RX}$ is the same length as $\overline{ST}$ (4), and that $\overline{XT}$ is the same as $\overline{RS}$ (8).

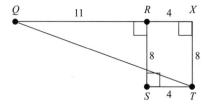

You now have the length of two of the legs of triangle QXT (15 and 8), and $\overline{QT}$ represents the hypotenuse. Use the Pythagorean theorem to find the length of $\overline{QT}$:

$$a^2 + b^2 = c^2$$
$$8^2 + 15^2 = c^2$$
$$64 + 225 = c^2$$
$$289 = c^2$$
$$c = \sqrt{289}$$
$$c = 17$$

The length of $\overline{QT}$ is 17 inches.

45. **The correct answer is C.** You are given that Jerry's bedroom is 2 meters wider than it is long. Therefore, $W = L + 2$. You are also given that the area of

his bedroom is 99 meters squared. Use the formula for area ($L \times W$) to solve:

$$A = L \times W$$
$$99 = L(L + 2)$$
$$99 = L^2 + 2L$$
$$L^2 + 2L - 99 = 0$$
$$(L + 11)(L - 9) = 0$$
$$L + 11 = 0 \text{ and } L - 9 = 0$$
$$L = -11 \text{ and } L = 9$$

Since the length of his bedroom cannot be a negative number, it must be 9 meters. The width is 2 more than the length, so his bedroom is 11 meters wide.

46. **The correct answer is G.** To solve this problem, draw a picture to give yourself a visual representation of what you need to find. You are given that the length of the diagonal is 17 units, and the length of one side is 15 units.

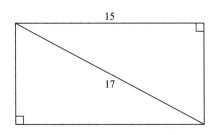

As you can see, the diagonal splits the rectangle into two equal right triangles. Use the Pythagorean Theorem to solve for the missing side:

$$a^2 + b^2 = c^2$$
$$a^2 + 15^2 = 17^2$$
$$a^2 + 225 = 289$$
$$a^2 = 64$$
$$a = \sqrt{64}$$
$$a = 8$$

To find the area of the rectangle, take the length times the width (15×8), which equals 120 square units.

47. **The correct answer is E.** The circumference of a circle is given by $C = \pi \times d$, where d is the diameter of the circle. For this problem, you are only given the area of the circle (25π). The area of a circle is given by $A = \pi r^2$. You can use this equation to find the radius of the circle:

$$25\pi = \pi r^2$$
$$25 = r^2$$
$$r = \sqrt{25}$$
$$r = 5$$

Since you know that the radius of the circle is 5, the diameter is twice that, which equals 10. Now you can solve for the circumference: $C = 10\pi$.

48. **The correct answer is H.** A fraction will have the value 0 if and only if the numerator is 0. If the denominator is 0, the fraction will be undefined. These statements are represented mathematically in answer choice H.

49. **The correct answer is B.** To solve this problem, first find the values of x and y. Start by taking one of the equations and solving for x in terms of y:

$$2x - 4y = -2.9$$
$$2x = 4y - 2.9$$
$$x = 2y - 1.45$$

Now, take this value of x and substitute it into the other equation to solve for y:

$$10x - 21.5 = -12y$$
$$10(2y - 1.45) - 21.5 = -12y$$
$$20y - 14.5 - 21.5 = -12y$$
$$20y - 36 = -12y$$
$$-36 = -32y$$
$$y = 1.125$$

Now that you have the numerical value of y, substitute this into one of the equations to find the numerical value of x:

$$2x - 4y = -2.9$$
$$2x - 4(1.125) = -2.9$$
$$2x - 4.5 = -2.9$$
$$2x = 1.6$$
$$x = 0.8$$

The problem asks you to determine the value of xy, which is 1.125×0.8, or 0.9.

50. **The correct answer is K.** The graph shows a solid line with the area below the line shaded. This tells you that y is less than (because the shaded region is below the line) or equal to (because the line is solid) in the inequality, so you would use the $\leq$ symbol. Eliminate answer choices F and G. Now you need to determine the slope and the y-intercept of the line. Since the line crosses the y-axis at (0, 4), the y-intercept (b) is 4. The two points of the line that you are given are (0, 4) and (−6, 0). You can use these to determine the slope (m) of the line:

$$m = \frac{0 - 4}{-6 - 0}$$
$$m = \frac{-4}{-6}$$
$$m = \frac{2}{3}$$

Finally, use the information you have found to write the inequality in slope-intercept form ($y = mx + b$):

$$y \le \frac{2}{3}x + 4$$

51. **The correct answer is E.** Using the given values in this problem, draw a picture and form a right triangle:

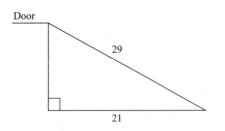

Since you are given two values of side lengths of the triangle, use the Pythagorean Theorem to find the missing value, which is the height of the start of the ramp:

$$a^2 + b^2 = c^2$$
$$a^2 + 21^2 = 29^2$$
$$a^2 + 441 = 841$$
$$a^2 = 400$$
$$a = \sqrt{400}$$
$$a = 20$$

The start of the ramp is 20 feet above the ground.

52. **The correct answer is G.** To solve the problem, first find the slope of the line that you are given by converting the equation to slope-intercept form:

$$2x + 6y = 11$$
$$6y = -2x + 11$$
$$y = -\frac{1}{3}x + \frac{11}{2}$$

The slope of this line is $-\frac{1}{3}$. To find the slope of a line perpendicular to this line, take the negative reciprocal of the first line's slope. The negative reciprocal of $-\frac{1}{3}$ is $-\frac{1}{3}$ divided by -1, which equals 3.

53. **The correct answer is D.** When dealing with an inequality that has an absolute value, you need to set up two separate inequalities, as shown next:

$$|3x - 5| > 13$$
$$3x - 5 > 13 \text{ or } 3x - 5 < -13$$
$$3x > 18 \text{ or } 3x < -8$$
$$x > 6 \text{ or } x < -\frac{8}{3}$$

54. **The correct answer is G.** To solve this problem, you first need to find some of the missing angle values. As you can see, there are two triangles within the larger triangle *WZY*. You are given that angles *WZY* and *ZXY* are 90° and that angle *ZWX* is 60°. Because angle *ZXY* is 90°, angle *ZXW* must also measure 90°, as the two form a line and therefore must add up to 180°. You now have two of the three angles in the smaller triangle (60° and 90°).

The three angles of a triangle must add up to 180°, so angle *WZX* must equal 30°. This also shows you that angle *XZY* equals 60°, as, when added to *WZX*, it equals 90° (the measurement of angle *WZY*). Because angle *XZY* equals 60°, angle *ZYX* equals 30°.

In a 30°-60°-90° triangle, the ratio of the measures of the sides are $1 - \sqrt{3} - 2$, respectively. You are asked to find the value of $\overline{XY}$, which is the side opposite the 60° angle. Since $\overline{ZY}$ is 6 units long, $\overline{XZ}$ must be 3 units long, and $\overline{XY}$ must be $3\sqrt{3}$ units long.

55. **The correct answer is E.** The best way to solve this problem is to use the given equation and test the answer choices to see which yields the greatest value. Replace a with each of the values in the answer choices, and solve the equations:

Answer choice A: $b = 19 - (5 + 19)^3$
$$b = 19 - (24)^3$$
$$b = 19 - 13,824$$
$$b = -13,805$$

Answer choice B: $b = 19 - (5 + 5)^3$
$$b = 19 - (10)^3$$
$$b = 19 - 1,000$$
$$b = -981$$

Answer choice C: $b = 19 - (5 + 1)^3$
$$b = 19 - (6)^3$$
$$b = 19 - 216$$
$$b = -197$$

Answer choice D: $b = 19 - (5 + (-5))^3$
$$b = 19 - (0)^3$$
$$b = 19 - 0$$
$$b = 19$$

Answer choice E: $b = 19 - (5 + (-19))^3$
$$b = 19 - (-14)^3$$
$$b = 19 - (-2,744)$$
$$b = 2,763$$

Answer choice E yields the greatest value.

56. **The correct answer is F.** If Chuck drinks 9 bottles of water in 2 days and continues drinking at this constant rate, the number of bottles he drinks in

d days can be expressed by $\frac{(9d)}{2}$. The problem asks you how many bottles he will drink in $2 + d$ days. Since you already know that he drinks 9 bottles in 2 days, and he will drink $\frac{(9d)}{2}$ bottles in *d* days, he will drink $9 + \frac{(9d)}{2}$ bottles in $2 + d$ days.

57. The correct answer is D. To solve this problem, use the equation $y_2 - y_1 = m(x_2 - x_1)$ using the points $(-4, 6)$ and $(x, 3)$ and the given slope, $-\frac{1}{3}$:

$$(3 - 6) = -\frac{1}{3}(x - (-4))$$

$$-3 = -\frac{1}{3}(x + 4)$$

$$-3 = -\frac{1}{3}x - \frac{4}{3}$$

$$4 = x + 4$$

$$5 = x$$

58. The correct answer is H. You are asked to find the difference in the areas of the two given figures, so you must first find the area of each figure. For the rectangle, you are given that the perimeter is 36 units and that its length is twice its width (this can be expressed as $L = 2W$). Use the formula for perimeter ($P = 2L + 2W$) to find the values of the length and the width:

$$36 = 2(2W) + 2W$$

$$36 = 4W + 2W$$

$$36 = 6W$$

$$6 = W$$

The length of the rectangle is $2W$, or 2×6, which equals 12. The formula for area of a rectangle is $A = L \times W$. For this rectangle, the area would be 6×12, or 72 square units.

Draw a picture of the triangle to help you visualize the problem:

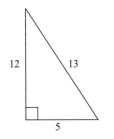

The area of a triangle is given by $A = \frac{1}{2}bh$, where $b = $ base and $h = $ height. In this triangle, the base is 5, and the height is 12, so the area is $\frac{1}{2}(5)(12)$, or 30 square units. The difference in the areas of the two figures is $72 - 30$, or 42 square units.

59. The correct answer is B. To solve this problem, write the numbers out in scientific notation, as follows:

$$3,000 = 3.0 \times 10^3$$

$$7,000,000,000 = 7.0 \times 10^9$$

The product of these two numbers can therefore be written as:

$$(3.0 \times 10^3)(7.0 \times 10^9) = 21.0 \times 10^{12}$$

Remember, when multiplying exponents with the same base, simply add the two numbers together.

Therefore, there are 12 zeros in the product of 3 thousand and 7 billion.

60. The correct answer is G. Recall that when $\frac{\pi}{2} < x < \pi$ on the unit circle, the point is in Quadrant II, which has negative values for cosine and positive values for sine. The value $\frac{\sqrt{2}}{2}$ corresponds with the angles 45°, 135°, 225°, and 315°, or $\frac{\pi}{4}, \frac{3\pi}{4}, \frac{5\pi}{4}$ and $\frac{7\pi}{2}$, respectively. These angles have sine and cosine values with the same magnitude, so you are left to determine the correct sign. As stated earlier, in Quadrant II, cosine values are negative and sine values are positive. Therefore, if the cosine is $-\frac{\sqrt{2}}{2}$, sine is $\frac{\sqrt{2}}{2}$. Tangent is defined as $\frac{\text{sine}}{\text{cosine}}$; therefore, $\tan x = \frac{\left(\frac{\sqrt{2}}{2}\right)}{\left(-\frac{\sqrt{2}}{2}\right)} = -1$.

PART IV

APPENDIXES

APPENDIX A

GLOSSARY OF MATHEMATICS TERMS AND FORMULAS

A

Absolute value:

The absolute value of a number is its distance on the number line from 0, without regard to its direction from 0. Therefore, absolute value will always be positive. Think of it as the distance from -10 to 0 on the number line, and the distance from 0 to 10 on the number line. Both distances equal 10 units.

$$\longleftrightarrow \quad \underset{-10}{\mid} \qquad \underset{0}{\mid} \qquad \underset{10}{\mid} \longrightarrow$$

The absolute value is indicated by enclosing a number within two vertical lines:

$$|-3| = 3, \text{ and } |3| = 3.$$

Absolute value inequalities:

To solve an absolute value inequality, you must set up two solutions. The way that you set these up depends on whether the inequality uses a less-than symbol (either $<$ or $\leq$), or a greater-than symbol (either $>$ or $\geq$). For a less-than symbol, you set up two parts to the solution with the connecting word *and*. For a greater-than symbol, you set up two parts to the solution with the connecting word *or*.

- If the symbol is $<$ or $\leq$ and $a > 0$, then the solutions to $|x| < a$ are:

  $x < a$ **and** $x > -a$.

- If the symbol is $<$ or $\leq$ and $a < 0$, then the solution to $|x| < a$ is all real numbers (because absolute value must be a positive number or 0, it is always greater than a negative number).
- If the symbol is $>$ or $\geq$ and $a > 0$, then the solutions to $|x| > a$ are:

  $x > a$ **or** $x < -a$.

- If the symbol is $>$ or $\geq$ and $a < 0$, then there is no solution (because absolute value must be a positive number or 0, it cannot be less than a negative number).

Acute angle:	An angle with a measurement less than 90 degrees.
Adjacent angle:	Either of two angles having a common side and a common vertex. For example, in the following figure, angles a and b are adjacent:

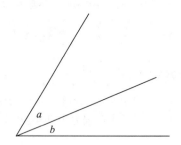

Arc:	A portion of the circumference of a circle. A circle has a major arc, which is the larger of two arcs between two points on a circle, and a minor arc, which is the smaller of the two arcs:

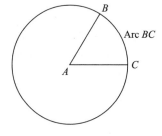

The complete arc of a circle has 360 degrees.

The equation used to find the arc of a circle is $s = r\theta$, where s is the arc length, r is the radius of the circle, and θ is the measure of the central angle in radians (angle A would be the central angle in the figure shown).

Area:	The number of square units that covers the shape or figure. The following are formulas for the area of some common figures:

- Square: side (s) squared — (s^2).
- Rectangle: length (l) times width (w) — ($l \times w$).
- Circle: π times the radius (r) squared — (πr^2).
- Triangle: one-half the base (b) times the height (h) — $\left(\frac{1}{2}b \times h\right)$.
- Parallelogram: base times height — ($b \times h$).

Arithmetic mean (see average):	The arithmetic mean is equivalent to the average of a series of numbers. Calculate the arithmetic mean by dividing the sum of all of the numbers in the series by the total count of numbers in the series. For example: a student received scores of 80%, 85%, and 90% on 3 math tests. The average, or mean score received by the student on those tests is $80 + 85 + 90$ divided by 3, or $\frac{255}{3}$, which is 85%.
Associative property:	According to this property, changing the grouping of numbers does not change the sum or the product. The associative property of multiplication can be expressed as $(a \times b) \times c = a \times (b \times c)$. Likewise, the associative property of addition can be expressed as $(a + b) + c = a + (b + c)$.

Average (see arithmetic mean):

The arithmetic mean of a group of values. Calculate the average by dividing the sum of all of the numbers in the series by the total count of numbers in the series. For example: a student received scores of 80%, 85%, and 90% on 3 math tests. The average score received by the student on those tests is $80 + 85 + 90$ divided by 3, or 255/3, which is 85%.

B

Base:

In geometry, the base is the bottom of a plane figure. For example, in the right triangle shown below, AC is the base:

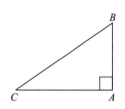

In algebra, the base is the number that is raised to various powers. For example, 4^2 indicates a base of 4 raised to the power of 2.

C

Circle:

The set of all points in a plane at a fixed distance, called the *radius*, from a given point, the center.

The following are properties of circles that are commonly tested on the ACT:

- The radius (r) of a circle is the distance from the center of the circle to any point on the circle.
- The diameter (d) of a circle is twice the radius.
- The area (A) of a circle is equivalent to πr^2. For example, the area of a circle with a radius of 3 is $3^2\pi$, or 9π.
- The circumference (C) of a circle is equivalent to $2\pi r$ or πd. For example, the circumference of a circle with a radius of 3 is $2(3)\pi$, or 6π.
- The equation of a circle centered at the point (h, k) is $(x - h)^2 + (y - k)^2 = r^2$, where r is the radius of the circle.
- The complete arc of a circle has 360°.

Circumference:

The distance around a circle. The circumference of a circle is equal to π times the diameter of the circle (πd). This can also be expressed as $2\pi r$, because the diameter, d, is twice the radius, r.

Collinear:

Refers to points that pass through or lie on the same straight line.

Commutative property:

According to this property, changing the order of numbers that you are either adding or multiplying does not change either the sum or the product. The commutative property of addition is expressed as $a + b = b + a$. Likewise, the commutative property of multiplication is expressed as $a \times b = b \times a$, or $ab = ba$.

Complementary angles:

Two angles that, when added together, equal 90°.

Congruent:

Any shapes or figures, including line segments and angles, with the same size or measure. For example, in the triangle below, sides *AB* and *BC* are congruent, and angles *A* and *C* are congruent.

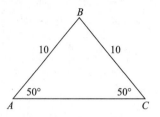

Coordinate plane:

A plane, typically defined with the coordinates *x* and *y*, where the two axes are at right angles to each other. The horizontal axis is the *x*-axis and the vertical axis is the *y*-axis, as shown in the following figure:

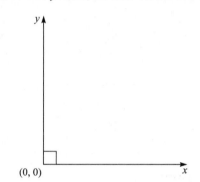

You can locate any point on the coordinate plane by an ordered pair of numbers. The ordered pair (0, 0), where the *x* and *y* axes meet, is the origin.

The coordinate plane is divided into four quadrants, as shown in the following figure:

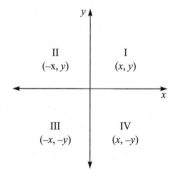

Cosecant (see trigonometric functions):

For an angle in a right triangle, the cosecant (csc) of an angle is defined as $\frac{1}{\sin}$.

Cosine (see trigonometric functions):

For an angle in a right triangle, cosine (cos) is defined as the ratio of the side adjacent the angle to the hypotenuse. $\text{Cos} = \frac{\text{adj}}{\text{hyp}}$.

Cotangent (see trigonometric functions):

For an angle in a right triangle, cotangent (cot) is defined as $\frac{\cos}{\sin}$, or $\frac{1}{\tan}$.

■ **D**

Decimal:

The point that separates values less than 1 from those greater than 1. In our number system, digits can be placed to the left and right of a decimal point. *Place value* refers to the value of a digit in a number relative to its position. Starting from the left of the decimal point, the values of the digits are ones, tens, hundreds, and so on. Starting to the right of the decimal point, the values of the digits are tenths, hundredths, thousandths, and so on.

When adding and subtracting decimals, be sure to line up the decimal points, as shown here:

$$
\begin{array}{r}
236.78 \\
+113.21 \\
\hline
349.99
\end{array}
\qquad
\begin{array}{r}
78.90 \\
-23.42 \\
\hline
55.48
\end{array}
$$

When multiplying decimals, it is not necessary to line up the decimal points. Just as you would do when multiplying whole numbers, start on the right and multiply each digit in the top number by each digit in the bottom number, and then add the products. Finally, place the decimal point in the answer by starting at the right and moving a number of places equal to the sum of the decimal places in both numbers that were multiplied. Refer to the following examples:

$$
\begin{array}{rl}
2.357 & \text{(3 decimal places)} \\
\times 0.78 & \text{(2 decimal places)} \\
\hline
18856 & \\
+164990 & \text{(5 decimal places)} \\
\hline
1.83846 &
\end{array}
$$

When dividing decimals, first move the decimal point in the divisor to the right until the divisor becomes an integer. Then move the decimal point in the dividend the same number of places:

$58.345 \div 3.21 = 5834.5 \div 321$. (The decimal point was moved two places to the right).

You can then perform long division with the decimal point in the correct place in the quotient, as shown below:

$$
\begin{array}{r}
18.17 \\
321\overline{)5834.50} \\
-321 \\
\hline
2624 \\
-2568 \\
\hline
565 \\
-321 \\
\hline
2440 \\
-2247 \\
\hline
193 \\
\text{and so on}
\end{array}
$$

Denominator:

The bottom part of a fraction. For example, in the fraction $\frac{2}{5}$, 5 is the denominator.

Diagonal: A line segment that connects two nonadjacent vertices in any polygon. In the following rectangle, AC and BD are diagonals:

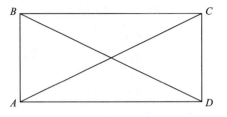

The lengths of the diagonals of a rectangle are congruent, or equal in length, so $AC = BD$.

Diameter: A line segment that joins two points on a circle and passes through the center of the circle, as shown in the following figure, where AB is the diameter:

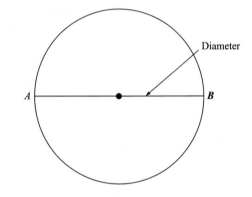

The diameter (d) of a circle is twice the radius (r).

Distance Formula: To find the distance between two points in the (x, y) coordinate plane, use the Distance Formula $\sqrt{([x_2 - x_1]^2 + [y_2 - y_1]^2)}$, where (x_1, y_1) and (x_2, y_2) are the two given points. For example, if you are given the points (2, 3) and (4, 5), you would set up the following equation to determine the distance between the two points:

$$\sqrt{(4 - 2) + (5 - 3)} = \sqrt{(4 - 2)^2 + (5 - 3)^2}$$
$$= \sqrt{2^2 + 2^2}$$
$$= \sqrt{16}$$
$$= 2\sqrt{2}$$

Distributive property: This property is used when an expression involves both addition and multiplication. The distributive property of multiplication is expressed as $a(b + c) = ab + ac$, where the variable a is distributed to the variables b and c. For example: $x(x + 3) = x^2 + 3x$.

Divisible: Capable of being divided, usually with no remainder. For example, 6 is divisible by 2, and the result is 3 with no remainder.

Domain: Refers to the x, or independent variable, values of a function. For example, take the function $y = 2x$. All of the various numbers that could go into x make up the domain of the function. The domain of this function would be all real numbers, since x could accept any real number.

▬ E

Equilateral triangle: A triangle in which all of the sides are congruent and each of the angles equals 60 degrees.

Exponent: A number that indicates the operation of repeated multiplication. A number with an exponent is said to be "raised to the power" of that exponent. For example, 2^3 indicates 2 raised to the power of 3, which equals $2 \times 2 \times 2$. In this example, 3 is the exponent.

The following are properties of exponents that are commonly tested on the ACT:

1. $a^m \times a^n = a^{(m+n)}$

   When multiplying the same base number raised to any power, add the exponents. For example: $3^2 \times 3^4 = 3^6$. Likewise, $3^6 = 3^2 \times 3^4$; $3^6 = 3^1 \times 3^5$; and $3^6 = 3^3 \times 3^3$.

2. $(a^m)^n = a^{mn}$

   When raising an exponential expression to a power, multiply the exponent and power. For example: $(3^2)^4 = 3^8$. Likewise, $3^8 = (3^2)^4$; $3^8 = (3^4)^2$; $3^8 = (3^1)^8$; and $3^8 = (3^8)^1$.

3. $(ab)^m = a^m \times b^m$

   When multiplying two different base numbers and raising the product to a power, the product is equivalent to raising each number to the power, and multiplying the exponential expressions. For example: $(3 \times 2)^2 = 3^2 \times 2^2$, which equals 9×4, or 36. Likewise, $3^2 \times 2^2 = (3 \times 2)^2$, or 6^2, which equals 36.

4. $\left(\dfrac{a}{b}\right)^m = \dfrac{a^m}{b^m}$

   When dividing two different base numbers and raising the quotient to a power, the quotient is equivalent to raising each number to the power, and dividing the exponential expressions. For example: $\left(\dfrac{2}{3}\right)^2 = \dfrac{2^2}{3^2}$, or $\dfrac{4}{9}$.

5. $a^0 = 1$, when $a \neq 0$

   When you raise any number to the power of 0, the result is always 1.

6. $a^{-m} = \dfrac{1}{a^m}$, when $a \neq 0$

   When you raise a number to a negative power, the result is equivalent to 1 over the number raised to the same positive power. For example: $3^{-2} = \dfrac{1}{3^2}$, or $\dfrac{1}{9}$.

▬ F

Factor: One of two or more expressions that are multiplied together to get a product. For example, in the equation $2 \times 3 = 6$, 2 and 3 are factors of 6. Likewise, in the equation $x^2 + 5x + 6$, $(x+2)$ and $(x+3)$ are factors. Common factors include all of the factors that two or more numbers share. For example: 1, 2, 4, and 8 are all factors of 8, and 1, 2, 3, and 6 are all factors of 6. Therefore, 8 and 6 have common factors of 1 and 2.

You may be required to find the factors or solution sets of certain simple quadratic expressions. A factor or solution set takes the form $(x \pm$ some number$)$. Simple quadratic expressions will usually have 2 of these factors or solution sets. For example, the solution sets of $x^2 - 4$ are $(x + 2)$ and $(x - 2)$.

To find the common factor, simply look for the element that two expressions have in common. For example, in the expression $x^2 + 3x$, the common factor is x: $x(x + 3)$ is the factored form of the original expression.

FOIL method:

A method of multiplying two binomials, such as $(x + 2)$ and $(x + 3)$, according to the following steps:

*F*irst: Multiply the first terms together: $(x)(x) = x^2$.
*O*utside: Multiply the outside terms together: $(x)(3) = 3x$.
*I*nside: Multiply the inside terms together: $(2)(x) = 2x$.
*L*ast: Multiply the last terms together: $(2)(3) = 6$.

Now, combine like terms to get $x^2 + 5x + 6$.

Fraction:

An expression that indicates the quotient of two quantities. For example, $\frac{2}{3}$ is a fraction, where 2 is the numerator and 3 is the denominator. The following are properties of fractions and rational numbers that are commonly tested on the ACT:

* To change any fraction to a decimal, divide the numerator by the denominator. For example, $\frac{3}{4}$ is equivalent to $3 \div 4$, or 0.75.
* Equivalent fractions are fractions that name the same amount. For example, $\frac{1}{3} = \frac{2}{6} = \frac{3}{9} = \frac{4}{12}$, and so on.
* Multiplying and dividing both the numerator and the denominator of a fraction by the same nonzero number will result in an equivalent fraction. For example, $\frac{1}{4} \times \frac{3}{3} = \frac{3}{12}$, which can be reduced to $\frac{1}{4}$. This is true because whenever the numerator and the denominator are the same, the value of the fraction is 1; $\frac{3}{3} = 1$.
* When adding and subtracting like fractions (fractions with the same denominator), add or subtract the numerators and write the sum or difference over the denominator. So, $\frac{1}{8} + \frac{2}{8} = \frac{3}{8}$, and $\frac{4}{7} - \frac{2}{7} = \frac{2}{7}$.
* To simplify a fraction, find a common factor of both the numerator and the denominator. For example, $\frac{12}{15}$ can be simplified into $\frac{4}{5}$ by dividing both the numerator and the denominator by the common factor 3.
* To convert a mixed number to an improper fraction, multiply the whole number by the denominator in the fraction, add the result to the numerator, and place that value over the original denominator. For example, $3\frac{2}{5}$ is equivalent to $(3 \times 5) + 2$ over 5, or $\frac{17}{5}$.
* When multiplying fractions, multiply the numerators to get the numerator of the product, and multiply the denominators to get the denominator of the product. For example, $\frac{3}{5} \times \frac{7}{8} = \frac{21}{40}$.
* When dividing fractions, multiply the first fraction by the reciprocal of the second fraction. For example, $\frac{1}{3} \div \frac{1}{4} = \frac{1}{3} \times \frac{4}{1}$, which equals $\frac{4}{3}$, or $1\frac{1}{3}$.

Frequency distribution: Frequency distribution is often a more convenient way to express a set of measurements. A frequency distribution table or graph shows the frequency of occurrence of each value in the set. Following is an example of a frequency distribution table:

Rank	Degree of agreement	Number of students
1	Strongly agree	23
2	Somewhat agree	31
3	Somewhat disagree	12
4	Strongly disagree	7

Function: A set of ordered pairs where no two of the ordered pairs has the same x value. In a function, each input (x value) has exactly one output (y value). An example of this relationship would be $y = x^2$. Here, y is a function of x because for any value of x, there is exactly one value of y. However, x is not a function of y because, for certain values of y, there is more than one value of x. The *domain* of a function refers to the x-values, while the *range* of a function refers to the y-values. For example: $f(x) = 2x + 3$. If $x = 3$, then $f(x) = 9$. For every x, only one $f(x)$, or y, exists. If the values in the domain correspond to more than one value in the range, the relation is not a function.

G

Greatest Common Factor (GCF): The largest number that will divide evenly into any 2 or more numbers. For example: 1, 2, 4, and 8 are all factors of 8, and 1, 2, 3, and 6 are all factors of 6. Therefore, the greatest common factor of 8 and 6 is 2.

H

Hexagon: A six-sided figure, as shown below:

The sum of the interior angles of a hexagon is $(6 - 2)(180°)$, or $720°$.

Hypotenuse: The leg of a right triangle that is opposite the right angle. For example, in the right triangle shown in the following figure, *BC* is the hypotenuse:

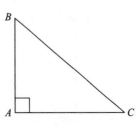

The hypotenuse is always the longest leg of a right triangle.

I

Inequality: A mathematical expression that shows two quantities are not equal. For example, $2x < 8$ is an inequality that means that $2x$ is less than 8. Likewise, $3a > 17$ is an inequality that means that $3a$ is greater than 17.

The following are properties of inequalities that are commonly tested on the ACT:

- Inequalities can usually be worked with in the same way equations are worked with. For example, to solve for x in the inequality $2x > 8$, simply divide both sides by 2 to get $x > 4$.
- When an inequality is multiplied by a negative number, you must switch the sign.

     For example, follow these steps to solve for x in the inequality $-2x + 2 < 6$:

$$-2x + 2 < 6$$
$$-2x < 4$$
$$-x < 2$$
$$x > -2$$

Integer: The following are properties of integers commonly tested on the ACT:

- Integers include both positive and negative whole numbers.
- Zero is considered an integer.
- Consecutive integers follow one another and differ by 1. For example, 6, 7, 8, and 9 are consecutive integers.
- The value of a number does not change when multiplied by 1. For example, $13 \times 1 = 13$.

Interior angle: An angle inside two adjacent sides of a polygon. The sum of the interior angles in a triangle is always 180 degrees. The sum of the interior angles of a parallelogram is always 360 degrees.

Irrational number: A number that cannot be exactly expressed as the ratio of two integers. In other words, if a number cannot be written as a fraction, it is an irrational number. Numbers such as $\sqrt{2}$ and Π (pi) are irrational numbers.

Isosceles triangle: A triangle in which two sides have the same length, as shown below:

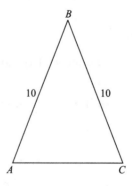

L

Least Common Denominator (LCD):   The smallest multiple of the denominators of two or more fractions. For example, the LCD of $\dfrac{3}{4}$ and $\dfrac{2}{5}$ is 20.

Least Common Multiple (LCM):

The smallest number that any two or more numbers will divide evenly into. For example, the common multiples of 3 and 4 are 12, 24, 36 and so on; 12 is the smallest common multiple, and is, therefore, the LCM of 3 and 4.

Like terms:

Terms that contain the same variables raised to the same power. For example, $3x^2$ and $10x^2$ are like terms that can be added to get $13x^2$; $-x$ and $4x$ are like terms that can be added to get $3x$; and $\dfrac{1}{11} + \dfrac{5}{11}$ are like terms that can be added to get $\dfrac{6}{11}$.

Line:

A straight set of points that extends into infinity in both directions, as shown in the following figure:

Line segment:

Represents two points on a line, and all the points in between, as shown in the following figure:

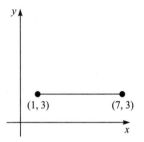

Logarithm:

A logarithm of a number x in a base b is a number n such that $x = b^n$, where b must not be 0 or a root of 1. This is most often written as a logarithmic equation, which looks like $\log_b(x) = n$.

The following are properties of logarithms commonly tested on the ACT:

- Logarithms are the inverse of exponentials. The logarithmic equation $\log_b(x) = n$ is equivalent to the exponential equation $b^n = x$. For example: $\log_x 81 = 4$ is equivalent to $x^4 = 81$.
- In any base, the logarithm of 1 is 0 ($\log_b 1 = 0$).
- In any base, the logarithm of the base itself is 1 ($\log_b b = 1$).

▇ M

Median:

The middle value of a series of numbers when those numbers are in either ascending or descending order. In the series (2, 4, 6, 8, 10), the median is 6. To find the median in an even set of data, find the average of the middle two numbers. In the series (3, 4, 5, 6), the median is 4.5.

Midpoint:

The center point of a line segment. To find the midpoint of a line given two points on the line, use the formula $\left(\dfrac{[x_1 + x_2]}{2}, \dfrac{[y_1 + y_2]}{2} \right)$.

For example, you would set up the following equation to determine the midpoint of the line between the two points (2, 3) and (4, 5):

- $\dfrac{(2+4)}{2} = \dfrac{6}{2} = 3$; the x-value of the midpoint is 3.

- $\dfrac{(3+5)}{2} = \dfrac{8}{2} = 4$; the y-value of the midpoint is 4.
- Therefore, the midpoint of the line between the points (2, 3) and (4, 5) is (3, 4).

Mode: The number that appears most frequently in a series of numbers. In the series (2, 3, 4, 5, 6, 3, 7) the mode is 3, because 3 appears twice in the series and the other numbers each appear only once in the series.

Multiple: A number is a multiple of another number if it can be expressed as the product of that number and a second number. For example: $2 \times 3 = 6$, so 6 is a multiple of both 2 and 3.

Common multiples include all of the multiples that two or more numbers share. For example:

Multiples of 3 include: $3 \times 4 = 12$; $3 \times 8 = 24$; $3 \times 12 = 36$.
Multiples of 4 include: $4 \times 3 = 12$; $4 \times 6 = 24$; $4 \times 9 = 36$.

Therefore, 12, 24, and 36 are all common multiples of both 3 and 4.

 N

Number line: The line on which every point represents a real number.
The following are properties of a number line commonly tested on the ACT:

- On a number line, numbers that correspond to points to the right of 0 are positive, and numbers that correspond to points to the left of 0 are negative.
- For any two numbers on the number line, the number to the left is less than the number to the right.
- If any number n lies between 0 and any positive number x on the number line, then $0 < n < x$; in other words, n is greater than 0 but less than x. If n is any number on the number line between 0 and any positive number x, including 0 and x, then $0 \leq n \leq x$, which means that n is greater than or equal to 0, and less than or equal to x.
- If any number n lies between 0 and any negative number x on the number line, then $-x < n < 0$; in other words, n is greater than $-x$ but less than 0. If n is any number on the number line between 0 and any negative number x, including 0 and $-x$, then $-x \leq n \leq 0$, which means that n is greater than or equal to $-x$, and less than or equal to 0.

Numerator: The top part of a fraction. For example, in the fraction $\dfrac{2}{5}$, 2 is the numerator.

 O

Obtuse angle: An angle that is greater than 90 degrees and less than 180 degrees.

Octagon: An eight-sided figure, as shown below:

The sum of the interior angles of an octagon is $(8 - 2)(180^\circ)$, or $1{,}080^\circ$.

Ordering (see inequality):

The process of arranging numbers from smallest to greatest or from greatest to smallest. The symbol $>$ is used to represent "greater than," and the symbol $<$ is used to represent "less than." To represent "greater than or equal to," use the symbol $\geq$; to represent "less than or equal to," use the symbol $\leq$.

▮ P

Parallel:

When two distinct lines lie in the same plane and do not intersect, they are parallel. Two lines are parallel if and only if they have the same slope. For example, the two lines with equations $2y = 6x + 7$ and $y = 3x - 14$ have the same slope (3), and are therefore parallel.

Parallelogram:

A quadrilateral in which the opposite sides are of equal length, and the opposite angles are equal, as shown in the following figure:

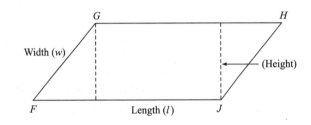

$$GH = FJ$$
$$GF = HJ$$
$$\angle F = \angle H$$
$$\angle G = \angle J$$

The sum of the angles in a parallelogram is always 360 degrees.

The area (A) of a parallelogram is equivalent to (base)(height). The height is equal to the perpendicular distance from an angle to a side. In the parallelogram shown above, the height is the distance from G to the bottom side, or base, or the distance from J to the top side, or base. The height is **not** the distance from G to F or the distance from H to J.

PEMDAS

An acronym that describes the correct order in which to perform mathematical operations. The acronym PEMDAS stands for Parentheses, Exponents, Multiplication, Division, Addition, Subtraction. It should help you to remember to do the operations in the correct order, as follows:

1. **P** – First, do the operations within the *parentheses*, if any.
2. **E** – Next, do the *exponents*, if any.
3. **M** – Next, do the *multiplication*, in order from left to right.
4. **D** – Next, do the *division*, in order from left to right.
5. **A** – Next, do the *addition*, in order from left to right.
6. **S** – Finally, do the *subtraction*, in order from left to right.

For example, $\dfrac{2(4+1)^2 \times 3}{5} - 7$ would be solved in the following order:

$$\dfrac{2(5)^2 \times 3}{5} - 7$$

$$= \dfrac{2(25) \times 3}{5} - 7$$

$$= \dfrac{50 \times 3}{5} - 7$$

$$= \dfrac{150}{5} - 7$$

$$= 3 - 7 = -4$$

Pentagon: A five-sided figure, as shown below:

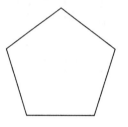

The sum of the interior angles of a pentagon is $(5-2)(180°)$, or $540°$.

Percent: Refers to one part in one hundred. A percent is a fraction whose denominator is 100. The fraction 25/100 is equal to 25%. To calculate the percent that one number is of another number, set up a ratio, as shown below:

What percent of 40 is 5?
5 is to 40 as x is to 100

$$\dfrac{5}{40} = \dfrac{x}{100}$$

Cross-multiply and solve for x:

$$40x = 500$$
$$x = \dfrac{500}{40} = 12.5$$

5 is 12.5% of 40

If a price is discounted by p percent, then the discounted price is $(100-p)$ percent of the original price.

Perimeter: The distance around any shape or object. Following are the formulas for the perimeter of some common figures:

- The perimeter (P) of both a parallelogram and a rectangle is equivalent to $2l + 2w$, where l is the length and w is the width.
- The perimeter (P) of other polygons is the sum of the lengths of the sides.
- The perimeter (P) of a triangle is the sum of the lengths of the sides.

Perpendicular: Two distinct lines are perpendicular if their intersection creates a right angle. Two lines are perpendicular if and only if the slope of one of the lines is the negative reciprocal of the slope of the other line. In other words, if line a has a slope of 2 and line b has a slope of $-\frac{1}{2}$, the two lines are perpendicular. The figure below shows two perpendicular lines:

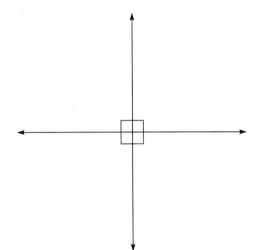

Point:

A location in a plane or in space that has no dimensions.

Point-slope form (see slope-intercept form):

The equation of a line in the form $y = mx + b$, where m is the slope and b is the y-intercept (that is, the point at which the graph of the line crosses the y-axis).

Polygon:

A closed plane figure made up of at least three line segments that are joined. For example, a triangle, a rectangle, and an octagon are all polygons.

Polynomial:

A mathematic expression consisting of more than two terms. $2x^2+4x+4$ is a simple quadratic equation, and is also a polynomial.

Prime number:

Any number that can only be divided by itself and 1: 1 and the number itself are the only factors of a prime number. For example: 2, 3, 5, 7, and 11 are prime numbers.

Probability:

The likelihood that an event will occur. For example: Jeff has three striped and four solid ties in his closet; therefore, he has a total of seven ties in his closet. He has three chances to grab a striped tie out of the seven total ties, because he has three striped ties. So, the likelihood of Jeff grabbing a striped tie is 3 out of 7, which can also be expressed as 3:7, or $\frac{3}{7}$.

Two specific events are considered independent if the outcome of one event has no effect on the outcome of the other event. For example, if you toss a coin, there is a 1 in 2, or $\frac{1}{2}$ chance that it will land on either heads or tails. If you toss the coin again, the probability of it landing on heads or tails will be the same as in the first toss. To find the probability of two or more independent events occurring together, multiply the outcomes of the individual events. For example, the probability that both coin-tosses will result in heads is $\frac{1}{2} \times \frac{1}{2}$, or $\frac{1}{4}$.

Product:

The result of multiplication. For example, 32 is the product of 8 and 4.

Proportion:	Indicates that one ratio is equal to another ratio. For example, $\frac{1}{5} = \frac{x}{20}$ is a proportion.
Pythagorean Theorem:	This theorem applies only to finding the length of the sides in right triangles, and states that $a^2 + b^2 = c^2$, where c is the hypotenuse (the side opposite the right angle) of the right triangle and a and b are the two other sides of the triangle.

▄ Q

Quadratic equation:	An equation of the form $ax^2 + bx + c$, where $a \neq 0$. $2x^2 + 4x + 4$ is a simple quadratic equation.
Quadratic formula:	Given a quadratic equation of the form $ax^2 + bx + c$, the quadratic formula can be used to solve. It is written as: $x = \dfrac{-b \pm \sqrt{b^2 - 4ac}}{2a}$. To solve, substitute the given values for a, b, and c in the quadratic equation into the formula. Keep in mind that the $\pm$ sign indicates that there will be both a negative and a positive solution to the equation.
Quadrilateral:	A four-sided polygon with four angles. A parallelogram, a rectangle, a square, and a trapezoid are all examples of quadrilaterals.
Quotient:	The result of division. For example, 3 is the quotient of 18 and 6.

▄ R

Radian:	A unit of angular measure. A circle has 2π radians, so $1^\circ = \dfrac{\pi}{180}$. To convert a degree measurement to radians, multiply by $\dfrac{\pi}{180}$. For example, 90° in radians is equal to $90\left(\dfrac{\pi}{180}\right)$, or $\dfrac{\pi}{2}$.
Radius:	The distance from the center of a circle to any point on the circle, as shown in the following circle with center C:

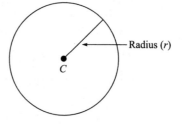

Range:	The y values of a function.
Ratio:	Expresses a mathematical comparison between two quantities. A ratio of 1 to 5, for example, is written as either $\frac{1}{5}$ or 1:5. When working with ratios, be sure to differentiate between part-to-part and part-to-whole ratios. For example, if two components of a recipe are being compared to each other, it is a part-to-part ratio (2 cups of flour:1 cup of sugar). On the other hand, if one group of students is being compared to the entire class, it is a part-to-whole ratio (13 girls: 27 students).
Rational number:	A fraction whose numerator and denominator are both integers and the denominator does not equal zero.

Real number: Any rational or irrational number, used to express quantities, lengths, amounts, and so on. All real numbers except zero are either positive or negative. All real numbers correspond to points on the number line, as shown below:

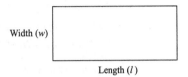

On a number line, such as that shown above, numbers that correspond to points to the right of zero are positive, and numbers that correspond to points to the left of zero are negative.

Reciprocal: Given a number, n, the reciprocal is expressed as 1 over n, or $\dfrac{1}{n}$. The product of a number and its reciprocal is always 1. In other words, $\dfrac{1}{3} \times \dfrac{3}{1} = \dfrac{3}{3}$, which is equivalent to 1.

Rectangle: A polygon with four sides (two sets of congruent, or equal, sides) and four right angles. All rectangles are parallelograms. Shown below is an example of a rectangle:

Width (w)

Length (l)

- The sum of the angles in a rectangle is always 360 degrees, because a rectangle contains four 90-degree angles.
- The perimeter (P) of a rectangle is equivalent to $2l + 2w$, where l is the length and w is the width.
- The area (A) of a rectangle is equivalent to $(l)(w)$.
- The lengths of the diagonals of a rectangle are congruent, or equal in length.
- A square is a special rectangle where all four sides are of equal length. All squares are rectangles.
- The length of the diagonals of a square are equivalent to the length of one side times $\sqrt{2}$. So, for example, a square with a side length of x would have diagonals equal to $x\sqrt{2}$.

Reflection: A reflection flips an object in the coordinate plane over either the x-axis or the y-axis. When a reflection occurs across the x-axis, the x-coordinate remains the same, but the y-coordinate is transformed into its opposite. When a reflection occurs across the y-axis, the y-coordinate remains the same, but the x-coordinate is transformed into its opposite. The object retains its shape and size. The figures below show a triangle that has been reflected across the y-axis:

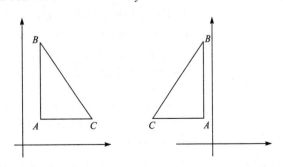

Right angle: An angle that measures 90 degrees.

██ **S**

Scientific notation:

When numbers are very large or very small, they are often expressed using scientific notation. Scientific notation is indicated by setting a positive number, N, equal to a number greater than or equal to 1, and less than 10, then multiplying that number by 10 raised to an integer. The integer depends on the number of places to the left or right that the decimal was moved. For example, 667,000,000 written in scientific notation would be 6.67×10^8, because the decimal was moved 8 places to the left, and 0.0000000298 written in scientific notation would be 2.98×10^{-8} because the decimal was moved 8 places to the right.

Secant (see trigonometric functions):

For an angle in a right triangle, secant is $\dfrac{1}{\cos}$.

Sequence:

The following are properties of arithmetic and geometric sequences that are commonly tested on the ACT:

- An *arithmetic* sequence is one in which the difference between one term and the next is the same. For example, the following sequence is an arithmetic sequence because the difference between the terms is 2: 1, 3, 5, 7, 9. To find the nth term, use the formula $a_n = a_1 + (n - 1)d$, where d is the common difference.
- A *geometric* sequence is one in which the ratio between two terms is constant. For example, $\dfrac{1}{2}$, 1, 2, 4, 8..., is a geometric sequence where 2 is the constant ratio. To find the nth term, use the formula $a_n = a_1(r)^{n-1}$, where r is the constant ratio.

Set:

The following are properties of number sets that are commonly tested on the ACT:

- A set is a collection of numbers. The numbers are elements or members of the set. For example: {2,4,6,8} is the set of positive, even integers less than 10.
- The union of two sets includes all of the elements in each set. For example: if Set A = {2,4,6,8} and Set B = {1,3,5,7,9}, then {1,2,3,4,5,6,7,8,9} is the union of Set A and Set B.
- The intersection of two sets identifies the common elements of two sets. For example: if Set A = {1,2,3,4} and Set B = {2,4,6,8}, then {2,4} is the intersection of Set A and Set B.

Similar triangles:

Triangles in which the measures of the corresponding angles are equal, and the corresponding sides are in proportion, as shown in the following figure:

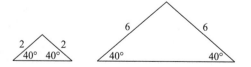

Sine (see trigonometric functions):

For an angle in a right triangle, sine (sin) is the ratio of the side opposite the angle to the hypotenuse. $\mathrm{Sin} = \dfrac{\mathrm{opp}}{\mathrm{hyp}}$.

Slope:

The change in y coordinates divided by the change in x coordinates from two given points on a line. The formula for slope is $m = \dfrac{(y_2 - y_1)}{(x_2 - x_1)}$ where (x_1, y_1) and (x_2, y_2) are the two given points. For example, the slope of a line that contains the points (3, 6) and (2, 5) is equivalent to $\dfrac{(6 - 5)}{(3 - 2)}$, or $\dfrac{1}{1}$, which equals 1.

A positive slope will mean the graph of the line will go up and to the right. A negative slope will mean the graph of the line will go down and to the right. A horizontal line has slope 0, while a vertical line has an undefined slope, because it never crosses the y-axis. See the figures below.

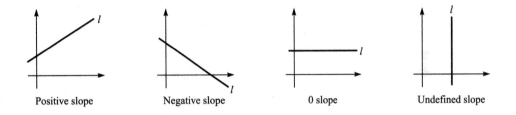

Positive slope   Negative slope   0 slope   Undefined slope

Slope-intercept form (see point-slope form):

The slope-intercept (standard) form of the equation of a line is $y = mx + b$, where m is the slope of the line and b is the y-intercept (that is, the point at which the graph of the line crosses the y-axis).

SOH CAH TOA (see trigonometric functions):

An acronym that can assist you in remembering the basic trigonometric functions:

(SOH) SIN = **OPPOSITE/HYPOTENUSE**
(CAH) COS = **ADJACENT/HYPOTENUSE**
(TOA) TAN = **OPPOSITE/ADJACENT**

Special triangles:

Triangles whose sides have special ratios. The following are angle measures and side lengths for special right triangles:

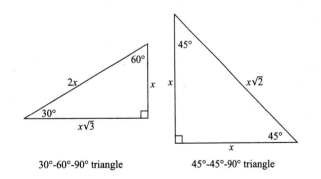

30°-60°-90° triangle   45°-45°-90° triangle

The sides of a 3-4-5 Special Right Triangle have the ratio 3:4:5.

Square: A number multiplied by itself. The following are properties of squares that are commonly tested on the ACT:

- Squaring a negative number yields a positive result. For example, $-2^2 = 4$.
- A number is considered a perfect square when the square root of that number is a whole number. The polynomial $a^2 \pm 2ab + b^2$ is also a perfect square because the solution set is $(a \pm b)^2$.

Square root: The square root of a number, n, is written as $\sqrt{n}$, or the nonnegative value a that fulfills the expression $a^2 = n$. For example, "the square root of 5" is expressed as $\sqrt{5}$, and $(\sqrt{5})^2 = 5$. A square root will always be a positive number.

Standard deviation: Calculated by finding the arithmetic mean of the data set, finding the difference between the mean and each of the n values of the data set, squaring each of the differences, finding the average of the squared differences, and taking the nonnegative square root of this average. This calculation is used infrequently on the ACT.

Surface area: The surface area of a rectangular solid (shown below) is the sum of the area $(l \times w)$ of the six faces of the solid. Think of each face as a square or a rectangle. The formula for the surface area of a rectangular solid is $A = 2(wl + lh + wh)$, where l = length, w = width, and h = height.

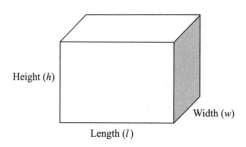

The equation for the surface area of a sphere with radius $r = 4\pi r^2$.

System of equations: A collection of two or more equations with the same set of unknowns. In solving a system of equations, find values for each of the unknowns that satisfy every equation in the system.

T

Tangent: A line perpendicular to the radius of a circle that touches the circle at one point.

In trigonometry, the tangent (tan) of an angle in a right triangle is the ratio of the side opposite the angle to the side adjacent to the angle (see definition for **trigonometric functions**). $\text{Tan} = \dfrac{\text{opp}}{\text{adj}}$.

Translation: A translation slides an object in the coordinate plane to the left or right, or up or down. The object retains its shape and size, and faces in the same direction. In the figure below, the triangle in the first graph is translated 4 units down in the second graph:

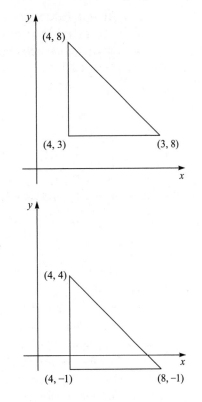

Transversal:

A line that intersects two other lines. In the following figure, line n is the transversal:

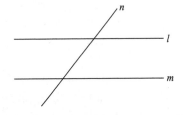

When two parallel lines are cut by a transversal, each parallel line has four angles surrounding the intersection, that are matched in measure and position with a counterpart at the other parallel line. The vertical (opposite) angles are congruent, and the adjacent angles are supplementary (they total 180°). See the figure below.

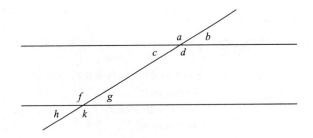

- Vertical angles: $a = d = f = k$
- Vertical angles: $b = c = g = h$
- Supplementary angles: $a + b = 180°$
- Supplementary angles: $c + d = 180°$

• Supplementary angles: $f + g = 180°$
• Supplementary angles: $h + k = 180°$

Trapezoid: A quadrilateral with exactly one pair of parallel sides, called the bases of the trapezoid (b_1 and b_2). The height of the trapezoid is the perpendicular distance between the two bases (h). Shown below is an example of a trapezoid:

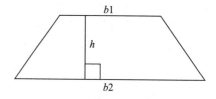

The area of a trapezoid is equal to the average of the bases times the height, expressed as:

$$A = \frac{(a+b)h}{2}$$

Triangle: A polygon with three vertices and three sides that are straight line segments.

The following are properties of triangles that are commonly tested on the ACT:

• In an equilateral triangle, all three sides have the same length, and each interior angle measures 60 degrees.
• In an isosceles triangle, two sides have the same length, and the angles opposite those sides are congruent.
• In a right triangle, one of the angles measures 90 degrees. The side opposite the right angle is the hypotenuse, and it is always the longest side.
• The sum of the interior angles in any triangle is always 180 degrees.
• The perimeter (P) of a triangle is the sum of the lengths of the sides.
• The area (A) of a triangle is equivalent to $\frac{1}{2}$(base)(height). The height is equal to the perpendicular distance from an angle to a side. Following are examples of the height of a given triangle:

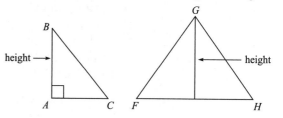

Trigonometric functions: Functions of an angle that are commonly defined as ratios of two sides of a right triangle containing the angle.

The following are properties of trigonometric functions that are commonly tested on the ACT (use the triangle below as a reference to the definitions):

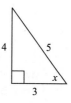

- In a right triangle, the *sine* (sin) of an angle is defined as the ratio of the leg opposite the angle to the hypotenuse (opposite/hypotenuse). In the triangle shown above, $\sin x = \frac{4}{5}$.
- In a right triangle, the *cosine* (cos) of an angle is defined as the ratio of the leg adjacent to the angle to the hypotenuse (adjacent/hypotenuse). In the triangle shown above, $\cos x = \frac{3}{5}$.
- In a right triangle, the *tangent* (tan) of an angle is defined as the ratio of the leg opposite the angle to the adjacent leg (opposite/adjacent). In the triangle shown above, $\tan x = \frac{4}{3}$.
- In a right triangle, the *cosecant* (csc) of an angle is defined as $\frac{1}{\sin}$. In the triangle shown above, $\csc x = \frac{5}{4}$.
- In a right triangle, the *secant* (sec) of an angle is defined as $\frac{1}{\cos}$. In the triangle shown above, $\sec x = \frac{5}{3}$.
- In a right triangle, the *cotangent* (cot) of an angle is defined as $\frac{\cos}{\sin}$, or $\frac{1}{\tan}$.
- In the triangle shown above, $\cot x = \frac{3}{4}$.

See SOH CAH TOA.

▬ V–Y

Vertical angle: One of two opposite angles that are formed by intersecting lines. Vertical angles are congruent. In the following figure, angles *a* and *b* are vertical angles:

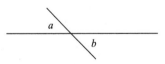

Volume: A measure of space or capacity of a three-dimensional object. The following are properties of volume that are commonly tested on the ACT:

- The formula for the volume of a rectangular solid is $V = lwh$, where l = length, w = width, and h = height.
- The formula for the volume of a cube is the length of a side (s) cubed (s^3).
- The formula for the volume of a sphere is $4\pi r^3$, where r is the radius of the sphere.

Word problem   A type of question on the ACT that uses words as well as, or sometimes instead of, mathematical symbols. When solving word problems, translate the verbal statements into algebraic expressions. For example:

- "greater than," "more than," and "sum of" means addition ($+$).
- "less than," "fewer than," and "difference" means subtraction ($-$).
- "of," "by" and "product" means multiplication ($\times$).
- "per" means division ($\div$).

Y-intercept   The point at which a line crosses the y-axis in the x, y coordinate plane. In the figure below, the y-intercept is 2:

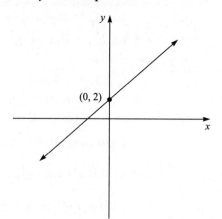

APPENDIX B

QUICK REVIEW SHEET

This review contains useful information about preparing for the ACT Mathematics Test. Be sure to read the book and take the practice tests before referring to this sheet. Review the information included on this sheet prior to entering the testing center, paying close attention to the areas in which you feel you need the most review. This sheet should not be used as a substitute for actual preparation; it is simply a review of important information presented in detail elsewhere in this book.

GENERAL TEST-TAKING STRATEGIES

1. Relax.

   - Don't panic if you are having a hard time answering the questions! You do not have to answer all the questions correctly to get a good score.
   - Take a few moments to relax if you get stressed during the test. Put your pencil down, close your eyes, take some deep breaths, and stop testing. When you get back to the test, you will feel better.

2. Do the easy stuff first.

   - You don't have to do the questions from each section in order. Skip the hard ones and come back to them later.
   - Keep moving so that you don't waste valuable time. If you get stuck on a question, move on!

3. Manage the answer sheet.

   - Do not go to your answer sheet after each question. Mark your answers in the book, and then transfer them

every one to two pages. Pay attention to question numbers, especially if you skip a question. Your score depends on what is filled in on your answer sheet.

4. Use the test booklet.

   - Do the math! Draw pictures to help you figure out problems and use the space available to write down your calculations.
   - Circle your answer choices, cross out answers you eliminate, and mark questions that you need to come back to later. If you cannot eliminate an answer choice, but think that it might work, underline it.

5. Be aware of time.

   - Pace yourself. You learned in practice which questions you should focus on and which questions you should skip and come back to later if you have the time.
   - Time yourself with a watch. Do not rely on the proctor's official time announcements.
   - You have only a limited amount of time. Read and work actively through the test.
   - Stay focused. Ignore the things going on around you that you cannot control.
   - Check over your answers if you have time remaining.

6. Guess Effectively.

   - *Never* leave a question blank; make educated guesses when you can, and fill in your random guessing choice on the remaining questions.

- Eliminate answer choices that you know are wrong. The more you can eliminate, the better your chance of getting the question right.

7. Don't Change Your Mind.

- Do not second-guess yourself. Your first answer choice is more likely to be correct. If you're not completely comfortable with your first choice, place a question mark next to your answer and come back to it later if you have time.
- Only change your answer when you are sure that it's wrong.

MATH CONCEPTS AND STRATEGIES

Following are general math concepts and strategies, as well as specific strategies for the multiple-choice questions.

General Math Concepts

1. The area of a circle is $A = \pi r^2$, where r is the radius of the circle.
2. The circumference of a circle is $C = 2\pi r$, where r is the radius of the circle. The circumference can also be expressed as πd because the diameter is always twice the radius.
3. The area of a rectangle is $A = lw$, where l is the length of the rectangle and w is the width of the rectangle.
4. The area of a triangle is $A = \frac{1}{2}bh$, where b is the base of the triangle and h is the height of the triangle.
5. The volume of a rectangular prism is $V = lwh$, where l is the length of the rectangular prism, w is the width of the rectangular prism, and h is the height of the rectangular prism.
6. The volume of a cylinder is $V = \pi r^2 h$, where r is the radius of one of the bases of the cylinder and h is the height of the cylinder.
7. The perimeter is the distance around any object.
8. The Pythagorean Theorem states that $c^2 = a^2 + b^2$ (or $a^2 + b^2 = c^2$) where c is the hypotenuse of the triangle and a and b are two sides of the triangle.

9. The following are angle measures and side lengths for special right triangles:

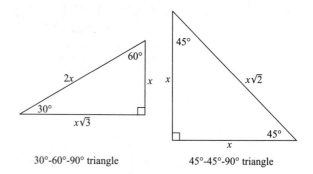

30°-60°-90° triangle   45°-45°-90° triangle

10. In an equilateral triangle, all three sides have the same length.
11. In an isosceles triangle, two sides have the same length.
12. The complete arc of a circle has 360°.
13. A straight line has 180°.
14. A prime number is any number that can be divided only by itself and 1.
15. Squaring a negative number yields a positive number.
16. To change any fraction to a decimal divide the numerator by the denominator.
17. If two numbers have one or more divisors in common, those are the common factors of the numbers.
18. To calculate the mean, or average, of a list of values, divide the sum of the values by the number of values in the list.
19. The median is the middle value of a list, where the values are in either ascending or descending order.
20. The mode is the value that appears most often in a list.
21. A ratio expresses a mathematical comparison between two quantities ($\frac{1}{4}$ or 1:4).
22. A proportion is an equation involving two ratios. ($\frac{1}{4} = \frac{x}{8}$ or 1:4 = x:8).
23. When multiplying exponential expressions with the same base, add the exponents.
24. When dividing exponential expressions with the same base, subtract the exponents.
25. When raising one power to another power, multiply the exponents.

General Math Strategies

1. Draw pictures or create tables as necessary to help you figure out problems.
2. Look for a way to reason through the problem. Don't just go for your calculator.
3. When reading word problems, translate them into mathematical equations. (Jenny has 5 more CDs than Amy is equivalent to $J = A + 5$)
4. Paraphrase questions to make sure that you are answering what is asked. Cross out any irrelevant information given in the question.
5. Remember to estimate or predict answers when you can. It is often possible to eliminate all but the correct answer choice without doing any actual math.
6. Once you've eliminated an answer choice, cross it out.

Multiple Choice Question Strategies

1. Look at the format of the answer choices before you attempt to work through the problem. Remember that the answer choices will be in either ascending or descending order where appropriate.
2. Even if the format of the question is unfamiliar to you, read through it and reorder the answer choices carefully. You might know how to solve the problem.

Good Luck!

APPENDIX C
ADDITIONAL RESOURCES

The purpose of this book is to help you prepare for the ACT Mathematics Test. While this book provides you with helpful information about the tests and realistic practice materials to get you ready for the real thing, the following additional resources might be useful in your preparation:

ACT, INC.

The ACT website at http://www.act.org offers a wealth of up-to-date information about the ACT. Once you get to the "The Test" area of the website, you can find out when and where the tests are administered, try practice questions from past tests, and even access the ACT Student Blog, a special area designed to help you explore different majors, colleges, and careers.

The Real ACT Prep Guide (ISBN 0-7689-1975-4), published by ACT, is a great source of practice material. This book is usually available at all the major bookstores. You can order it online at http://AdvantageEd.com/hsbooks.htm

ADVANTAGE EDUCATION

Advantage Education offers many programs for college-bound students, including programs that prepare students for the PSAT, SAT, and ACT, as well as Admissions Counseling and College Preparation. To learn about individual tutoring, workshops, courses, and other programs for college-bound students, visit http://AdvantageEd.com

Advantage Education has also written *McGraw-Hill's ACT* (ISBN 0-07 149262-3) and *McGraw-Hill's 10 ACT Practice Tests* (0-07-14572-9), both available in bookstores and from the website (http://AdvantageEd.com/hsbooks.htm). These books include many additional simulated full-length practice tests.

TEXTBOOKS AND HUMAN RESOURCES

Middle school and high school textbooks are extremely valuable resources. The content areas tested on the ACT are the same content areas that you've been studying in school. Hence, textbooks cover many of the relevant skills and subjects you will need for success on the ACT. If you do not have your textbooks, your school library should have copies that you can use.

Don't forget to talk to teachers and older students who have some experience with the ACT. They might be able to shed some additional light on getting ready for the test. It is in your best interest to be as well prepared as possible on test day.